Pastoral Care 11–16

A companion website to accompany this book is available online at:
http://www.bloomsbury.com/uk/pastoral-care-11-16-9781441127488

Please type in the URL above to receive your unique password for access to the book's online resources.

If you experience any problems accessing the resources, please contact contact@bloomsbury.com

Also available from Bloomsbury Academic

A Pastoral Leader's Handbook: Strategies for Success in the Secondary School, Marilyn Nathan

Physical Education for Learning: A Guide for Secondary Schools, edited by Richard Bailey

Reflective Teaching: Evidence-informed Professional Practice (3rd edition), Andrew Pollard

Pastoral Care 11–16

A Critical Introduction

Edited by

Noel Purdy

BLOOMSBURY

LONDON · NEW DELHI · NEW YORK · SYDNEY

Bloomsbury Academic
An imprint of Bloomsbury Publishing Plc

50 Bedford Square   175 Fifth Avenue
London   New York
WC1B 3DP   NY 10010
UK   USA

www.bloomsbury.com

First published 2013

British Library Cataloguing-in-Publication Data
A catalogue record for this book is available from the British Library.

ISBN:HB: 9781441174284
    PB: 9781441127488
 e-Pub: 9781441117175
   PDF: 9781441181237

Library of Congress Cataloging-in-Publication Data
Pastoral care, 11–16 : a critical introduction / edited by Noel Purdy.
pages cm
Includes index.
ISBN 978-1-4411-2748-8 (pbk.) – ISBN 978-1-4411-7428-4 (hardcover) –
ISBN 978-1-4411-8123-7 (ebook (pdf)) – ISBN 978-1-4411-1717-5 (ebook (epub))
1. Educational counseling. 2. Church work with students. 3. Child care.
4. School psychology. I. Purdy, Noel.
LB1027.5.P326 2013
371.4–dc23
2012041406

Typeset by Newgen Imaging Systems Pvt Ltd, Chennai, India
Printed and bound in India

Contents

Contributors

Jo Bell is a Lecturer in the Department of Social Sciences at The University of Hull, UK. Jo completed her PhD on Adolescent Development in 2001. She has researched and published in the areas of self-harm and suicide in young people, young suicide bereavement, young parenthood and sexual behaviour in young people, domestic violence, excluded young people and school-based health education and prevention programmes. Her current research activity continues to engage these topics. Her most recent research interests are around young people's use of the internet and new media, and how internet use influences self-harming and suicidal behaviour.

Paula Hall is a British Association of Counselling and Psychotherapy (BACP) Accredited and United Kingdon Council for Psychotherapy (UKCP) Registered Relationship Psychotherapist who currently works in private practice in Warwickshire. She has worked with Relate for many years counselling adults, young people and families. She specializes in the impact of divorce and separation on children and young people and is author of the Relate Guide *Help Your Children Cope with Your Divorce* as well as a book for parents, *How to Have a Healthy Divorce*. Paula also provides training to counsellors and schools on the impact of divorce and separation on young people.

Christine Harrison is Associate Professor, Chair of the School of Health and Social Studies, and Director of the Centre for the Study of Safety and Well-being at the University of Warwick, UK. She is an experienced social worker and has co-ordinated and taught child care and child protection social work at qualifying and post-qualifying levels for the last 20 years. She teaches on programmes for other professionals, including health professionals, in the Warwick Medical School and elsewhere. She is consultant to a Sexually Inappropriate Behaviours Service for Children and Young People and works closely with the Survivors Trust, an NGO umbrella organization for dedicated sexual violence services. Research related to physical, emotional and sexual violence towards women and children, and the issues this raises for promoting their safety, is a theme running throughout various aspects of her work over recent years. She has undertaken teaching and developmental work in Thailand, Iceland, Taiwan and Australia on these issues. Her most recent work has focused on domestic violence and child contact; digital information and communication technologies and abuse of women and children; sexual violence and the experiences of survivors; domestic violence and child filicide.

Mary F. Lappin has been involved in the field of education for the past 25 years, working in England, Canada and Scotland. She currently teaches Religious Education at the University of Glasgow, UK, on a variety of undergraduate and postgraduate courses. She also has expertise in the field of Grief and Loss Education, providing professional development courses, guidance and consultancy to schools, pre-5 establishments and within a variety of health and well-being initiatives. She pioneered the programme 'Seasons for Growth' in Scotland and regularly provides training for professionals in using the programme within educational establishments. Her work within Grief and Loss Education extends beyond bereavement to work on children's experiences of separation and divorce, the needs of Looked After and Accommodated children and educational concerns relating to attachment difficulties within adopted and fostered children.

Bronagh McKee is currently Child Protection Co-ordinator and Senior Lecturer at Stranmillis University College, Belfast, UK. She is an early years specialist with a background in social work. Bronagh teaches and co-ordinates undergraduate and postgraduate modules in the areas of safeguarding and child protection, working with disadvantaged pupils, social work with children and families, pupils' mental health and well-being and improving outcomes for children and young people. Her research interests include pre-service child protection training and safeguarding education, preventative education and using arts-based education in learning and teaching activity. She co-ordinates Inter-Professional Education with colleagues in Queen's University Belfast, is a Director on Women's Aid Federation Northern Ireland Management Board, and sits on the Domestic Violence Research Special Interest Group and the

Regional Domestic Violence and Sexual Abuse Children and Young People Sub Group. Bronagh oversees the child protection and safeguarding education and training requirements for all students and staff, chairs the Joint Consultative Child Protection Committee and is the editor of the College Child Protection and Safeguarding newsletter.

Noel Purdy is Principal Lecturer and Head of Education Studies in the Department of Teacher Education at Stranmillis University College, Belfast, UK. Formerly he taught modern languages in two secondary schools in Northern Ireland where he was closely involved with pastoral care. In his current role, he lectures on pastoral care at undergraduate and postgraduate level. His recent research has focused on the professional development needs of Newly Qualified Teachers in inner-city schools, student teachers' knowledge and confidence in relation to disablist bullying, and the production of a teachers' guide to the law in relation to cyberbullying in schools. He is a member of the Northern Ireland Anti-Bullying Forum and the executive committee of the all-Ireland Standing Conference on Teacher Education North and South.

Peter K. Smith is Emeritus Professor of Psychology at the Unit for School and Family Studies, Goldsmiths, University of London, UK. He is co-author of *Understanding Children's Development* (Wiley-Blackwell, 5th edition 2011), and co-editor of *School Bullying: Insights and Perspectives* (Routledge, 1994), *Tackling Bullying in Your School: A Practical Handbook for Teachers* (Routledge, 1994), *The Nature of School Bullying* (Routledge, 1999), *Bullying in Schools: How Successful Can Interventions Be?* (CUP, 2004), the *Blackwell Handbook of Childhood Social Development* (2nd edition, Wiley-Blackwell, 2010) and *Cyberbullying in the Global Playground: Research from International Perspectives* (Wiley-Blackwell, 2012). He is editor of *Violence in Schools: The Response in Europe* (Routledge, 2002). He directed the Department for Education Sheffield Anti-Bullying project from 1991–4, advised on the Department for Education and Employment pack *Don't Suffer in Silence* (1994, 2nd edition, 2000), and has coordinated EU-funded projects on *The Nature and Prevention of Bullying* (1997–2001) and *Violence in Schools* (1999–2002). He chaired COST Action IS0801 on Cyberbullying (2008–2012).

Ravi K. Thiara is Principal Research Fellow at the Centre for the Study of Safety and Well-being, School of Health and Social Studies, University of Warwick, UK. She has conducted extensive national and international research on gender violence over the last 20 years. She has published widely and has a particular expertise in domestic violence and issues for Black and minority ethnic women and children.

Fran Thompson is a researcher at the Unit for School and Family Studies, Goldsmiths, University of London, UK. During her six years at the Unit she has focused on researching and evaluating anti-bullying interventions. She has co-authored three publications with Peter K. Smith: an article for the *British Journal of Educational Psychology*, 'Anti-bullying strategies in schools – What is done and what works'; a report for the DfE (2011) on *The Effectiveness of Anti-Bullying Strategies in Schools* (DfE: RR-098) and an online literature review for the Anti-Bullying Alliance (2008): *Tackling Bullying in Schools: A Mapping of Approaches.* She is in the process of writing a book on anti-bullying interventions with Peter K. Smith for Wiley-Blackwell.

Acknowledgements

Thanks are due first to Alison Baker (née Clark) and Rosie Pattinson from Bloomsbury who have provided invaluable support throughout this project, and also to each of the contributing authors for their time and extraordinary talents.

Introduction
Noel Purdy

What is pastoral care?

Pastoral care in schools is not glamorous work. It doesn't grab the head-lines like top examination results or sporting success often do. It can be challenging and offers little public reward. The range of pastoral issues which schools have to deal with also seems to be growing constantly in number, intensity and complexity. Consequently, some might argue that teachers should simply throw in the towel and leave pastoral care to 'the professionals', allowing teachers to get on with their 'real job' of delivering their subject. The very term pastoral care is being used less and less in schools, and traditional titles like 'Head of Year' are reportedly being replaced by new terms such as 'Director of Learning' and 'Progress Manager'. So, is it time to abandon ship? Should we acknowledge the overwhelming challenges of pastoral care work for an already busy class-room teacher, and bow out graciously? Should we just get on with deliv-ering the curriculum and raising attainment to meet the latest government targets? Is the pastoral role of the modern teacher simply one challenge too many? And is the very term 'pastoral care', with its religious origins, unsuited to the modern, increasingly secular secondary school context?

Emphatically, no! This book, while acknowledging and addressing the real challenges of providing pastoral care in schools, seeks to cele-brate this unsung work and would argue that there remains a very defi-nite place for pastoral care in all our secondary schools, despite the challenges. For there can be no denial of the reality of the many serious problems which children and young people are already facing or will encounter in their lives, and which schools are dealing with every day. Nor is it possible to forget that teachers are already under significant pressure, not least to meet targets, achieve levels and raise attainment, and that they often feel ill-prepared to deal with the complexity and severity of serious pastoral issues.

However, one of the core messages of this book is that schools are uniquely placed to offer understanding and practical support to pupils in times of need, and, crucially, teachers are uniquely skilled in relating to these same pupils at an age-appropriate level. When dealing with a pastoral issue, teachers are thus in the privileged position of already knowing their pupils and of already having developed a relationship with them. This is priceless. In severe cases, teachers must of course refer children on to external agencies for additional support. This is legally and morally right. However, as the first point of contact, and for all the non-critical but still very significant pastoral issues which arise, teachers have a vital and unrivalled pastoral role to play, and this volume offers advice to them in responding to some of the most common of these issues.

But pastoral care is much more than an emotional 'crutch' for troubled children to lean on in difficult times, and also more than a set of procedures or policies, important though they may be in ensuring that teachers' responses are considered and consistent. Fundamentally, it is about a whole-school atmosphere in which relationships are centrally important and are healthy and positive: between and among staff, pupils and the wider community. It is also about preparing children and young people through the curriculum for the realities of life today, and equipping them with the skills they will need to face challenging situations when (rather than if) they arise. In this way pastoral care in schools encompasses both reactive responses to issues which can arise in children's lives, but also preventative or educational strategies to enable children to be better prepared for current and future problems in their lives and in the lives of those around them at home and at school. This book therefore offers many suggestions for how teachers can address these issues in the curriculum, in traditional subject classrooms and also in tutor groups or subjects such as Personal, Social, Health and Economic education (PSHE).

The term pastoral care is notoriously difficult to define but there is no doubt that it can embrace a wide range of issues including those covered in this book but also school counselling, PSHE, behaviour management, mental health issues, eating disorders, alcohol/drug misuse and many more. For such an introductory volume, there has had to be a selection of some of the most significant issues in pastoral care. The selection was based on several years of listening to teachers and student teachers talking about their greatest concerns, but it would be foolish to suggest that these are any more or less important than the many other issues which have not found a place in this introductory volume.

How can this book help me?

In editing this volume, it was my aim that each chapter would give you lots of practical advice, but also to ensure that this practical advice was grounded in recent, international research evidence. This allows you to see the rationale behind the advice offered, and even to locate the original research studies and read the detail for yourselves. Thus, this book represents much more than a series of simple tips for the pastoral care teacher. Such simple tips and generalizations are, in any case, of limited value, given the individuality and complexity of the real cases encountered every day in our schools. This book therefore aims to be both practical and evidence-based, an objective which confirms the view of pastoral care in schools as a highly complex, evolving and challenging activity which demands the latest, and most reliable research evidence, rather than leaving teachers to respond in an ad hoc, instinct-led manner. The volume is unashamedly replete with references to research and policy, but each chapter also strives to apply that research to the everyday context of secondary schools and to the real problems faced by children and young people in our schools.

The book is intended to be of relevance to student teachers as you prepare for a pastoral role within the secondary school. Initial Teacher Education is often a very short, busy period, during which you will be learning about the curriculum, assessment, specifications and targets. You will most likely have to spend many hours planning and writing up lessons, resources and evaluations. However you will quickly learn that teaching is more than writing and delivering well-crafted lessons. Teaching involves interacting with and facilitating the learning of real children and young people. Each one will have different personalities, interests, aptitudes and, importantly, home backgrounds. Very soon you will discover that these children and young people have a life outside of school, a life which helps form attitudes and dispositions towards school, learning and other people. When the stability of that home life is disrupted, then there is an immediate and often enduring impact on the child's sense of security, well-being and happiness but also on their readiness to learn in school. Providing understanding and support for that child in need is one of the key elements of effective pastoral care in schools. Realizing your role as a teacher in helping to meet children and young people's pastoral needs is one of the most important things that you will learn during your Initial Teacher Education.

This book is however also intended as a useful resource for serving teachers and pastoral leaders in schools, who are busy dealing with the issues presented in these chapters on a daily basis, but who simply do not have the time to read an entire book on each topic. For you, this book is certainly a timely opportunity to read a brief, critical introduction to each issue, and quickly to gain an understanding of how your localized situation relates to the wider context, as presented by the analysis of national and international research and policy. In a brief number of pages you will gain a critical, introductory understanding of key issues facing pastoral care teachers in secondary schools today and will be directed to further resources, if you wish to read more. Realistically, given the busyness of your professional life, you may not have time to go any further than the chapters in this volume, and so it is hoped that each chapter in itself will give you a thorough grounding in each pastoral area, promoting deeper understanding and facilitating personal reflection.

What's in the book?

The book offers you the opportunity to read a concise, critical analysis of core pastoral issues faced by secondary schools, to reflect on the evidence provided and to consider how best to apply the recommendations to your individual setting.

In **Chapter 1** Noel Purdy considers the origins of pastoral care in relation to education, detailing a number of important definitions which have helped shape our understanding of this diffuse concept. It is contended that pastoral care remains a vital element in the twenty-first-century secondary school, and is characterized above all by the nature and quality of the relationships which exist within the school community. The chapter analyses the demanding and yet rewarding roles of the Form Tutor and the Head of Year which are central to pastoral care systems in most secondary schools, but also addresses the role of the classroom teacher. Here it is argued that, even though they may not have a named pastoral role in the school, the classroom teacher embodies the pastoral ethos of a school through their teaching, their relationships and their knowledge of the pastoral procedures of the school. In all of this work, there is a need to provide support and care for the pastoral care team, an area which is often overlooked by schools.

In **Chapter 2** Bronagh McKee examines the importance of Child Protection in secondary schools. The chapter begins by setting the legal and policy context for protecting, safeguarding and promoting the welfare needs of children and young people, with particular emphasis on the UK, Ireland, the US, Australia and New Zealand. The four main forms of abuse are then presented in detail: physical, emotional and sexual abuse and neglect. It is also argued that bullying and domestic violence fall within the definition of maltreatment within an educational context. This chapter highlights the development of the safeguarding role which teachers play in promoting children and young people's welfare, and illustrates the complexity of the task through a three-part case study. The chapter concludes with an analysis of the role which schools can play in helping to prevent abuse through recognizing early signs of abuse but also in teaching children through the curriculum about how to protect themselves. Challenges remain however in relation to the confidence of teachers to deliver such lessons and also in terms of the availability of appropriate training and resources.

Chapter 3 explores the nature of bullying in schools. Fran Thompson and Peter K. Smith address the many possible manifestations of bullying behaviour in schools (for example, physical, verbal, social exclusion, indirect and cyberbullying) and outline the nature of the different roles involved, including the bully, the victim and also the bystander. The chapter outlines proactive school strategies such as the development of effective policies, curricular approaches and assertiveness training, and considers a number of different peer support schemes. Attention is then focused on reactive strategies. Once again, research evidence is used to examine several different approaches, from the use of direct sanctions to restorative approaches and the support group method. The chapter concludes with an analysis of the effectiveness of school-based intervention programmes and argues that schools need to learn from both the successes and failures to date. Thompson and Smith contend that although there have been some important advances made in our understanding of bullying, there remains much work to be done.

Addressing the topic of domestic violence and abuse in **Chapter 4**, Christine Harrison and Ravi Thiara argue at the outset that schools can provide a haven for children and young people affected by domestic violence through the presence of positive relationships with peers and teachers, the gaining of a sense of achievement and the reassurance of a secure routine. The chapter analyses recent research into the extent and nature of domestic violence, its impact on children and young people (including post-separation violence) and the particular needs of children affected by domestic violence. As well as discussing the impact of domestic violence between adults, Harrison and Thiara also present research which highlights the prevalence of teenage relationship violence and the presence of condoning attitudes at an early age. In subsequent pages, the nature of school responses is discussed: on a primary level, schools can teach their pupils to develop healthy, non-abusive relationships and also to support children and young people who are living with the impact of domestic violence; on a secondary level, schools can help by providing support for children whose development is affected by any form of adversity, even if its source is not immediately identifiable; and, on a tertiary level, more intensive intervention, including referral to external specialist support agencies, can be offered to children and young people where it is known that they have experienced domestic violence.

In **Chapter 5** Paula Hall and Noel Purdy consider the complex question of how schools can respond to parental separation and divorce. Having first analysed the international social context where family structures are now more transient than ever before, the chapter examines the impact which parental separation can have on children and young people (e.g. feelings of shock, fear and guilt). A number of different roles are then presented (the Silent Child, the Angry Child, the Clingy Child, the Fragile Child and the Perfect Child), and it is highlighted that individual responses depend not just on developmental age, but also on a range of other mitigating factors. The chapter then examines the long-term consequences of parental separation, drawing evidence from longitudinal studies which reveal an enduring legacy in the lives and attitudes of many children of divorce, even after 25 years. The final section of this chapter offers suggestions as to how secondary schools can respond to separation and divorce, both on a whole-school level (through effective communication, policies and a supportive ethos) and also on an individual classroom level, where teachers can offer understanding and support in many different ways.

Chapter 6 tackles the sensitive issue of bereavement. Here Mary F. Lappin presents an overview of a number of leading international models of grief, and outlines the distinction between those which see grief as a linear process and those which see grief as more cyclical and complex. While acknowledging the individuality of children's responses to significant loss, the chapter describes common trends in children's developing concepts of death and responses to death. An introduction is then given to how bereaved young people can best be supported, illustrated by research examples and a case study. The chapter also considers how death can be integrated into the curriculum. In the final section, Lappin considers the challenges of dealing with ambiguous loss and disenfranchised grief, where children (as well as adults) can struggle to deal with instances which are less 'tidy' such as the loss of a soldier parent who is missing in action, presumed dead, the loss of an abusive parent, or situations where children feel unable to express their grief publicly. In conclusion, teachers are reminded of the important role which they can play in supporting bereaved young people through this particularly difficult period of loss and adjustment.

The final topic of self-harm and suicide is addressed by Jo Bell in **Chapter 7**. The chapter opens with some alarming UK and US statistics revealing the extent of the problem of suicide involving 11–16-year-olds. Research into the incidence of self-harm is also presented, examining motives and exploring popular misconceptions. Bell then considers how best schools can respond to self-harm and suicide, and highlights the importance of education and awareness-raising programmes in schools. Here it is argued that the key issue is not *whether* this should be discussed in schools, but *how* it should be done, and in this regard, teachers need to be well-prepared and have access to appropriate classroom resources (several school-based programmes are analysed in detail). The chapter then addresses how schools can respond to incidents or disclosures of self-harm when they arise. Given that self-harm and suicidal behaviour is now a major public health issue among young people, Bell concludes by arguing that schools should work hard to raise awareness, provide preventative programmes and know how to respond effectively to this challenging issue.

What are the key features of the book?

You may wish to read the entire book from cover to cover, but perhaps more realistically, you will choose to read one or more of the individual chapters on a theme which you are currently discussing as part of your Initial Teacher Education course, or are facing in the classroom as a teaching professional.

Each chapter has a number of pedagogical features. These are:

- Research Examples – providing a short, accessible summary of a piece of published research. These studies have been chosen because of their high impact in the field of research, and/or because of a particular methodological approach adopted.
- Case Studies – illustrating the challenges faced by schools in tackling often very complex, individual cases. These are based on real-life examples, but some details have been altered to ensure anonymity. Each case study is followed by some questions to facilitate individual or group reflection.
- Annotated Further Reading – offering opportunities for you to access additional reading resources. Each recommended title is followed by a summary of the content.
- Useful Websites – giving details of useful internet sites relevant to the respective topics, and with details of what each site has to offer.

Finally, the book is accompanied by a companion website available at http://education.purdy.continuumbooks.com, allowing readers to read further research examples, case studies and other resources related to each of the seven core chapters.

However you use this book, I hope that it will encourage and inspire you to become more effective in your crucial pastoral role as a secondary school teacher.

Pastoral Care: Origins, Definitions and Roles

Noel Purdy

1

Chapter Outline

Introduction

Pastoral care is a diffuse and elusive concept. Its etymology is rooted in agriculture (pascere – *Latin* to feed) and subsequent biblical references to Christ as the Good Shepherd tending his flock (e.g. Psalm 23 'The Lord in my Shepherd, I shall not want') but also to Pope Gregory I's *Liber Regulae Pastoralis* or *Cura Pastoralis*, written around the year 590, which outlined the responsibilities of bishops in caring for the 'souls' of believers. However as Carroll (2010) notes, the notion of pastoral care even within Christianity has been 'fairly fluid' (p. 146) through the centuries and between different denominations.

The history of pastoral care in schools dates back to the church's role in the nineteenth century in founding church schools and in instilling Christian values of care within these institutions. This often implicit concern for the welfare of the pupils became gradually more explicit through the first half of the twentieth century with the 1904 *Regulations for Elementary Schools* in England encouraging teachers to 'know', 'sympathize with' and 'touch the mind' of the pupils in striving to help them reach their 'full development as individuals' (Cunningham, 2002). However as Marland (2002) notes, the term pastoral care was not used consistently in the early part of the century, even though there was a growing realization of the need to provide support for the non-academic welfare of the pupils in schools. In 1937 the Board of Education noted that 'We realise more and more the importance of broadening the aims of education and of placing greater emphasis on the social development of children' (Board of Education, 1937). In the post-war era, the introduction to the London School Plan 1947 (which followed the Education Act 1944) stressed that 'It is now the duty of authorities to establish equality of opportunity for all children – a phrase that implies the provision for every pupil of a "place" in a school where his spiritual, physical, social and mental development can be properly nurtured' (London County Council, 1947, p. 7). Marland's account of the development of pastoral care from the fifties to the seventies is however a story of new comprehensive schools struggling to develop effective pastoral structures and where the House System (originating in private boarding schools where pupils lived in the same 'house' as a small group of other pupils under the personal care of a resident housemaster/mistress) failed to meet the needs of pupils in large, urban comprehensive day-schools, often becoming little more than a convenient way of organizing in-school sporting competitions.

It is far from clear when exactly the term 'pastoral care' was first used in relation to schools. Ribbins (1985) claims that it has been in use since the late 1940s; Armstrong (2008) dates its introduction to the 1950s; while Power (1996) suggests that it was as late as the 1960s or early 1970s before the term 'pastoral care' was consistently used, even though form groups and assemblies may have begun earlier. Calvert (2009) charts the evolution of pastoral care in schools over the past 50 years through 7 discernible 'ages': (i) *Pastoral Care as Disciplinary Control* characterized by hierarchical structures and a clear pastoral/academic dichotomy; (ii) *Pastoral Care as Individual Need* where ill-prepared Form Tutors were expected to offer a form of counselling, largely intended to bring the pupil's behaviour in line with the school's expectations; (iii) *Pastoral Care as Group Need* where Form Tutors were required, despite varying levels of skill and motivation, to meet individual needs through group activities delivered in short form periods at the start of the day; (iv) the *Development of the Pastoral Curriculum*, an ill-fated attempt to bring together all the school-based learning activities relating to personal and social development; (v) *Pastoral Care Post-implementation of the National Curriculum* when schools focused almost exclusively on a tightly prescribed range of subjects to be taught and assessed, and where non-statutory subjects had little or no value (vi) *Pastoral Care for Learning*, where a recognition emerged that higher grades could be achieved through the development of emotional intelligence and psychological well-being (vii) and finally, *Pastoral Care, the Wider Workforce and the Every Child Matters Agenda* (2003 to the present day) where there is greater diversity than ever before in England and Wales in the way in which schools organize their management structure, where year heads have often been replaced by learning managers and where there is more inter-agency working (with resulting differences of emphases) and greater dependence on paraprofessionals to perform tasks formerly associated with teachers such as in-class support, covering lessons, mentoring and careers guidance (see also Andrews, 2006; Edmond and Price, 2009). Calvert (2009, p. 276) concludes his account of the seven 'ages' by noting once again that 'clarity of what pastoral care means or might mean is long overdue'.

Since the introduction of the term 'pastoral care' in relation to schools there have been numerous attempts to define it. Among the earliest was Marland (1974, p. 8) who noted that pastoral care 'means looking after the total welfare of the pupil' and suggested that the broad area of pastoral care can be broken down into the following six separate but complementary aims:

i.   to assist the individual to enrich his *(sic)* personal life;
ii. to help prepare the young person for educational choice;
iii. to offer guidance or counselling, helping young people to make their own decisions – by question and focus, and by information where appropriate;
iv. to support the subject teaching;

v.   to assist the individual to develop his or her own lifestyle and to respect that of others;

vi. to maintain an orderly atmosphere in which all this is possible (Marland, 1974, p. 10).

Marland warned against any pastoral/academic split and concluded that schools must help the individual pupil to find meaning for their studies and their life. To achieve these goals, 'the central task of the school, its pastoral work, must be sensitive, warm, human, efficient, realistic and thorough' (1974, p. 12).

Four years later Hamblin's definition builds on this by highlighting the importance of pastoral care as an integral part of classroom teaching and by stressing the need for classroom 'modification' to support the particular learning needs of all pupils:

> Pastoral care is not something set apart from the daily work of the teacher. It is that element of the teaching process which centres around the personality of the pupil and the forces in his *(sic)* environment which either facilitate or impede the development of intellectual and social skills, and foster or retard emotional stability. The pastoral effort is also concerned with the modification of the learning environment, adapting it to meet the needs of individual pupils, so that every pupil has the maximum chance of success whatever his *(sic)* background or ability. (Hamblin, 1978, p. xv)

Hamblin continues that an effective pastoral care system is 'more than a device for providing emotional first-aid for adolescent tensions in a complex society, or a welfare activity for alleviating poor home conditions' (Hamblin, 1978, p. 1). Instead, Hamblin argues for a carefully planned integration of the pastoral and the curricular aspects of the school, suggesting that the 'failure' of the secondary school lies in poor teaching and inappropriate methods in the classroom, which in turn prohibits positive teacher–pupil relationships. Like Marland, Hamblin notes the irony that while arguing for pastoral-academic integration it is still necessary 'to isolate the pastoral task for the purposes of exposition' (Hamblin, 1978, p. xvi).

A comprehensive definition, the result of an inspection of pastoral care in 27 comprehensive schools by Her Majesty's Inspectorate, was provided by DES (1989) in which, rather than limiting the work to a designated team of pastoral specialists, the whole-school responsibility for pastoral care is made clear:

> Pastoral care is concerned with promoting pupils' personal and social development and fostering positive attitudes: through the quality of teaching and learning; through the nature of relationships amongst pupils, teachers and adults other than teachers; through arrangements for monitoring pupils' overall progress, academic, personal and social; through specific pastoral structures and support systems; and through extra-curricular activities and the school ethos. Pastoral care, accordingly, should help a school to achieve success. In such a context it offers support for the learning, behaviour and welfare of all pupils, and addresses the particular difficulties some individual pupils may be experiencing. (DES, 1989, p. 3)

More recently Best (1999a; 2002) provided a more specific model in which he outlined five objectives of pastoral care in schools: (i) reactive care where, for instance the Form Tutor responded to pupils' personal, social, emotional or behavioural difficulties; (ii) proactive care where teachers used form assemblies to educate and pre-empt some of the most commonly perceived difficulties through helping pupils to make wise choices; (iii) developmental care comprising the school's PSHE programmes; (iv) the promotion and maintenance of an orderly and supportive environment through a positive whole-school ethos; and (v) the management and administration of pastoral care through effective systems established to monitor and support individual pupils.

A further definition is provided by the Education and Training Inspectorate of Northern Ireland whose guidance on the evaluation of pastoral care notes that:

> Through its pastoral care arrangements and provision a school demonstrates its continuing concern for the personal and social development of all of its pupils, regardless of their age or ability, as individuals and as secure, successful and fully participating members of the school and its wider community. (ETI, 2008, p. 5)

Here there is a clear acknowledgement of the need to focus on pupils as individuals but there is also an inclusive concern that pupils should be fully participating within the school and wider community, irrespective of their age or (more importantly) their ability. Many would argue that there remains in schools an undue focus on attainment levels (league tables are still published annually in England though not in Wales, Northern Ireland and Scotland) and on *Pastoral Care for Learning* whose main purpose is to facilitate academic attainment, rather than purely pupil well-being.

Finally, most recently Carroll (2010) provides a definition which resists the temptation to list multiple aspects of provision but instead draws attention to the focus on individual need:

> One common element to many descriptions of pastoral care, whether in an educational context or otherwise, is that it is concerned with the welfare of the person as an individual. That is, there is an implicit recognition that each person is unique and that care, if it is to be pastoral, should thus recognise individual and not merely communal need. (Carroll, 2010, p. 147)

In relation to research in this field McLaughlin (2010, p. 257) comments on her period as Editor of the journal *Pastoral Care in Education* from 1999–2010 and notes that over this period there has been a 'shift in nomenclature' with the very terms 'pastoral' and 'care' being used less and less in the titles of published research articles. McLaughlin argues that this is due in part to the fact that, in many cultures, pastoral care is not linked to school systems of support and instead has predominantly 'religious overtones' (p. 257), and also due in part to international policy developments which have seen 'the rise of specialists as opposed to generalists' (p. 257) and emerging areas of focus such as mental health and emotional well-being. This has led to what McLaughlin refers to as the 'atomisation of the field' (p. 258) in relation to the research being reported in recent times (leading to greater focus and detail but less overview), and the regrettable situation where 'It is very hard to find a substantial text on pastoral care in education beyond 1990 as well as large-scale research on it' (p. 258).

Such a situation in which the very term pastoral care is less commonly used is regrettable. For instance it is not mentioned once in the Training and Development Agency for Schools' *Professional Standards for Teachers* (TDA, 2007) and while there is a page on the

Department for Education's website devoted to pastoral care, the content is minimal – for instance, among the ten resources, there is information about managing medicines, drug use and teenage relationship abuse, but nothing at all in relation to the many different strands normally associated with pastoral care and nothing concerning the still vital roles of Form Tutor, Head of Year or Head of Pastoral Care (DfE, 2012).

Notwithstanding the confusion regarding its precise definition, the near invisibility of the term 'pastoral care' in recent government policy and the atomization of its field of research, the term is still very commonly used and indeed broadly understood by many schools, teachers, pupils and parents. To talk of pupil health and well-being (e.g. TDA, 2007) is important but is limiting in its scope. It is therefore time to revive the usage of the term 'pastoral care', a term which has an enduring resonance with the perception of teaching as a fundamentally and unashamedly caring profession.

Pastoral care thus remains a vital element in the twenty-first-century school. Indeed it is more vital than ever, and so as Jones (2006, p. 66) makes clear, despite the 'ideological battle' between the pressure to raise standards of attainment and the responsibilities to meet the broader needs of young people, 'Pastoral staff should not feel guilty about having to justify the time spent on pastoral work in schools'. Pastoral care is a fundamental part of the ethos of any successful school; it is facilitated by the policies and procedures of the pastoral care system but, importantly, it is embodied above all in the person of the teacher whose *relationship* with an individual child or young person is at the core of the entire system, offering advice, support, guidance and reassurance on a daily basis, helping them make progress academically but also socially, providing the link between home and school, referring serious problems to experts who can help, and knowing and valuing the child or young person as an individual irrespective of background, age or ability. As one head teacher explained, 'It all comes down to relationships; if you get those right, all else follows. If you don't then you won't achieve very much of anything' (cited in Best, 1995, p. 5).

Case Study: What is Pastoral Care?

St. Colm's High School, a co-educational Catholic-maintained secondary school with around 650 pupils, is situated on the outskirts of Belfast in one of the most socially disadvantaged areas of the UK. Known as 'Twinbrook', the estate surrounding the school was built in the 1970s, rehousing many Catholic families intimidated out of their homes in the inner city at the height of the 'Troubles'. Although the 'Troubles' have since ended, Twinbrook remains an estate beset by significant social problems (including vestigial paramilitary influences) and a lack of employment opportunities. Over half of the pupils at St. Colm's High School receive Free School Meals and almost two-thirds are currently on the SEN register. Faced with such challenges and despite thwarted attempts to secure government funding for a much-needed new school building, the school is highly successful. In an inspection carried out in 2010 by the Education and Training Inspectorate for Northern Ireland (ETINI), St. Colm's was praised for 'the outstanding quality of pastoral care, guidance and support for all of the pupils' and 'the commitment and perseverance of the teachers and support staff who have developed exceptionally good working relationships with the pupils'. This is matched by staggering GCSE performance gains over the past decade: in 2010–11, 62 per cent of the pupils achieved five or more GCSEs (A*-C) compared to just 23 per cent in 1999–2000.

So what's the secret of St. Colm's success? Principal Imelda Jordan (who has taught at the school for 35 years) says it's simple: 'It's all about relationships here. It is not simply about policies, procedures and structures – people make the difference. Relationships need to be right at all levels: that's the starting point. Pastoral care is central to everything we do, but it can't be separated from the curriculum. It has to be symbiotic. For us, pastoral care is based on achievement, on our pupils getting real qualifications, because that's their only way out of the cycle of deprivation in this community. So pastoral care means having and instilling high expectations; giving our pupils a second and a third and a fourth chance; encouraging them to learn from their mistakes; and helping them achieve their full potential. It is threaded through absolutely everything we do and is integral to our Catholic ethos. Pastoral care is the real magic, the stardust in our school which turns eleven year olds – many with significant challenges – into confident, positive and achieving GCSE pupils.'

Questions

1. How important do you think positive relationships are to effective pastoral care in schools?
2. Do you agree that the curriculum and pastoral care should be 'symbiotic'?

The organization of pastoral care in schools

It is self-evident that schools must have a structure to make pastoral care a reality. Indeed for Marland, 'the school *is* its pastoral organization' (1974, p. 11), the implications of which are spelt out:

> Some schools seem to set up a 'pastoral system' within, or even, as it were, beside the main structure – rather like the plumbing in a building. This ultimately proves unsatisfactory, because it is not the main structure, and there is a 'dis-location' between the teaching and the caring. (1974, p. 11)

Similarly Best (1995) notes that for many teachers, pastoral care is more easily and more commonly identified with structures and roles rather than with its actual outworking through daily interactions and relationships which in turn are determined by attitudes and values. Clearly it is crucial that, while structures are important to facilitate the provision of pastoral care, they should neither come to represent that care nor to become so institutionalized that they become immutable.

Notwithstanding this caveat, there are five essential elements to the organization of pastoral care in schools: a pastoral ethos across the school, a pastoral care policy, effective systems, committed staff and support and training for pastoral teams:

(i) A *pastoral ethos* provides the foundation for all of the subsequent pastoral care work of a school. A school with a strong pastoral ethos has a distinctive atmosphere (almost tangible on arrival) characterized by positive relationships among all staff, all pupils and between staff and pupils, where pupils feel safe, secure and valued, and where parents have confidence in the pastoral arrangements.

(ii) All schools require a *pastoral care policy* which is comprehensive in its detail of the structure and procedures of pastoral care in the school, which has been developed through whole-school participation, which is widely distributed and consistently followed, and which is reviewed on a regular basis. The formulation of clear and understood procedures is core to the efficient management of the pastoral care.

(iii) Schools must ensure that there are *effective systems* in place to allow the needs of the children and young people to be met without undue delay. Roles must be clear; communication must be swift and unambiguous; and appropriate action must be taken promptly when necessary. In most schools a hierarchical model persists with a Vice-Principal or Head of Pastoral Care overseeing the work of Heads of House or Heads of Year who in turn supervise the work of a team of Form Tutors. The precise detail of the structure itself and the many variations of titles are less important than the degree to which staff and children are able to use the structures effectively.

(iv) *Committed staff* are required to embody the pastoral ethos of a school, and this begins with the head teacher whose ability to articulate a consistent and coherent pastoral ethos plays a vital role. In many schools there remain outdated models of pastoral care where all teachers are expected to lead a form group, irrespective of their commitment or suitability for this aspect of their role. Much damage can be done by such teachers, and it is much better to select and reward only those who are suitably motivated and competent for all roles within the system.

(v) *Support and training for pastoral teams* is an absolute necessity. As outlined below, the pastoral demands of the Form Tutor or Head of Year are great, and the range of issues to deal with increasingly diverse. The leadership of a school must therefore match its commitment to the pastoral care of its pupils with an acknowledgement that its pastoral staff will require continuing professional development and will themselves need structures established to care for the carers (see below).

The following sections outline the nature of the key roles within the pastoral system: the Form Tutor, the Head of Year and the Classroom Teacher.

The role of the Form Tutor

At the core of the pastoral system in post-primary schools stands the Form Tutor. Marland and Rogers describe the tutor as the champion of the student:

> The tutor is the heart of the school, the specialist whose specialism is bringing everything together, whose subject is the pupil herself, who struggles for the tutee's entitlement, and who enables the pupil to make best use of the school and develop her person. The tutor will be successful to the extent that he keeps this central vision in mind and builds out of it an over-arching pattern to which all the details relate. (Marland and Rogers, 1997, p. 12)

This seminal description of the role of the tutor gives the role of the Form Tutor an elevated status which, many would argue, is belied by the lack of emphasis given to the role in Initial Teacher Education, the lack of opportunities for Continuing Professional Development, the lack of recent guidance on this role and the lack of recognition of the importance by schools themselves or by government (see Carnell and Lodge, 2002; Marland, 2002). Indeed Marland provides a damning account of the development of the role of the tutor from its roots in the role of the public school boarding housemaster (residential, small groups, individual attention, vertical family structure) through to its modern-day administrative role. Marland (1974) defines the polarity of the modern role where, at its best, the 'tutor ascendant' has full information about the pupils, feels a primary responsibility for the pupils' welfare and plays a major advisory role in educational and vocational decisions, liaising with parents, teachers and external agencies, but where, at its worst, the 'tutor subordinate' is reduced to merely marking the register and is neither privy to any other information about the pupil nor involved in any communication with parents or other teachers.

Despite Marland's claim that 'this first-level pastoral figure is arguably the most important person in the school' he bemoans the fact that detailed planning and focus for the role of tutor is too often 'left to chance or tradition' (1974, p. 74). More recently Marland and Rogers (2004, p. 3) note that, given the limited preparation for their role and its incessant demands, the tutor can become 'an overloaded functionary, reeling from problems and rarely in a position to look ahead'. Rather than purely reacting to events, Marland and Rogers argue that the role of tutor should also be about helping pupils to 'look to the future, both immediate and distant, and to take control of their inner, their social and their learning lives' (2004, p. 3).

The role of the modern-day tutor therefore should be more proactive than reactive, should focus on the pupil as an individual ('whose subject is the pupil herself') and should aim to support that individual child in whatever way necessary to facilitate their well-being and their learning. Being a Form Tutor is not the same as being a social worker, however, even though the range of problems facing pupils (which Form Tutors will thus encounter) is equally broad. As Rosenblatt (2002, p. 22) explains, 'the key difference between social work and tutoring is that the latter recognizes how the problem impacts on the students' education and helps establish conditions for learning'. If it can be assumed, therefore, that the aim of the tutor is to support the individual child in such a way that they are able to participate fully in their education, then Rosenblatt argues that tutors need to receive more targeted staff development, be given more time to work with their tutees (and fewer administrative tasks), and be encouraged to evaluate their own work while sharing their best practice with colleagues.

In seeking to understand better the role of the modern Form Tutor, five experienced Form Tutors were approached and asked first what their role entails. Their responses highlight the sheer breadth of the role of the Form Tutor whose duties were judged to fall into five main categories: *administrative tasks* such as marking the register and collecting permission slips and/or money for trips; *rule enforcement* such as addressing absenteeism, poor behaviour or carrying out checks on school uniform; *collating information* such as reports on behaviour or academic progress from class teachers or work for a pupil who is off sick for a short period; *listening to pupils' concerns* when they come forward with questions or issues relating to their home or school life; and *liaising with parents and other teachers* in relation to personal circumstances (e.g. parental separation) or problems they are encountering with their learning.

When asked what skills were needed to be a good Form Tutor, the most commonly cited responses reflected the diversity of tasks associated with the post: there was a need to be organized and to know the school's policies and procedures (to accomplish the administrative elements) but also to be approachable and a good listener, to be patient, caring and understanding and, importantly, to have high expectations of your tutor group. As one Form Tutor explained:

> I personally feel that encouragement is one of the most important aspects of being a form tutor – praising the pupils when they have achieved something. This may be something relatively small such as remembering all their books that day. Whatever it might be, pupils thrive on praise and encouragement. I often tell my form class just how proud I am of them and they love to feel valued.

The tutors were then asked what they found most challenging about their role. One of the main challenges to emerge was the lack of time with the tutor group itself (to develop relationships and to discuss issues) and also the lack of time (and energy) to follow up properly with parents, teachers and the pupils themselves. Many of the tutors spoke of the challenge of getting to know a whole class and of the danger that their attention would be focused predominantly on the most vocal or troublesome. Another tutor spoke of the challenge of dealing with more serious pastoral issues despite limited professional development:

> Whether it is parents or siblings or living conditions or eating disorders or self-harm or depression, the home and personal life of the pupils makes a big difference to their attitude towards school and to their readiness to learn. And it is very difficult not to become emotionally invested in the lives of your form class if you are a good form tutor. Dealing with those parents or personal issues can be stressful and despite your best efforts, you can often feel helpless.

However, despite these challenges, each of the tutors spoke of the many satisfying aspects of their role. These include being able to provide support for a pupil who is experiencing a serious problem and seeing the positive impact this can have on a pupil's well-being; working alongside parents; seeing the form group grow from shy 11-year-olds to confident, mature 16-year-olds; getting to know a group of pupils as individuals and also letting the pupils get to know 'the human side' of the tutor. One tutor referred to the role as being like a parent. Several of the tutors also spoke of the 'privilege' of the role, as the following comment illustrates:

> For me it's about the trust that is built up between a form tutor and their form class. Being a pupil's first port of call is a wonderful position. It is a real privilege that pupils in your form class come to you if they are worried, excited, stressed or happy and want to share their emotions with you. Frequently they share with you the happiest and the saddest times in their life – what a responsibility, but also what a pleasure!

Case Study: Introducing a Vertical Tutor System

The following case study shows how one school has recently introduced a vertical tutor system with very encouraging initial results:

Glengormley High School (an ICT specialist academy) is a large, mixed, all-ability post-primary school on the outskirts of Belfast with 950 pupils including 250 in the sixth form. In September 2010 a vertical tutor system was introduced

⇨

throughout the entire school. Unique in Northern Ireland, the system comprises five Pastoral Learning Groups (each with its own Pastoral Learning Leader), sub-divided into eight form groups (each with a Form Tutor). Each form group (of 25 pupils) includes three or four pupils from each year group within the school but is also mixed in terms of gender and academic ability. In addition, siblings are customarily placed within the same form group, and efforts are made to ensure that Year 8 (English Year 7) pupils entering the school for the first time have at least one other pupil from the same feeder primary school in their form group. Form groups meet every morning for 15 minutes with one day set aside for a meeting of the entire Pastoral Learning Group.

Although the creation of five large groupings within the school bears an initial resemblance to a traditional House system, the choice of the title Pastoral Learning Groups was a deliberate attempt to focus attention on the two complementary aims of the system: pastoral care and pupil learning (and away from the devalued notion of Houses devoted purely to sporting competitions). Pastoral Vice-Principal, Colin Millar, explains that in the two years since the inception of the vertical tutor system there have already been many discernible benefits: 'The vertical tutor system helps all pupils to develop a whole-school identity and facilitates the creation of friendships across traditional year group divisions. While some schools have to artificially create opportunities for year groups to meet to facilitate buddy systems or peer mentoring schemes, in Glengormley High School peer mentoring is an inherent part of the pastoral structure.' The system has also led to a significant reduction in bullying between year groups as older pupils develop a greater affinity with their younger counterparts and build natural friendships, and as younger pupils entering the school for the first time grow more quickly in confidence. For staff too, the vertical tutor system allows them to gain a greater understanding of the pastoral and learning needs of pupils of all ages, rather than being limited to a particular year group.

The new system has already been extensively evaluated and the results are very encouraging: at the end of the first year 77 per cent of the pupils and 94 per cent of the teaching staff preferred the new system to the previous year group model. There are of course challenges associated with a vertical tutor system, not least in terms of the preparation of activities for integrated tutor groups, but it is clear that this highly innovative development of a vertical tutor system at Glengormley High School has breathed new life into a tried and tested pastoral model.

Questions

1. What do you see as the main advantages and disadvantages of the vertical tutor group structure?
2. How important do you think it is to evaluate the effectiveness of pastoral structures?

The role of the Head of Year

The position of Head of Year has been described as representing 'the hardest position in the middle management of secondary schools' and as constituting 'the engine room of a school' (Carline, 2007, p. xii). However the role has developed significantly over the past two decades, with the very title of Head of Year (or Year Head) often being super-seded in the 1990s by terms such as Year Curriculum Coordinator, Progress Manager or Director of Learning (Lodge, 1999, 2006; Nathan, 2011).

Where once there was a very clear distinction in schools between the academic and pastoral development of pupils (see discussion above), the emergence of the new titles reflects a growing appreciation of the necessary interdependence of the two overlapping dimensions, and an acknowledgement of the role of schools in promoting and facilitating learning. Lodge (1999) notes that this shift in emphasis was broadly wel-comed by pastoral post holders, who had hitherto struggled with the 'discipline fixation' of their roles, the 'watered-down welfare' that was being offered to a small number of problem families, the administra-tive overload created by schools using pastoral time to perform routine tasks and the lack of communication between the pastoral and academic teams.

Although this shift in emphasis has been widely reported (Lodge, 1999, 2006; Nathan, 2011), the extent to which schools across the UK and beyond have fully embraced the spirit of these changes is far from clear. While some schools have radically restructured their pastoral care sys-tems and redistributed burdensome administrative duties, Lodge (1999) herself admits that many schools have simply expanded the role of Head of Year to include the monitoring of curricular progress, thus adding additional activities onto an already over-stretched role. It is also clear that the structural divide between Heads of Department (with responsi-bility for academic progress) and Heads of Year (with pastoral responsi-bility) persists in many schools with continued confusion regarding the precise remit of each role. There is clearly a need for further research across the UK to assess the full picture and to discern the reality behind the rhetoric in terms of the burgeoning workload of pastoral team lead-ers (irrespective of their title).

It must also be acknowledged that even if the role of Head of Year has been reconceptualized in many schools to include the monitoring of overall learning progress and the addressing of the broader learning needs of pupils, there remains a need to balance that element of the role with the ever-present daily demands of leading a year group (and a team of tutors) with very real needs. This equates with Best's (1999) description of the enduring pastoral functions of schools and with Lodge's (2006) argument that the established functions served by Heads of Year address a persistent need in schools to support young people. Perhaps it also reflects the 'inherent conservatism' in the organizational structures of schools as institutions as well as the reluctance among more experienced staff to embrace significant change (Lodge, 1999). Carline (2007), for instance, a former Head of Year, lists the duties associated with the post of Head of Year and includes the need to have a watching brief over the academic progress of individual students and to have strategies in place for dealing with underachievement, to manage and review target-setting processes for the year group and to coordinate records of student academic performance. However these represent only three of the 24 duties listed for a Head of Year. The other perennial duties include overseeing the team of Form Tutors, liaising with parents and outside agencies, forming the link between Form Tutors and senior management, organizing year assemblies and PSHE resources and overall responsibility for behaviour in the year group. The variety of the role is considerable and the workload immense as Carline (2007, p. xii) describes, 'You will be doctor, disciplinarian and detective one day, you will be arbitrator, motivator and facilitator the next.' Although the varied demands of the role of Head of Year undoubtedly do help the incumbent develop useful skills ideal for progression to senior management (Carline, 2007, p. xiii), the risk of overload appears undeniable.

One of the key challenges identified in the role of Head of Year is leading a team of Form Tutors. Here it is clear that much depends on the particular members of the team and, in particular, on their level of experience, skill, prior training and, perhaps crucially, motivation to meet the demands of the role. Nathan (2011) acknowledges that the role of Form Tutor, for most members, is not the most important aspect of their jobs ('They regard it as an additional burden on an already pressurized workload' – p. 42) and notes that this can lead to a reluctance to commit the required level of energy to the role, as well as taking up a dispro-portionate amount of the Head of Year's time in 'getting these horses to water' (Nathan, 2011, p. 42). Carline bemoans this fact too:

> One very common issue you will have to deal with is that some teachers feel being a form tutor is an imposition. They believe they are paid to teach their subject specialism and they really haven't the time to bother with all of this pastoral nonsense. They weren't trained as form tutors and so why should they bother? This minority group is, perhaps, the most challenging of all tutors you are likely to meet. (Carline, 2007, p. 27)

This reluctance to engage must be addressed by the Head of Year; how-ever, their concerns must also be heard and relayed to senior manage-ment, for the reality remains that, in many cases, the untrained and unqualified Head of Year is responsible for the provision of pastoral care through their leadership of a team of similarly untrained and unqualified Form Tutors who often have many other competing demands on their time, who are generally not rewarded financially for their very signifi-cant endeavours, and who often have had no choice in their allocation to the role of Form Tutor. For there is a very obvious paradox in most post-primary schools that the preparation, resourcing, training, support and rewards for Form Tutor work are wholly inadequate. As Carline notes, the Head of Year is therefore charged with raising the morale of the team of Form Tutors and of boosting confidence for those (espe-cially less experienced) Form Tutors struggling with the demands of the role which is often ill-defined and for which they feel ill-prepared.

Being a successful Head of Year involves meeting the parallel demands of being an effective manager and leader. Nathan (2011) addresses the particular challenges and argues that both are essential elements of the role of Head of Year. Heads of Year need first to be effective manag-ers through the establishment of effective systems, structures and pro-cedures which enable the Form Tutors to know what to do and when. Meetings should be focused, purposeful and well chaired with no time wasted on irrelevant discussions. Tasks should be delegated fairly and appropriate support offered. Reporting systems (now usually electronic) should be used wherever possible to allow staff to access appropriate information quickly. The Head of Year must also monitor and evaluate regularly the work of the team of tutors to ensure that there is coherence across the year group. While 'good systems and structures rarely turn people on' (Nathan, 2011, p. 52) they represent the necessary foundation for effective pastoral work to take place. True commitment and motivation however comes from the second element: leadership. Given the reality of the low status role of the Form Tutor, there is a very real need for the Head of Year to define and articulate a positive vision for the pastoral work and to demonstrate a blend of energy, enthusiasm and commitment while remaining realistic about expectations from team members.

The role of Head of Year has undoubtedly changed and will continue to change with a sharper emphasis on monitoring and improving pupil attainment, a growing number of non-teaching staff now in such positions and the development of closer links between schools and outside agencies following the Every Child Matters suite of policy initiatives (Lodge, 2006). However despite a raft of contextual changes throughout the UK, the need for this middle management post remains undiminished.

Research Example: Towards a De-professionalization of Pastoral Care in Schools?

In this article Edmond and Price (2009) report the enormous growth in the number of support staff employed in schools in England and Wales over the past 40 years but, in particular, provide a critique of the model of professionalization of staff contributing to pastoral care over the past decade.

In recent years the role of Teaching Assistant has developed to include more pedagogical functions (teaching individual children, small groups and at times whole classes) but a number of new roles have also emerged which encompass specific pastoral functions such as 'Learning Mentors' (often working with the most disadvantaged pupils) or 'Parent Support Advisors' (supporting struggling parents in engaging with their child's learning and development). Edmond and Price report that there is however no national requirement for support staff to have a qualification and that, consequently, there is a lack of training and preparation for these key roles. The consequences of these changes are significant in terms of the undesirable dis-integration of the academic and the pastoral, the resulting marginalization of the pastoral, and the status differential between teaching staff and non-teaching staff in pastoral roles, which reduces the likelihood of inter-professional dialogue and joint decision-making.

Despite the government's avowed intention of providing more care and support for pupils through the expansion of the school workforce, this article exposes the 'de-professionalization' of the pastoral care function, as teachers concentrate on teaching and learning and as responsibility for pastoral care is increasingly delegated onto a body of non-teaching staff for whom there are still no qualification requirements. Edmond and Price conclude that although there are many committed non-teaching individuals working in these pastoral roles who are making a positive impact on children and their families, there is a need to reverse the perceived segmentation and marginalization of pastoral care in schools, and an accompanying need to empower non-teaching pastoral care workers through quality professional development and supervision within integrated professional teams.

Reference

Edmond, N. and Price, M. (2009), 'Workforce re-modelling and pastoral care in schools: A diversification of roles or a de-professionalisation of functions?' *Pastoral Care in Education*, 27(4): 301–11.

The role of the Classroom Teacher

As McGuiness (1989) makes clear, there is no 'opting out' of the pastoral dimension in the role of the teacher. Much earlier Marland (1974, p. 8) had noted that 'All pastoral care has a teaching element, and the converse is equally true: you cannot "teach" at all effectively without establishing some form of relationship. The pedagogic concern inevitably has a personal element'.

To suggest that pastoral care is restricted to Form Tutors or Heads of Year would be to deny the value of the role of the classroom subject teacher, because every teacher, including those without a named role within a defined pastoral system, has a duty of care towards the pupils in their class and a responsibility to meet basic standards in relation to the health and well-being of the pupils (see Chapter 2 in this volume). These standards are outlined in the Training and Development Agency for Schools' *(Core) Professional Standards for Teachers* (TDA, 2007) and state that a teacher should:

- Know the current legal requirements, national policies and guidance on the safeguarding and promotion of the well-being of children and young people. (Competence 22)

- Know the local arrangements concerning the safeguarding of children and young people. (Competence 23)
- Know how to identify potential child abuse or neglect and follow safeguarding procedures. (Competence 24)
- Know how to identify and support children and young people whose progress, development or well-being is affected by changes or difficulties in their personal circumstances, and when to refer them to colleagues for specialist support. (Competence 25)

These standards are of course valuable but it is clear that they fall far short of encompassing the breadth or depth of what is meant by the term pastoral care as it relates to the classroom teacher. There is undoubtedly much more to pastoral care than purely safeguarding procedures and more to be done than simply reacting to 'changes or difficulties in their personal circumstances'.

Much has been written about the setting of targets and the raising of standards in schools in the UK over the past two decades. The TDA's (Core) *Professional Standards for Teachers* (TDA, 2007) states that teachers should have a commitment 'to establishing fair, respectful, trusting, supportive and constructive relationships' with children and young people, but apart from this, there has been little written about the need for teachers to relate to the individual child, to develop a positive professional rapport and to display an emotional warmth in daily interactions. These are however central to the work of any successful teacher and go hand in hand with the more instrumental aspects of the teacher's role in curriculum delivery and in the raising of academic standards.

Moreover, a subject teacher who has a genuine concern for the well-being of pupils will marry their ability to relate effectively to their class with a conscientious and sustained desire to prepare appropriate, well-resourced, confidently delivered and rigorously evaluated lessons. Ill-prepared teaching by poorly motivated, unenthusiastic and distant teachers is the very antithesis of good pastoral care. It is clear therefore that for *every* classroom teacher, pastoral care is embodied first and foremost in the quality of their teaching on a day by day, lesson by lesson basis. For as Hall (1998, p. 57) outlines, there is a very clear association between progress in pupil learning and teacher–pupil relationships:

> The pastoral dimension of the teaching role is enacted on a day-to-day basis through the delivery of the curriculum, as well as in the more

subtle but pervasive sense of the quality of the interpersonal relationships between teachers and students. The quality of those relationships is inextricably linked, both positively and negatively, to the learning outcomes in the classroom. (Hall, 1998, p. 57)

Therefore the classroom teacher plays a vital role in helping create and maintain the pastoral ethos of a school through the quality of their teaching, the quality of their relationships and their knowledge of pastoral procedures within the school, so that every pupil can feel valued, respected and safe in any classroom environment and so that any serious pastoral concerns can be passed on swiftly to those who do have a more explicit and clearly defined pastoral responsibility.

Care for the pastoral carers

As long ago as 1985 Lawley highlighted the importance of providing effective pastoral care for teachers. Lawley noted that 'the pastoral care of teachers is a rarely considered notion' (p. 202) and added that there was a fundamental contradiction between the actions of a school which cared deeply about its pupils but neglected the needs of its teachers. To remedy the situation Lawley proposed a model of staff pastoral groupings, shadowing the pastoral groupings of the tutor group structure, so that teachers would meet in groups of around ten to help staff deal more effectively with 'potentially volatile incidents' in the classroom but also to offer targeted support for new teachers. Responsibility for the provision of these care structures for teachers would thus lie with middle management (for instance, the Head of Year). In his response to Lawley's proposal, Dunham (1987) rejected the suggestion that this should be purely the responsibility of the already stretched middle management of schools, suggesting instead that the work be multi-dimensional and shared by everyone. Dunham also surveyed 52 teachers on their pressures and coping strategies. The results showed a group of pastoral teachers who were heavily burdened and over-stretched, who were doing their best to implement effective coping strategies but who at times also experienced physical and emotional symptoms of stress. Crucially, the three main recommendations made by the pastoral teachers a quarter of a century ago were to be given more time to complete their pastoral work properly, more training and more support. It is hard to imagine any different recommendations emerging today.

It is important to acknowledge the particular challenge for the pastoral teacher who through their work is listening to and dealing with accounts by pupils of, at times, highly traumatic experiences (such as self-harming or sexual abuse). Griffiths and Sherman (1991, p. 141) highlight the emotional impact which this has on pastoral teachers: 'To listen to such a story is harrowing; it churns the emotions; it hurts. It produces feelings of rage and frustration.' They further note it is not just the tutor who needs support professionally, 'but the "person" – sensitive and vulnerable to stress – behind the role' (p. 141). Hall (1998) recounts her own experience as a newly appointed Head of Year dealing with a Year 7 girl in an abusive home. Feelings of despair, uselessness, sadness, depression and incompetence in dealing with the girl's chaotic home life were compounded by pressures from other teachers to ensure that homeworks were being handed in on time and by self-imposed pressures to be seen by colleagues to be resolving the highly complex problem.

However, all too often, there remains in schools a perception that a teacher who asks for help and support is a failing teacher. Nothing could be further from the truth. As the stigma associated with mental health gradually dissipates, so too teachers should be provided with appropriate support structures and should in no way feel embarrassed about availing of that support whenever necessary. Griffiths and Sherman (1991) and Hall (1998) note many different models of support including co-tutoring, more thorough induction processes, supportive supervision, mentoring, buddy systems and, finally, taking the time to exercise and eat healthily. More recently Carroll (2010) suggests that Local Education Authorities (LEAs) might be best placed to appoint officers with pastoral responsibility for the pastoral care of teachers who could develop programmes within schools and facilitate the sharing of best practice between different schools. However in today's climate of financial austerity, it is hard to see this worthy idea becoming a reality. A number of LEAs now also offer their employees access to free, confidential counselling services accessed by telephone. Clearly there is a need for further, large-scale research into the pastoral care of teachers and into the effectiveness of various models of support, both in-school support methods and external solutions. Only then will we move from the current piecemeal provision to properly address this very real issue.

Summary

This chapter has explored:

- The origins of the use of the term pastoral care in education
- A range of significant definitions of pastoral care in education
- The organization and structural systems of pastoral care in schools
- The challenges and opportunities associated with the role of the Form Tutor in secondary schools
- The demands of the role of the Head of Year as a pastoral team leader
- The role of the Classroom Teacher in promoting pastoral care through the delivery of the curriculum and also by establishing positive classroom relationships
- The importance of considering the pastoral care of teachers themselves, so that those on the front line of pastoral care are themselves supported in their work.

Annotated further reading

Carline, B. (2007), *How to be a Successful Head of Year*. London: Continuum.

This is a very accessible account of the challenges and opportunities of being a Head of Year written by a teacher with over 30 years' experience. The book addresses many of the key aspects of the role including leading the year group, managing a team of tutors, working with parents and dealing with common pastoral problems.

Marland, M. and Rogers, R. (2004), *How to be a Successful Form Tutor*. London: Continuum.

The authors provide a very realistic guide to the vital role of the Form Tutor, replete with practical suggestions from the authors' own extensive experience of pastoral care in schools. The book gives advice on tutorial activities, relating to families, working with others within the school and looks at the role and style of the Form Tutor in the secondary school.

Nathan, M. (2011), *A Pastoral Leader's Handbook – Strategies for Success in the Secondary School*. London: Continuum.

In this comprehensive publication, Nathan sets out the roles and responsibilities of the modern pastoral leader, offering advice and guidance on becoming more effective in their role, getting the best out of their tutor team, working with external agencies and handling difficult or hard-to-reach parents.

Useful website

www.napce.org.uk

This is the website of the National Association for Pastoral Care in Education (NAPCE). NAPCE aims to support and inform those who have a professional concern for pastoral care; to promote the theoretical study of pastoral care in education; to disseminate good practice in pastoral care in education; to promote the education, training and development of those engaged in pastoral care; and to liaise with other organizations who have similar objectives. NAPCE operates through its journal *Pastoral Care in Education* and an annual conference.

References

Andrews, D. (2006), 'Non-teachers' moving into roles traditionally undertaken by teachers: Benefits and challenges – for whom?' *Pastoral Care in Education*, 24(3): 28–31.

Armstrong, A. C. (2008), 'Pastoral Care', in G. Crook (ed.), *Routledge International Encyclopaedia of Education*. London: Routledge, pp. 428–9.

Best, R. (1995), 'Concepts in Pastoral Care and PSE', in R. Best, P. Lang, C. Lodge and C. Watkins (eds), *Pastoral Care and Personal-Social Education – Entitlement and Provision*. London: Cassell.

— (1999a), 'Pastoral Care and the Millenium', in U. Collins and J. McNiff (eds), *Rethinking Pastoral Care*. London: Routledge.

— (1999), 'The impact of a decade of educational change on pastoral care and PSE: A survey of teacher perceptions'. *Pastoral Care in Education*, 17(2): 3–13.

— (2002), *Pastoral Care and Personal-social Education*. Southell, Notts: BERA.

Board of Education (1937), *Handbook of Suggestions for the Consideration of Teachers and Others Concerned in the Work of Public Elementary Schools*. London: HMSO.

Calvert, M. (2009), 'From pastoral care to care: Meanings and practices'. *Pastoral Care in Education*, 27(4): 267–77.

Carline, B. (2007), *How to be a Successful Head of Year*. London: Continuum.

Carnell, E. and Lodge, C. (2002), 'Support for students' learning: What the Form Tutor can do'. *Pastoral Care in Education*, 20(4): 12–20.

Carroll, M. (2010), 'The practice of pastoral care of teachers: A summary analysis of published outlines'. *Pastoral Care in Education*, 28(2): 145–54.

Cunningham, P. (2002), 'Primary Education', in R. Aldrich (ed.), *A Century of Education*. London: Routledge Falmer, pp. 9–30.

Department for Education (2012), *Pastoral Care*. Available at www.education.gov.uk/schools/pupilsupport/pastoralcare.

Department of Education and Science (1989), *Pastoral Care in Secondary Schools: An Inspection of Some Aspects of Pastoral Care in 1987–88*. London: DES.

Dunham, J. (1987), 'Caring for the pastoral carers'. *Pastoral Care in Education*, 5(1): 15–21.

Edmond, N. and Price, M. (2009), 'Workforce re-modelling and pastoral care in schools: A diversification of roles or a de-professionalisation of functions?' *Pastoral Care in Education*, 27(4): 301–11.

Education and Training Inspectorate (2008), *Evaluating Pastoral Care*. Bangor: ETI.

Griffiths, P. and Sherman, K. (1991), *The Forum Tutor: New Approaches to Tutoring in the 1990s*. Oxford: Blackwell Education.

Hall, C. (1998), 'Fitness for Purpose: Self-Care and the Pastoral Tutor', in M. Calvert and J. Henderson (eds), *Managing Pastoral Care*. London: Cassell.

Hamblin, D. H. (1978), *The Teacher and Pastoral Care*. Oxford: Basil Blackwell.

Jones, P. (2006), 'Status of pastoral care in schools in the 21st century'. *Pastoral Care in Education*, 24(2): 64–6.

Lawley, P. (1985), 'The pastoral care of teachers'. *Pastoral Care in Education*, 3(3): 202–7.

Lodge, C. (1999), 'From Head of Year to Year Curriculum Coordinator and back again?' *Pastoral Care in Education*, 17(4): 11–16.

— (2006), 'Beyond the Head of Year'. *Pastoral Care in Education*, 24(1): 4–9.

Marland, M. (1974), *Pastoral Care (Organising the Care and Guidance of the Individual Pupil in a Comprehensive School)*. London: Heinemann Educational Books.

— (2002), 'From form teacher to tutor: The development from the fifties to the seventies'. *Pastoral Care in Education*, 20(4): 3–11.

Marland, M. and Rogers, R. (1997), *The Art of the Tutor: Developing your Role in the Secondary School*. London: Routledge Falmer.

— (2004), *How to be a Successful Form Tutor*. London: Continuum.

McGuinness, J. (1989), *A Whole-School Approach to Pastoral Care*. London: Kogan Page.

McLaughlin, C. (2010), 'Editorial reflections on the field and the journal'. *Pastoral Care in Education*, 28(4): 257–9.

Nathan, M. (2011), *A Pastoral Leader's Handbook – Strategies for Success in the Secondary School*. London: Continuum.

Power, S. (1996), *The Pastoral and the Academic: Conflict and Contradiction in the Curriculum*. London: Cassell.

Ribbins, P. (1985), 'Editorial: Three reasons for thinking more about schooling and welfare', in P. Ribbins (ed.), *Schooling and Welfare*. Lewes: Falmer Press.

Rosenblatt, M. (2002), 'Effective tutoring and school improvement'. *Pastoral Care in Education*, 20(4): 21–6.

Training and Development Agency for Schools (2007), *Professional Standards for Teachers*. Available online at www.tda.gov.uk/teacher/developing-career/professional-standards-guidance/~/media/resources/teacher/professional-standards/standards_a4.pdf.

2 Child Protection in Schools

Bronagh McKee

Introduction

This chapter is written from a children's rights perspective as enshrined in the *United Nations Convention on the Rights of the Child* [UNCRC] (UN, 1989), which enables it to be viewed in an international context. The chapter defines child protection as a distinct yet complementary pastoral care issue contained within the wider safeguarding remit of schools and explores the legal and policy context, what constitutes childhood maltreatment, the impact on pupils' learning and development and what teachers need to do if they are concerned about a child or young person. The chapter concludes by highlighting how schools can begin to address maltreatment proactively.

The legal and policy context

Child protection as a specific and separate aspect of pastoral care in post-primary education is not a new concept, but the relatively recent shift towards safeguarding and promoting children and young people's welfare has, on the one hand, contributed to professional understanding of child protection, and, on the other, added to the complexity of the issue. The legal and policy context is also somewhat confusing and can be ambiguous even to those most familiar with the legalities of child protection practice. For example, in the US, mandatory reporting of suspected maltreatment was first introduced in the 1960s and in less than one decade all states had passed child abuse reporting statutes (Rodriguez, 2002). After the Child Abuse Prevention and Treatment Act [CAPTA] of 1974, procedures for identification, reporting and intervention of maltreatment were clarified. This legislation is applicable to everyone who works with children and young people (Beyer, Higgins and Bromfield, 2005) and includes, among other professionals, school teachers and school counsellors. This legislation was amended by the CAPTA Reauthorization Act 2010, however states may choose to put forth an expanded definition of child abuse and neglect that builds on that provided by CAPTA, and implementation of the Act remains highly state specific. The Australian Commonwealth Government has responsibility for family support and parent and relationship education, as well as child maltreatment response contained within the Care and Protection of Children Act 2007 (Northern Territory Government, 2010). Established by State and Territory legislation and sourced in a common law duty of care, teachers now have a legal duty to report maltreatment in every Australian State and Territory. However, similar to CAPTA in the US, the *type* of abuse and *reason* for reporting still rests with individual States or Territories (Australian Institute of Health and Education [AIHE], 2011).

In the UK and Ireland there is no single piece of legislation concerning child protection, and no single suite of legislation covers all jurisdictions. The current legal child protection system is based on the Children Act 1989 (England and Wales); the Children (Northern Ireland) Order 1995 and Safeguarding Vulnerable Groups (Northern Ireland) Order 2007 (Northern Ireland); the Children (Scotland) Act 1995, the Protection of

Children (Scotland) Act 2003 and the Protection of Vulnerable Groups (Scotland) Act 2007 (Scotland); and the Child Care Act 2006 (Republic of Ireland). More recently, the Children Act 2004 (England and Wales) and the Safeguarding Board (Northern Ireland) Act 2011 (Northern Ireland) provide the legal framework for multi-agency safeguarding practice across all childcare services, including education.

This legal emphasis on protection and safeguarding also features prominently in international policy and practitioner guidance documents for example *A Canada Fit for Children* in Canada (Government of Canada, 2004); *Every Child Counts* (Ministry of Social Development, 2004) and *Safer Communities* (Ministry of Justice, 2004) in New Zealand; *National Safe Schools Framework* in Australia (Department for Education and Early Childhood Development, 2009); and *Breaking the Silence on Child Abuse* in the US (US Department of Health and Human Services, 2011). In England and Wales, the *Every Child Matters Outcomes Framework* (DCSF, 2008) and the *Working Together to Safeguard Children* (HM Government, 2010), in Scotland *Safe and Well* (Scottish Executive, 2005), in Northern Ireland, the *Ten Year Strategy for Children and Young People* (OFMDFM, 2006) and *Pastoral Care in Schools: Child Protection* (DENI, 1999), and in the Republic of Ireland the *Children First* (Department of Health and Children [DHC], 2011a) national guidance documents all require that teachers and schools can demonstrate that they are enabling children and young people to be safe from all forms of harm, from accidental injury and death, and that they have security, stability and are cared for.

While the legal and policy framework has become increasingly one of complex interconnections, the expectations of governments at a global level consistently place schools, in partnership with others, as a central agent for meeting the holistic needs of children and young people. As well as addressing educational achievement traditionally associated with the work of schools, teachers are now required to consider the safety and physical and psychological well-being of pupils.

Defining maltreatment

Internationally teachers have a legal and moral duty to protect pupils from physical, sexual and emotional abuse; physical, emotional, educational and medical neglect; bullying by an adult or peer – physically, verbally or emotionally; and to respond to the needs of pupils living with, or experiencing violence at home or in a relationship. Collectively, these forms of harm are known as maltreatment. A 'child', by international definition, is anyone up to and including 17 years (UN, 1989; World Health Organisation [WHO], 2006).

Child abuse and neglect

Since this is a very complex area of work, this section of the chapter can only provide an overview of the various types of harm. For detailed help and guidance about particular child protection issues, readers are advised to refer to related guidance applicable to their own area of work and their own national guidelines. All school personnel, including non-teaching staff, should be familiar with early indicators of maltreatment and, while the definitions provided below are presented separately, the national guidance outlined above is clear that a child or young person may be subjected to one or more forms of harm at any given time and that different children may react to different forms of harm in different ways (DHC, 2011b; OFMDFM, 2006). The first four definitions (physical abuse, emotional abuse, sexual abuse and neglect) are provided by HM Government (2010, pp. 38–9).

> **Physical Abuse** is any form of non-accidental injury or injury which results from wilful or neglectful failure to protect a child or young person. It may involve hitting, shaking, throwing, poisoning, burning or scalding, drowning, suffocating or otherwise causing physical harm to a child. Physical harm may also be caused when a parent or carer fabricates the symptoms of, or deliberately induces, illness in a child. A large number of children who experience physical abuse suffer both short and long-term consequences.
>
> **Emotional Abuse** is normally to be found in the relationship between an adult and a child or young person and is rarely manifested in terms of physical symptoms. It is defined as the persistent emotional maltreatment of a child such as to cause severe and persistent adverse effects on the child's emotional development. It may involve conveying to children that they are worthless or unloved, inadequate or valued only insofar as they meet the needs of another person. It may include not giving the child opportunities to express their views, deliberately silencing them or making

fun of what they say or how they communicate. It may feature age or developmentally inappropriate expectations being imposed on children. These may include interactions that are beyond the child's developmental capability, as well as overprotection and limitation of exploration and learning, or preventing the child participating in normal social interaction. It may involve seeing or hearing the ill-treatment of another. It may involve serious bullying (including cyberbullying), causing children frequently to feel frightened or in danger, or the exploitation or corruption of children. Some level of emotional abuse is involved in all types of maltreatment of a child, though it may occur alone.

Sexual Abuse involves forcing or enticing a child or young person to take part in sexual activities, not necessarily involving a high level of violence, whether or not the child is aware of what is happening. The activities may involve contact, including assault by penetration (e.g. rape or oral sex) or non-penetrative acts such as masturbation, kissing, rubbing and touching outside of clothing. Sexual abuse may also include non-contact activities, such as involving children in looking at, or in the production of, sexual images, watching sexual activities, encouraging children to behave in sexually inappropriate ways or grooming a child in preparation for abuse (including via the internet). Sexual abuse is not solely perpetrated by adult males. Women can also commit acts of sexual abuse, as can other children.

Neglect is the persistent failure to meet a child's basic physical and/ or psychological needs, likely to result in the serious impairment of the child's health or development. Neglect may occur during pregnancy as a result of maternal substance abuse. Once a child is born, neglect may involve a parent or carer failing to: provide adequate food, clothing and shelter (including exclusion from home or abandonment); protect a child from physical and emotional harm or danger; ensure adequate supervision (including the use of inadequate care-givers); or ensure access to appropriate medical care or treatment. It may also include neglect of, or unresponsiveness to, a child's basic emotional needs.

Bullying

Bullying is explored in more detail in Chapter 3 but from a child protection point of view, there is increasing recognition that bullying behaviour can be harmful to both the bully and the victim, and indeed the broadest definition of abuse in the educational context usually includes bullying (Ma, 2001). As well as the inclusion of bullying (including cyberbullying) within the emotional abuse definition provided above by HM Government (2010), the NSPCC (2009, p. 2) refers specifically to bullying in their national guidance on *Definitions and Signs of Child Abuse*, defining it as:

> . . . deliberately hurtful behaviour, usually repeated over a period of time, where it is difficult for those bullied to defend themselves. It may take many forms, but the three main types are physical (e.g. hitting, kicking, theft), verbal (e.g. racist or homophobic remarks, threats, name calling) and emotional (e.g. isolating an individual from the activities and social acceptance of their peer group).

Domestic violence

Internationally, research with a focus on 'child protection in education' has recently begun to include domestic violence as a child protection concern because of the developmental and psychological impact on children and young people (Lazenbatt, 2010; McKee and Holt, 2011). Furthermore, domestic violence has been strongly associated with children involved in the child protection system (Devaney, 2008), and further research has shown that children exposed to domestic violence are at increased risk of other forms of abuse and neglect (Holt et al., 2008). Like bullying, domestic violence is now included in most child protection guidance documents for schools for example HM Government (2010, p. 38), refers to 'seeing or hearing the ill-treatment of another' in the definition of emotional abuse and the Republic of Ireland's guidance *Child Protection in Post-Primary Schools* (DHC, 2011b, p. 38) includes 'living with or experiencing domestic violence' in their descriptors of child abuse and neglect.

Prevalence and impact

Like all research that involves statistics, a word of caution is required when considering prevalence (proportion of a defined population during a specified period of time) and incidence (number of new cases occurring in a defined population over a year) data related to child maltreatment. Studies of this kind can be problematic due to definitional complexities within and between countries and the different study methods employed. As awareness of this global problem grows, the incidence rate increases (Creighton, 2004); however, available international data are likely to be an underestimation of the true extent of the problem (Australian Institute of Health and Welfare [AIHW], 2011). A useful starting point for consideration is provided by the *UN Secretary General's Study on Violence Against Children* (World Health Organisation [WHO], 2006), one of the first comprehensive global studies on all forms of violence against children, which found that child maltreatment takes place in every country of the world, in every culture and ethnic group, whether families are educated or not, and whether they are rich or poor.

Physical abuse

According to the WHO (2006), an estimated 80 per cent of the world population experience physical abuse to some extent and at some point during childhood. Although the impact of childhood physical abuse on adult behaviours is controversial and often contradictory in terms of prevalence, persistent physical abuse during childhood can lead directly to neurological damage, physical injury, disability or, in the extreme, death (Laming, 2009). For example, of the 53,000 children who died during 2002 as a result of maltreatment, a large percentage experienced physical abuse (WHO, 2006). Other evidence suggests a link between childhood physical abuse and lifetime psychological distress (Hughes et al., 2007), and physically abused children can often have poor physical and intellectual development, and can display more difficult and aggressive behaviour, compared to their non-abused peers (Creighton, 2004). The physical abuse of children frequently coexists with domestic violence (HM Government, 2010).

Emotional abuse

Young people in school can show signs of emotional abuse by their behaviour (e.g. withdrawal or unexplained or unusual demands for attention, or avoidance of a family member); by their emotional state (e.g. low self-esteem or general unhappiness); or by their development (e.g. inability to concentrate on tasks). It has been proposed that emotionally abused children are significantly more likely to show attachment, emotional and/or behavioural problems (Lazenbatt, 2010), school-related problems in ability and academic achievement, and in comparison to demographically matched controls, have significantly lower levels of social competence and social adjustment (Perry and Hambrick, 2008).

Sexual abuse

Globally, approximately 150 million girls and 73 million boys experience sexual abuse at some point in childhood, nearly 2 million children are forced into prostitution and pornography and just over 1 million children are victims of trafficking annually (WHO, 2006). A theme that recurs in the research area of child sexual abuse has been a concern that exposure to this type of abuse has been associated with a number of short- and long-term consequences, including adult psychiatric and substance use disorders, increased sense of isolation, and increased levels of depression, social anxiety and personality disorders (Allnock, 2010; Gilbert et al., 2009). It may be expected that such difficulties with social functioning will be associated with disturbances in behaviour, in developing relationships in the school setting and in some aspects of academic learning (Cole et al., 2005).

Neglect

Neglect has consistently been shown to have higher incidence rates than all other types of harm (DHSSPS, 2010) and often results in more profound developmental deficits (Dubowitz, 2007). However, teachers' knowledge of the impact of neglect on learning may be restricted because it seems to be the least studied form of child abuse (McSherry, 2007). One of the main difficulties with substantiating neglect is that it is 'the absence of a desired set of conditions or behaviours, as opposed to the presence of an undesirable set of behaviours' (English et al., 2005, p. 191). Neglect is a likely consequence of parents not providing children with basic care but it is not restricted to young children (Cleaver et al., 2011). In a review of research by Stein et al. (2009), for example, there was evidence that neglect during adolescence was associated with poorer educational achievement, anti-social behaviour, bullying, poorer mental health and well-being, and risky health behaviours. Neglect has also been cited as one of the reasons for self-harm among young people, although it is important to recognize that self-harm is not usually triggered by one isolated event (Underwood, 2009). Like physical abuse, a significant number of child fatalities have been attributed to neglect (Parton and Frost, 2009). In many cases, professionals have failed to recognize the risk of neglect posed to pupils and despite increased awareness of the effects of neglect, early recognition and intervention is 'inconsistent and referrals to services are often triggered by other events or concerns about vulnerable children' (Daniel et al., 2009, p. 1).

Bullying

It is important that teachers are aware of their school's policy on how to deal with bullying and that for more serious incidents where the bullying behaviour is regarded as potentially abusive, the school should consult with external agencies with a view to drawing up an appropriate response. There is increasing recognition that victims of bullying can experience severe and long-term adversities, for example increased problems with social skills, lower self-esteem and higher emotional loneliness, lower academic achievement and feelings of being unsafe and, at worst, suicide (Marr and Field, 2001). It is also possible that pupils who bully can continue their behaviour into adulthood. For instance Save the Children (2006) suggests that schools should make a clear link between bullying and their child protection policy to help avoid future bullying or abusive behaviour in adulthood. In the most recent report for the UK, the UN Committee on the Rights of the Child [CRC] (CRC, 2008, p. 15) also raised concern that bullying remained prevalent and that it 'may hinder children's attendance at school and successful learning'. Solberg et al. (2007) warn that teachers who fail to recognize and respond to bullying early may subsequently fail some children and young people deemed to be at risk of other forms of abuse.

Domestic violence

US studies suggest that between 3.3 and 10 million children and young people experience domestic violence annually (Radford et al., 2011). In the UK, estimates of children and young people living with domestic violence range from 200,000 (Laming, 2009) to 400,000 (Radford et al., 2011), placing them at increased risk of physical injury (either by accident or because they attempt to intervene), distress at the physical and emotional suffering of a parent, and anxiety which may express itself in anti-social and criminal behaviour. Adolescents exposed to domestic violence may live in constant fear of violent arguments, being threatened, or actual violence towards a parent or themselves, impacting negatively on their emotional, behavioural and intellectual development. In some cases young people try to intervene to protect their abused parent and have been known to encourage parental separation in the hope that the violence will stop. However, separation is not a simple solution to this global concern. Three-quarters of domestic violence murder reviews involved separation and at least 29 children were killed in the last decade by their fathers post-separation (Saunders, 2004, cited in Cleaver et al., 2011). In such cases it is most likely that the teacher will be the first to observe the subsequent deterioration in performance and behaviour of a pupil living with domestic violence and, for some children, a safe and responsive environment such as school may help buffer the impact of violence in the home.

Despite the development of an international child protection system over the last few decades, the prevalence of child abuse and neglect, and family violence remains high. Enduring problems such as anxiety, relationship difficulties, low academic achievement and poor social skills are common long-term consequences of maltreatment. These problems are significant because they can interfere with academic, behavioural and social performance, and in many cases, complicate a pupil's reintegration into the school system following a child protection investigation. Although causal factors for such problems are difficult to determine and indeed it is beyond the scope of this chapter to discuss reasons and theories behind abuse in any depth, the definitions provided and the impact on pupils' learning and development merit on-going attention from researchers, school personnel and society at large.

Child protection as a safeguarding or pastoral care concern

In adopting the above definitions and understanding the impact of maltreatment on children, there are few who would deny that schools have a significant role to play in child protection, but there is also a need for teachers to understand its 'locality' within current pastoral care systems in schools as well as within a wider safeguarding agenda. It could be argued that most safeguarding practice for the past half century has been grounded in a paradigm that sees children as vulnerable and in need of protection, and views parents as either abusive or neglectful, or as protective and nurturing (Sidebotham and Appleton, 2012), an approach which usually focuses on the protection and provision rights of children as enshrined in the UNCRC (UN, 1989). While appropriate and helpful for effective protection of vulnerable children, the relatively recent shift towards safeguarding *all* children challenges these views and places greater emphasis on engagement with and involvement of parents and families in protecting their own children, on improving children's and young people's life experiences more generally and on prevention in particular.

Safeguarding is a broad term and is commonly held to be a more inclusive concept than that of child protection. It refers to the importance of acknowledging a child who may be in need and then providing appropriate intervention to mitigate a range of unfavourable outcomes. While terminology may vary between countries, there is international recognition that at the centre of safeguarding is pupils' well-being, demonstrating a link to, and overlaps in, the pastoral care role of schools. Guided by *A Canada Fit for Children*, professionals are expected to 'respect the rights and ensure the wellbeing of all children' in Canada (Government of Canada, 2004, p. 15) and a primary aim of *Every Child Counts* in New Zealand is that well-being is recognized as central to all policy for, and practice with, children and young people (Ministry of Social Development, 2004). Australian teachers, guided by the *National Safe Schools Framework,* are expected to enhance safety and students' well-being and, as part of a whole school approach, must focus on school values, ethos, structures and student welfare (Ministerial Council for Education, Early Childhood Development and Youth Affairs, 2011).

Direct links between safety (protection) and well-being also feature prominently in UK guidance for example *Every Child Matters* [ECM] (DfES, 2003), *Working Together to Safeguard Children* (DfES, 2006),

Ten Year Strategy for Children and Young People in Northern Ireland (OFMDFM, 2006) and a cross-departmental safeguarding statement on the *Protection of Children and Young People* (OFMDFM, 2009). This shift in thinking and practice is illustrated in revised national guidance for England and Wales (HM Government, 2010, p. 34) which includes four elements in the safeguarding definition to ensure professionals are:

- 'protecting children from maltreatment;
- preventing impairment of children's health or development;
- ensuring that children are growing up in circumstances consistent with the provision of safe and effective care; and
- undertaking their role to enable children to have optimum life chances and to enter adulthood successfully.'

The above definition demonstrates the range of activities and services encompassed within the term safeguarding but these can equally be linked to five pastoral care tasks previously described by Best (1999; 2002). The first task, described as the role of school staff when responding to children 'who present problems of a personal, social, emotional or behavioural kind' (Best, 1999, p. 19) is referred to as the Reactive pastoral care role. According to Best (1999), this tends to take place on a one-to-one basis and because it includes referring pupils to outside agencies, also involves child protection recognition and response. The second Proactive task involves activities of a preventative nature and focuses on 'the development of practical knowledge and coping skills' of pupils (Best, 1999, p. 19). The aim of this task is to pre-empt 'critical incidents' and is clearly linked to secondary prevention, but the extent to which this is achievable depends on the experience and preparation of school personnel.

This led to the third task, the Developmental Curriculum, where the aim is to promote the 'social, moral, spiritual and cultural development and wellbeing of children' (Best, 2002, p. 251) which, more recently, is referred to as Personal, Social, Health and Economic education [PSHE] or the social and emotional aspects of learning [SEAL] and can be delivered as part of the curriculum (DfES, 2005). In 2002 the Promotion and Maintenance of an orderly and supportive environment and the

Management and Administration of pastoral care were added (Best, 2002). The first of these is described as the 'supportive systems and positive relationships between all members, and the promotion of a pervasive ethos of mutual care and concern' (Best, 2007, p. 251) and the final task refers simply to the methods used to facilitate and achieve the first four tasks, illustrating the importance of a whole school approach. This model, proposed and developed by Best (1999, 2002, 2007), suggests that the delivery of pastoral care is underpinned by a genuine concern for the welfare and well-being of pupils. Equally, this genuine concern for the welfare and well-being of pupils is central to safeguarding practice in schools which, as already outlined, includes 'protecting children from maltreatment' (HM Government, 2010, p. 38).

Thus, while pastoral care has been core to the professional identify of teachers and a source of professional satisfaction for some time (Day et al., 2006), within a wider safeguarding remit teachers and other school personnel now have a legal responsibility to ensure that effective pastoral care includes recognizing and responding to child protection concerns, providing child protection education to pupils through the curriculum, and that such practice is supported by a whole school approach. It seems that teachers and schools can no longer 'choose' which aspects of pastoral care to provide. In order to meet the protection needs of pupils effectively, child protection professionals rely on others, such as teachers, who are in contact with more children for longer periods of time, allowing them to get to know their pupils and to recognize any changes in behaviour and appearance which might indicate maltreatment. There is no doubt that the renewed emphasis on early intervention and prevention is to be welcomed, but until it is valued by the wider education community (from pre-service preparation to practice) and formalized in all schools, teachers must be prepared for and understand two key elements of practice, recognition and response, to ensure the sharp focus on child protection is not lost within a wider safeguarding remit and that it remains a key component of pastoral care systems in schools.

Using a case study approach by way of illustration, readers are encouraged to reflect on these elements of practice in 'Sarah's Story' and to consider potential harm (recognition) and decisions to be made (response).

Case Study: Sarah's Story

Sarah was a bright yet reserved Year 10 pupil. She had not presented with any problems during the first three years of her post-primary education. The first indication that something might be wrong came through an essay written for an English homework in which she described a very emotionally charged and potentially worrying situation at home. She wrote that her dad had been violent towards her mum, that he had recently left the family home, and that her mum was taking it badly. From her account, Sarah's mum had been drinking quite heavily to cope, had threatened to kill herself and appeared to be relying on Sarah for support. The essay was well written, sounded genuine and seemed to fit in with recent changes – Sarah had lost weight recently and looked tired and pale, had become much more withdrawn and didn't seem to take part in any of her usual after-school activities. Other teachers had reported that Sarah had become quite 'sullen' and was known to be uncooperative in class. The English teacher decided to talk to Sarah about her essay and she admitted that everything she wrote was true and that the situation at home had deteriorated. Sarah told the teacher that she thought her mum was drinking because she was scared that her dad would come back for them but that her mum had refused to speak to anyone else about the situation. Sarah was very worried about the teacher talking to her mum because it would make the situation worse, her mum would lose trust in her and her mum might do something to harm herself.

Questions

1. Is this a child protection concern? Explain your answer.
2. What would you do in this situation?

Disclosure to teachers can be rare but when it does occur, for many, the first instinct is to reassure the child that everything will be alright. In the case outlined above, was the teacher in a position to do this? If they [the teacher] had, could it have had a detrimental impact on Sarah? The rationale behind developing child protection practice in schools (and other organizations) derives primarily from two themes which are well documented historically but have received renewed emphasis in recent times: public anxiety about the state's ability to guarantee the safety of all children; and the importance of enhancing childhood experiences to positively influence longer-term outcomes. Unfortunately, many teachers claim to feel ill-equipped to respond to child maltreatment disclosures and often express anxiety and concern about what to do, which makes it more difficult for them to positively influence longer-term outcomes. Additionally, because traditional notions of 'family' consider domestic violence to be a private matter, thus allowing it to evade scrutiny and intervention, teachers may be hesitant about involving themselves in such cases (Taylor and Lloyd, 2001).

The main difficulty for the teacher in Sarah's story lies in the interpretation of the situation and whether it constitutes 'maltreatment'. Teachers are not expected to make a 'diagnosis' of maltreatment or become involved in formal child protection investigations but they *are* expected to have a sound knowledge and understanding of definitions of harm, the impact of this harm on pupils, and what to do about it. In this situation and to understand and identify potential harm to a child or young person, the professional is advised to consider:

- The nature of harm in terms of maltreatment or failure to provide adequate care;
- The impact on the child's health and development;
- The child's development within the context of their family and wider environment;
- Any special needs, such as medical conditions, communication impairment or disability, that may affect the child's development and care within the family;
- The capacity of parents to meet adequately the child's needs; and
- The wider and environmental family context (HM Government, 2010, p. 37).

It must be pointed out that knowledge related to the above alone does not ensure that an appropriate report is made. Internationally, there is evidence that teacher, school, child (personality traits, resilience, age and development) and case (type, seriousness, duration and extent of harm) characteristics all have a role to play in terms of teachers' ability to recognize maltreatment and in their decisions to report it.

Teacher characteristics are more complex and warrant ongoing attention in research, pre-service preparation and practice. In New Zealand, for example, Rodriguez (2002) explored professionals' reporting decisions and found that personal and professional experiences, previous and current social interactions, and, in particular, attitudes about child and case characteristics may all contribute to whether teachers report abuse or not. In other words, when professionals perceived the abuse to be less serious, such as neglect, they were less likely to report it. Walsh

et al. (2006) found that in Australia, where reporting of abuse is mandatory, pre-service and in-service child protection preparation and educators' knowledge and understanding of the situation (e.g. type of abuse,
impact on the child, duration of harm, ability to recognize indicators
etc.) can all contribute to reporting. They add that gender, parental status, years of experience and previous reporting behaviour may also predict whether teachers will report abuse or not.

In a similar vein, Webster et al. (2005) involved 480 teachers in Ohio
to explore the relationship between recognition of abuse and subsequent
reporting behaviours and found that discrepancies between recognition
and reporting were related to case, teacher and school characteristics.
In terms of school characteristics, the authors found that rural schools
and those with a greater number of pupils were more likely to under-
report abuse compared to schools with a lower number of teachers. It
seems that management styles and supports available to staff, as well
as geographical location and size of school are contributing factors in
the reporting debate, highlighting the importance of a whole school
approach to child protection. Clearly professional understanding must
go beyond informing teachers of their legal duty to report maltreatment
and providing them with a helpline to do so. Training and preparation,
for example, must help teachers to look at themselves as the first line of
defence against child maltreatment, how to recognize the early indicators of maltreatment, and ways to avoid external issues, such as those
outlined above, which might impact on decisions not to report abuse.
If teachers overlook recognized abuse and fail to report it to the appropriate agencies, they run the risk of leaving vulnerable pupils without
protection and, in some international communities, are themselves
accountable by law (Laskey, 2008).

Case Study: Sarah's Story Develops

The teacher informed the Designated Teacher (DT) who decided that Sarah and
her mum should be invited into the school to talk to them about the content of
the essay. When the DT informed Sarah of this decision, she started to cry and
said that some of the things in her essay were untrue. During the conversation,
she admitted that her mum and dad still lived together at home but that her
dad had recently had an affair and that it was for this reason that her mum was

⇨

drinking heavily and finding it hard to cope. She pleaded with the DT not to arrange the meeting because she knew her mum would be very embarrassed and probably very cross with Sarah for speaking out about the affair. Sarah also admitted that she had exaggerated how much her mum was drinking and that she was very sorry to have caused any concern. Over the next few weeks, Sarah's character and behaviour changed. A number of teachers reported that she had been hostile to them and to her peers during class, and that on one occasion she had been aggressive towards a younger child in the school. The DT asked Sarah if she wanted to talk about it and during the course of the conversation Sarah stated that she could not cope any longer, that she did not wish to go home and that she was very worried about her mum's drinking.

Questions

1. Did the DT make the correct decision to listen to Sarah and allow her (Sarah) to contribute to 'decisions made' regarding the meeting?
2. How important was it for other teachers to record their concerns based on observations of Sarah's behaviour?

In this situation, the DT listened to Sarah and initially allowed Sarah to contribute to decisions made regarding the meeting between school and home. But these decisions cannot, and indeed morally and legally, must not be made lightly. The requirements of Article 12 of the UNCRC (UN, 1989) in relation to participation and the voice of the child are particularly relevant in this debate. Teachers must be able to achieve a balance between a child's right to participate in decisions that might impact on their lives and the child's right to protection which, for obvious reasons, they may not be able to achieve themselves. The Munro Report (2011) refers also to the centrality of forming relationships with children and families and recommends that children and young people's rights, wishes, feelings and experiences inform and shape the provision of service response. Teachers must remember that the 'client' of the school is the pupil and not the parent and even though parents have a right to be included in discussions about their child, this should only occur when it will not impact on the pupil's safety.

However, despite the legal and policy focus on child protection in schools, research shows continued barriers to effectiveness, including confusion and concern about information sharing and understanding legal responsibilities (HM Government, 2010). Some teachers also lack confidence in their ability to recognize an abusive situation and can be uncertain about the consequences for the child and family following a report (Webster et al., 2005). Others have found that teachers fail to report recognizable child maltreatment cases because of concerns about family disruption or retaliation and, in the extreme, lack of evidence (Kenny, 2001). These concerns about recognizing abuse and whether to report a concern were also identified among pre-service teachers (McKee and Dillenburger, 2009).

Understandably, decision-making is a difficult process, especially for those who feel they are not prepared for their extensive child protection role in schools, but it is for this very reason that teachers should receive pre-service child protection training and that procedures should be in place so that teachers receive the help they require to make decisions to forward concerns to appropriate agencies *without delay.*

Case Study: Sarah's Story Unfolds

The DT told Sarah that they were genuinely concerned about her situation and that the school would need to seek further advice from child and family social services. Although reluctant to involve others, Sarah agreed that this was the best course of action. The social worker recorded the information and advised the DT to invite Sarah and her parents into the school to discuss the concerns raised about Sarah's change in character and her sudden change in behaviour, as well as the content of the English essay. Sarah's dad was unable to attend the meeting due to work commitments but her mum agreed to attend. At the meeting, Sarah's mum seemed genuinely shocked and concerned about Sarah's situation in school and said that she had not noticed any changes in Sarah at home. Sarah's mum denied that her husband had had an affair and could not understand why Sarah would say such a thing as their relationship was very good. She admitted that she did take a few drinks with her evening meal but that Sarah was obviously exaggerating about the amount taken. It was agreed that all adults would continue to observe Sarah and that the school would offer her the use of the counselling services to commence immediately. During the first session of counselling, Sarah admitted that her dad had been sexually abusing her since she was 8 years old, that he had stopped abruptly 2 months ago, and that her main concern was that her dad would now start to abuse her younger sister who had recently turned 7.

⇨

> ## Questions
>
> 1. What might have happened if the school had not provided a counselling service for Sarah?
> 2. Why did it take Sarah so long to reveal the true nature of the situation?

Sexual abuse in children is probably one of the most difficult types of abuse to recognize, mainly because the young person will go to great lengths to keep the abuse hidden. It is also one aspect of child protection work which many teachers find particularly difficult to deal with. Skinner (1999), for example, interviewed 14 teachers to see how they coped with reporting child sexual abuse. Their responses detailed the complexities of dealing with the child and demonstrated the discrepancies between whatever training and preparation they had been given and the reality of the experiences the teachers had faced. All participants claimed to experience increased stress and highlighted the importance of support from the school and other external agencies. In particular, the most difficult issue to deal with was the direct disclosure of abuse.

As in the case of Sarah, some young people eventually find the courage to disclose sexual abuse to a trusted adult when their concern for a younger sibling becomes greater than the concern for themselves. Unfortunately the negative consequences of childhood maltreatment of any kind are often further exacerbated by children's and young people's reticence to report abusive experiences and seek help early (Allnock, 2010). Primary research with children and young people who have experienced maltreatment indicates a number of reasons why children and young people find it difficult to disclose their experiences, including concerns about being believed, and the stigma and consequences of telling. It is also significant and clearly of greater concern that sometimes children do not recognize that childhood maltreatment experiences are in fact abusive (Children's Commissioner for Wales, 2004). International research confirms that the reason for uncertainty about abuse during childhood is because children and young people are not usually taught the appropriate knowledge or skills necessary to protect themselves either in the home or in the school environment (Wurtele, 2009). There are, however, other opportunities for schools to ensure that young people feel confident enough to seek help through relationships with teachers and other support staff, preventative education taught through the curriculum and a positive whole school ethos which focuses on protecting and safeguarding all pupils.

Intervention and strategies

The Munro Report on Child Protection in the UK (Munro, 2011) contends that responsibility for the primary prevention of violence and harm against children and young people lies with, among other services, education. There is also international evidence that teachers are increasingly recognized as front-line practitioners with a tri-fold role to play in child protection: recognition, response and prevention. It is the third role, prevention, which this final part of the chapter explores.

School-based preventative education programmes are one of the most widely applied strategies and have been incorporated into the regular school curriculum across the globe. These programmes are generally designed to teach pupils how to recognize threatening situations and to provide them with the skills and knowledge to protect themselves from danger. More recently, as pastoral care and safeguarding have taken on a broader application to include prevention, there has been a growing emphasis on preventative education as a whole-school responsibility, which demands the involvement of all teachers, rather than just specialists. In complying with the health and welfare standards laid out by the UNCRC (UN, 1989) and the safety expectations of various international education policies (e.g. DEECD, 2009; DfES, 2003; Ministry of Justice, 2004; OFMDFM, 2006), schools are well placed to focus on primary prevention by offering children and young people a more detailed, structured education in staying safe.

However, primary prevention must work in tandem with other community and nationwide strategies to shift the attitudes and social norms that support violence and abuse, to promote non-violent norms, and to challenge the unequal and disrespectful relationships that are often the context for violence and abuse. School-based prevention programmes therefore must be centred on promoting respectful relationships characterized by non-violence, equality, mutual respect and trust.

In Australia, New Zealand, Canada, the US and the Republic of Ireland schools are required to provide a personal safety skills curriculum to all children from pre-school through to post-primary, although there are considerable differences in terminology. In the US, schools have been using the *Protective Behaviour* programmes for a number of years and recent evaluations show significant gains for pupils, teachers, parents and even communities. A similar approach is adopted in New Zealand where the *Keeping Ourselves Safe* programme is provided legal support to help schools fulfil their duty to teach children and young people how to keep safe (Russell, 2008). Using evidence from both programmes, the Republic of Ireland adopted the *Stay Safe* programme to use in schools from junior infants through to post-primary education. Evaluations of this approach also suggest significant gains, in particular in terms of teachers' response to disclosure but also in preventing abuse in the first place (MacIntyre et al., 2000). By infusing the post-primary curriculum with a greater understanding of the broad principles of parenting and the impact of maltreatment and other adversities on the developing child, schools can easily contribute to early intervention and prevention.

This point of view was also a central theme of the Allen Report (2010), a UK government-commissioned report to examine the role and importance of early intervention to make lasting improvements in the lives of children and young people. The Report identified a small number of specific and generic early intervention programmes guided by current government policy. While the overall approach is that the 0–3 age group is the primary target, the Report emphasized that *all* children from birth to 18 years should receive the knowledge and support that they require in order to be good parents and for post-primary pupils in particular to receive 'pre-parenting programmes' (Allen, 2010, p. 74), adding that:

> . . . there are also opportunities to help create excellent parents for future generations by continuing to build a social and emotional bedrock up to the age of 18 and by responding to . . . the first glimmer of anti-social behaviour in secondary schools or the first indicators of relationship problems in early adulthood. (Allen, 2010, p. 41)

National guidance (HM Government, 2010) also highlights the role schools can play in making children and young people aware of inappropriate behaviour towards them as well as how they can keep themselves safe. Pupils should be given information on:

- the availability of advice and support in their local area and online;
- recognizing and managing risks in difficult situations, including on the internet, and deciding how to respond to child protection concerns;
- judging what kind of physical contact is acceptable and unacceptable; and
- recognizing when pressure from others (including people they know) threatens their personal safety and wellbeing and developing effective ways of resisting pressure (HM Government, 2010, p. 79).

The Child Protection Support Services in Schools [CPSSS] and Department of Education [DE] also highlight that school policy across Northern Ireland should include evidence of the school's approach to the preventative curriculum and how 'safeguarding messages are actively promoted with children and young people within the curriculum and through other activities' (CPSSS and DE, 2010, p. 19).

Clearly the time demands on the school curriculum are increasing. In addition, there is growing recognition that child maltreatment prevention is too complex for schools, or any one sector, to manage alone. However, explicit education on non-violent conflict resolution, problem-solving and parenting techniques needs to be widely available to pupils for two main reasons: a reduction in corporal punishment and abuse; and the disruption of the intergenerational cycle of violence (pupils would acquire skills not involving violence). Such education could be incorporated into existing life-skills programmes in schools and school-based counselling services, indicating the ineffectiveness of corporal punishment and providing instruction in alternative positive parenting and relationships, as well as conflict resolution strategies.

Central to such education, regardless of what it is called, is the importance of relationships. This is particularly significant in child protection matters since a central characteristic of any abuse is the dominant position of the abuser and the abuse of trust, power and relationships. As Adams (2002, p. 177) explains:

The power of the adult is based first and foremost upon size and strength but it is also related to the authority over children which society gives to adults in general and to some adults – parents and teachers spring to mind – in particular.

Research Example: Implementing Relationships and Sexuality Education in Schools

In this study Mayock et al. (2007) set out to explore the barriers and facilitators to optimum implementation of Relationships and Sexuality Education (RSE) from the perspective of key stakeholders. Using a multi-method design, the study involved questionnaires to schools (n=187), interviews with Government officials (n=27), school case studies (n=9) using interviews and focus groups with staff, parents and pupils (n=164), and interviews with external facilitators (n=4). The study found widespread support for the principles and content of RSE from all participants: school staff and department officials felt it should be a compulsory requirement of all schools because young people find it difficult to talk to their parents about sex and relationships; parents wanted schools to address, not avoid, the real issues confronting young people; and young people recognized how RSE helped them to learn about and understand wider issues such as bullying, conflict and abusive or coercive relationships. However, the study also revealed potential barriers to success, including teacher characteristics (lack of preparation, training, confidence and positive attitudes), school characteristics (lack of a supportive whole-school environment, ethos and leadership), time constraints and lack of resources, and the need to consider the use of external facilitators for support. Since positive relationships are central to safeguarding and protection, addressing RSE effectively in schools will help pupils to develop the necessary skills, knowledge and understanding to keep themselves safe and prepared for the demands and challenges of adult and working life.

Reference

Mayock, P., Kitching, K. and Morgan, M. (2007), *Relationships and Sexuality Education (RSE) in the Context of Social, Personal and Health Education (SPHE)*. Dublin: Department of Education and Science, and Crisis Pregnancy Centre.

By virtue of their training and understanding of how children and young people learn and grow holistically, coupled with their unique position to develop relationships with pupils and subsequent ability to recognize changes in behaviour or learning over time, teachers have been involved in secondary prevention long before the relatively recent emphasis on primary prevention. The fact that schools have an important role in the primary prevention strand of child protection as a pastoral care responsibility is also without question, since preventative education aims to make 'children and young people aware of behaviour towards them that is not acceptable, and of how they can keep themselves safe' (DfES, 2006, pp. 67–8) while at the same time signposting sources of help and informing pupils that it is acceptable to talk about their problems to school staff (HM Government, 2010, p. 79). No other services or organizations can ensure that these messages are delivered to the whole child population, a fact which places teachers in a unique position to recognize and respond to child protection concerns but also to contribute proactively to prevention. Schools need to address aspects of maltreatment so that they can 'contribute through the curriculum by developing children's understanding, awareness and resilience' (DfES, 2006, p. 67). To narrowly focus on core curriculum content ignores the impact that maltreatment has on learning, behaviour and relationships within education.

Conclusion

Despite the increased focus on schools as agents for child protection and safeguarding, teachers admit to being confused as to what constitutes abuse, how to fulfil their safeguarding role and how to integrate preventative measures into the school curriculum. Additionally, it has also been suggested that the steady rise in abuse and violence against children and young people often goes unrecognized by teachers. Clearly school personnel have a significant role in child protection and safeguarding and those in charge of teacher education have important decisions to make about pre-service child protection preparation. Teachers can help all children and young people by creating a positive and supportive environment in school and can help to identify welfare concerns and indicators of maltreatment at an early stage, but it is important to remember that this relies heavily on the support of a whole-school approach as well as quality teaching *and* quality teachers. The precise form that a country's child protection and education system takes will vary according to context, needs and other factors, but common components include a legal and policy framework based on children's rights, early intervention and prevention and, probably above all else, a highly skilled and knowledgeable workforce. Staff in schools should not themselves investigate possible maltreatment; their key role is to refer child protection concerns, to contribute to an assessment of need where appropriate and to contribute to prevention positively and proactively. This will enable pupils to develop and leave school with the motivation and knowledge and skills to ensure they stay safe, keep healthy, enjoy and achieve and make a positive contribution to society. As such, pupils are more likely to enjoy economic and social well-being in the future.

Summary

This chapter has explored:

- the international legal and policy context for child protection.
- the definitions, prevalence and impact of maltreatment on children and young people.
- child protection as a safeguarding and pastoral care concern.
- preventative education as a proactive intervention strategy for schools.

Annotated further reading

Baginsky, M. (2008), *Safeguarding Children and Schools*. London: Jessica Kingsley Publishers.

This book is presented in three parts and explores Policy: context, role of outside agencies and a case study of an Integrated Community school in Scotland; Practice: looked after children, children with disabilities, harmful sexual behaviour, mental health and counselling services in schools and preventative education; and Training: a whole school approach to training, a case study from Australia and an overview of how every school matters in relation to safeguarding children.

Harries, J. (2006), *Promoting Personal Safety in PSHE*. London: Paul Chapman.

Developed in consultation with young people, this book is a resource for post-primary teachers on how to integrate keeping safe messages into the PSHE curriculum. Key issues include: emotional health and well-being; seeking help and support; and family, social and sexual relationships.

Raymond, A. (2009), *The Child Protection and Safeguarding Handbook for Schools: A Comprehensive Guide to Policy and Practice*. London: Optimus Education.

This is a useful tool-kit for teachers. It provides in-depth detail in relation to the context and impact of maltreatment, and practical responses in schools. Key issues include: the legal and policy framework, ethical considerations and child protection in practice; a practical approach to inter-agency working and shared responsibilities with partner agencies; incorporating preventative education into the school's curriculum with special attention to children with additional needs; inspection and self-evaluation; and staff support and training.

Useful websites

Child Welfare Information Gateway – www.childwelfare.gov/

A service of the US Department of Health and Human Services, this website provides comprehensive information, resources and research to help professionals (including education professionals) to protect children and young people and strengthen families.

NSPCC Inform – www.nspcc.org.uk/inform/

This is a separate section of the national NSPCC website which provides an excellent range of child protection and safeguarding related resources, literature, policy briefings and press releases, and will be useful to anyone working with children or young people.

References

Allen, G. (2010), *Early Intervention: The Next Steps*. London: HM Government.

Allnock, D. (2010), *Children and Young People Disclosing Sexual Abuse: An Introduction to the Research*. London: NSPCC.

Australian Institute of Health and Welfare [AIHW] (2011), *Child Protection Australia 2009–10*. Canberra: AIHW.

Best, R. (1999), 'The impact of a decade of educational change on pastoral care and PSE: A survey of teacher perceptions'. *Pastoral Care in Education*, 17(2): 3–13.

— (2002), *Pastoral Care and Personal-Social Education: A Review of UK Research Undertaken for the British Educational Research Association [BERA]*. London: BERA.

— (2007), 'The whole child matters: The challenges of "Every Child Matters" for pastoral care'. *Education 3–13*, 35(3): 249–50.

Beyer, L. R., Higgins, D. J. and Bromfield, L. M. (2005), *Understanding Organisational Risk Factors for Child Maltreatment: A Review of the Literature*. Australia: Institute of Family Studies.

Children's Commissioner for Wales (2004), *Clywch: Report of the Examination of the Children's Commissioner for Wales into Allegations of Child Sexual Abuse in a School Setting*. Swansea: Children's Commissioner for Wales.

Cleaver, H., Unell, I. and Aldgate, J. (2011) (2nd edition) *Children's Needs – Parenting Capacity. Child Abuse: Parental Mental Illness, Learning Disability, Substance Misuse, and Domestic Violence*. London: TSO.

Cole, S. F., Greenwald O'Brien, J., Gadd, G., Rustuccia, J., Wallace, L. and Gregory, M. (2005), *Helping Traumatized Children Learn: Supportive Schools Environments for Children Traumatized by Family Violence*. Boston, MA: Harvard Law School and Task Force on Children Affected by Domestic Violence.

Committee on the Rights of the Child [CRC] (2008), *Consideration of Reports Submitted by State Parties under Article 44 of the Convention: United Kingdom of Great Britain and Northern Ireland*. Geneva: UN.

CPSSS and DE (2010), *School Governors Handbook on Child Protection and Safeguarding*. Belfast: CPSSS and DE.

Creighton, S. J. (2004), *Prevalence and Incidence of Child Abuse: International Comparisons*. Leicester: NSPCC.

Daniel, B., Taylor, J. and Scott, J. (2009), *Noticing and Helping the Neglected Child Literature Review*. London: DCSF.

Day, C., Kington, A., Stobart, G. and Sammons, P. (2006), 'The personal and professional selves of teachers: Stable and unstable identities'. *British Educational Research Journal*, 32(4): 601–16.

Department for Children, Schools and Families [DCSF] (2008), *Every Child Matters Outcomes Framework*. London: DCSF.

Department for Education and Early Childhood Development (2009), *Respectful Relationships Education: Violence Prevention and Respectful Relationships Education in Victorian Secondary Schools*. Available online at eduweb.vic.gov.au/edulibrary/public/stuman/well-being/respectful_relationships/respectful-relationships.pdf.

Department for Education and Skills (DfES) (2003), *Every Child Matters*. London: DfES.

— (2005), *PSHE in Practice. Resource Pack for Teachers in Secondary Schools*. London: DfES.

— (2006), *Working Together to Safeguard Children*. London: DfES.

Department of Education Northern Ireland (1999), *Pastoral Care in Schools: Child Protection*. Belfast: DENI.

Department of Health and Children (2011a), *Children First: Guidelines for the Protection and Welfare of Children*. Dublin: DES.

— (2011b), *Child Protection Guidelines and Procedures for Post-Primary Schools*. Dublin: DES.

Department of Health, Social Services and Public Safety [DHSSPS] (2010), *Children Order Statistical Trends for Northern Ireland 2005/06 to 2010/11*. Belfast: DHSSPS.

Devaney, J. (2008), 'Inter-professional working in child protection with families with long-term and complex needs'. *Child Abuse Review*, 17(3): 242–61.

Dubowitz, J. (2007), 'Understanding and addressing the "neglect of neglect": Digging into the molehill'. *Child Abuse and Neglect: the International Journal*, 31(6): 603–6.

English, D. J., Thompson, R., Graham, J. C. and Briggs, E. C. (2005), 'Towards a definition of neglect in young children'. *Child Maltreatment*, 10(2): 190–206.

Gilbert, R., Spatz Widom, C., Browne, K., Fergusson, D., Webb, E. and Janson, S. (2009), 'Burden and consequences of child maltreatment in high-income countries'. *The Lancet*, 373: 68–81.

Government of Canada (2004), *A Canada Fit for Children*. Canada: Government of Canada.

HM Government (2010), *Working Together to Safeguard Children: A Guide to Inter-agency Working to Safeguard and Promote the Welfare of Children*. Norwich: The Stationary Office.

Holt, S., Buckley, S. and Whelan, S. (2008), 'The impact of exposure to domestic violence on children and young people: A review of the literature'. *Child Abuse and Neglect, the International Journal*, 33(7): 797–810.

Hughes, T. L., Johnson, T. P., Wilsnack, S. C. and Szalacha, L. A. (2007), 'Childhood risk factors for alcohol abuse and psychological distress among adult lesbians'. *Child Abuse and Neglect: The International Journal*, 31(7): 769–89.

Kenny, M. C. (2001), 'Child abuse reporting: Teachers' perceived deterrents'. *Child Abuse and Neglect: The International Journal*, 25(1): 81–92.

— (2004), 'Teachers attitudes toward and knowledge of child maltreatment'. *Child Abuse and Neglect*, 28(12): 1311–19.

Laming, Lord H. (2009), *The Protection of Children in England: A Progress Report*. London: TSO.

Laskey, L. (2008), 'Training to safeguard: Lessons from the Australian experience', in M. Baginsky (ed.), *Safeguarding Children and Schools*. London: Jessica Kingsley Publishers.

Lazenbatt, A. (2010), *The Impact of Abuse and Neglect on the Health and Mental Health of Children and Young People*. Belfast: NSPCC.

Ma, X. (2001), 'Bullying and being bullied: To what extent are bullies also victims?' *American Educational Research Journal*, 38(2): 351–70.

MacIntyre, D., Carr, A., Lawlor, M. and Flattery, M. (2000), 'Development of the Stay Safe Programme'. *Child Abuse Review*, 9: 200–16.

Marr, N. and Field, T. (2001), *Bullycide: Death at Playtime: An Expose of Child Suicide Caused by Bullying*. London: Screen Unlimited.

McKee, B. E. and Dillenburger, K. (2009), 'Child abuse and neglect: Training needs of student teachers'. *International Journal of Educational Research*, 48(5): 320–30.

McKee, B. E. and Holt, S. (2011), *Domestic Abuse – Using Arts-based Education to Help Student Teachers Learn about the Context and Impact on Children*. Armagh: SCoTENS.

McSherry, D. (2007), 'Understanding and addressing the "neglect of neglect": Why are we making a mole-hill out of a mountain?' *Child Abuse and Neglect: The International Journal*, 31(6): 607–14.

Ministerial Council for Education, Early Childhood Development and Youth Affairs (2011), *National Safe Schools Framework*. New Zealand: MCEECDYA.

Ministry of Justice (2004), *Safer Communities: Action Plan to Reduce Community and Sexual Violence*. New Zealand: Ministry of Justice.

Ministry of Social Development (2004), *Every Child Counts*. New Zealand: Ministry of Social Development.

Munro, E. (2011), *The Munro Review of Child Protection Interim Report: The Child's Journey*. Available online at www.education.gov.uk/munroreview.

Northern Territory Government (2010), *Growing them Strong, Together: Promoting the Safety and Wellbeing of the Northern Territories Children Summary Report of the Board of Inquiry into the Child Protection System in the Northern Territory 2010*. Australia: Northern Territory.

NSPCC (2009), *Child Protection Fact Sheet: The Definitions and Signs of Child Abuse*. Leicester: NSPCC.

OFMDFM (2006), *Our Children and Young People, Our Pledge. A Ten Year Strategy for Children and Young People in Northern Ireland*. Belfast: OFMDFM.

— (2009), *Safeguarding Children: A Cross-departmental Statement on the Protection of Children and Young People by the Northern Ireland Executive*. Belfast: OFMDFM.

Parton, N. and Frost, N. (2009), *Understanding Children's Social Care: Politics, Policy and Practice*. London: Routledge.

Perry, B. D. and Hambrick, E. (2008), 'The neurosequential model of therapeutics'. *Reclaiming Children and Youth*, 17(3): 38–43.

Radford, L., Corral, S., Bradley, C., Fisher, H., Bassett, C., Howat, N. and Collishaw, S. (2011), *Child Abuse and Neglect in the UK Today*. London: NSPCC.

Rodriguez, C. M. (2002), 'Professionals' attitudes and accuracy on child abuse reporting decisions in New Zealand'. *Journal of Interpersonal Violence*, 17(3): 320–42.

Russell, N. (2008), *What Works in Sexual Violence Prevention and Education: A Literature Review*. New Zealand: Task Force for Action on Sexual Violence.

Save the Children (2006), *Anti-Bullying Week 2006 'Don't just stand there' Highlighting the Role of the Bystander*. Belfast: Save the Children.

Scottish Executive (2005), *Safe and Well*. Scotland: Scottish Executive.

Sidebotham, P. and Appleton, J. V. (2012), 'Revolutions in safeguarding?' *Child Abuse Review*, 21(1): 1–6.

Skinner, J. (1999), 'Teachers coping with sexual abuse issues'. *Educational Research*, 41(3): 329–39.

Solberg, M. E., Olweus, D. and Endresen, I. M. (2007), 'Bullies and victims at school: Are they the same pupils?' *British Journal of Education Psychology*, 77: 441–64.

Stein, M., Rees, G., Hicks, L. and Gorin, S. (2009), *Neglected Adolescents – Literature Review. Research Brief*. London: DCSF.

Taylor, S. and Lloyd, D. (2001), *Mandatory Reporting and Child Sexual Abuse: Contextualising Beliefs and Attitudes*. Victoria, Australia: School of Education, University of Ballarat.

Underwood, A. (2009), *Child Protection Research Briefing. Young People Who Self-harm: Implications for Public Health Practitioners*. Leicester: NSPCC.

United Nations [UN] (1989), *The Convention on the Rights of the Child, Adopted by the General Assembly of the United Nations 20 Nov 1989*. Geneva: Defence for Children International (DCI).

US Department of Health and Human Services [DHHS] (2011), *Breaking the Silence on Child Abuse*. United States: US DHHS.

Walsh, K., Farrell, A., Bridgstock, R. and Schweitzer, R. (2006), 'The contested terrain of teachers' detecting and reporting child abuse and neglect: The need for empirical research in an Australian state with unique reporting laws'. *Journal of Early Childhood Research*, 4(1): 65–76.

Webster, S. W., O'Toole, R., O'Toole, A. W. and Lucal, B. (2005), 'Overreporting and underreporting of child abuse: Teachers' use of professional discretion'. *Child Abuse and Neglect, the International Journal*, 29(11): 1281–96.

World Health Organisation [WHO] (2006), *UN Secretary General's Study on Violence Against Children*. Geneva: WHO.

Wurtele, S. K. (2009), 'Preventing sexual abuse of children in the twenty-first century: Preparing for challenges and opportunities'. *Journal of Child Sexual Abuse*, 18(1): 1–18.

3

Bullying in Schools

Fran Thompson and Peter K. Smith

Chapter Outline

Introduction

Bullying in school has become a topic of international concern over the last 20 years (Smith et al., 1999; Jimerson et al., 2010). This chapter discusses what we mean by 'bullying'; summarizes some research findings on the nature of bullying; discusses the results of large-scale school-based interventions; and raises issues for future research and practice.

Although there is no universally agreed definition, there is some consensus in the Western research tradition that bullying refers to repeated intentional aggressive acts against someone who cannot easily defend themselves (Olweus, 1993). A similar definition, with broader connotations, is that bullying is a 'systematic abuse of power' (Smith and Sharp, 1994; Rigby, 2002).

This definition is now widely accepted by researchers, although some studies tend to conflate 'bullying' with 'aggression', which may affect the findings obtained (Hunter et al., 2007). The definition of bullying has varied historically with the inclusion of indirect bullying in the 1990s and cyberbullying in the 2000s. It also varies with age. Younger children have a broader definition of bullying as nasty things that happen to you (Monks and Smith, 2006). There are also issues around applying this definition to cyberbullying (see below). Nevertheless the criteria of repetition, intention and a systematic imbalance of power are accepted for most types of bullying, and understood by many older children and adults. They make bullying a particularly nasty and undesirable form of aggression.

The increase in international concern about school bullying appears to reflect an increase in concern for rights issues through the twentieth century (Greene, 2006). This has been evidenced by an awareness of, and legislation against, forms of discrimination due to, for example, sex, race, age, religion, disability and sexual orientation – a process that is still continuing. *Bullying* or *victimization* refers to discrimination that is usually on a more individual basis.

Bullying can happen in many contexts – within personal relationships, the home, the workplace, residential children's homes, the armed forces and prisons (Monks and Coyne, 2011). In school, too, we can think of teacher–teacher, teacher–pupil, pupil–teacher as well as pupil–pupil bullying. However, it is mainly pupil–pupil bullying which has been the focus of research up until now, and which is discussed here.

Types of bullying

Some main types of bullying are:

- *Physical:* hitting, kicking, punching, taking or damaging belongings
- Verbal: teasing, taunting, threatening
- Social exclusion: systematically excluding someone from social groups
- Indirect and relational: spreading nasty rumours, telling others not to play with someone
- *Cyberbullying:* involving the use of mobile phones or the internet.

Boys and girls have a similar understanding of what bullying is, but they do differ in the types they use, and experience. Boys use more physical forms; girls use more indirect bullying, social exclusion and other relational forms. Direct bullying is face-to-face; indirect bullying is via a third party, for example, nasty rumour spreading.

Identity-based bullying or bias bullying refers to bullying on the basis of a broader identity or grouping rather than just individual characteristics (Tippett et al., 2011); sexual or sexist bullying (Duncan, 1999); race, religion or culture-based bullying (Tippett et al., 2011); bullying related to sexual orientation or gender identity (Hunt and Jensen, 2007); and bullying relating to special educational needs or disability (Mishna, 2003). Other forms of bullying can involve family background, for example cared-for or adopted children and children from gypsy, Roma or traveller families (Tippett et al., 2011).

Awareness of cyberbullying has developed greatly in the last decade (Tokunaga, 2010; Smith, 2012). This describes forms of bullying using mobile phones and the internet. Smith et al. (2008) identified seven types of cyberbullying: text message bullying; mobile phone call bullying; picture/video clip bullying (via mobile phone cameras); email bullying; chat-room bullying; bullying through instant messaging; and bullying via websites. New forms of cyberbullying are appearing as electronic technologies develop further (e.g. smartphones; 3G phones), and social networking sites become more popular in adolescents (Patchin and Hinduja, 2010).

There are some distinctive features of cyberbullying (Smith, 2012). It depends on some degree of technological expertise: although it is easy enough to send emails and text messages, more sophisticated attacks such as masquerading (pretending to be someone else posting denigrating material on a website) require more skill. It is primarily indirect rather than face-to-face; thus there is some 'invisibility' of those doing the bullying. A perpetrator may try to withhold identification in text or internet postings to maintain anonymity.

Relatedly, the perpetrator does not usually see the victim's reaction, at least in the short term. This can enhance moral disengagement from the victim's plight and thus might make cyberbullying easier; but, many perpetrators enjoy the feedback of seeing the suffering of the victim, and would not get this satisfaction so readily by cyberbullying. The variety of bystander roles in cyberbullying is more complex than in most traditional bullying: the bystander is with the perpetrator when an act is sent or posted; the bystander is with the victim when it is received; or the bystander is with neither, but receives the message or visits the relevant internet site. Relatedly, one motive for bullying is thought to be the status gained by showing (abusive) power over others, in front of witnesses; the perpetrator will often lack this in cyberbullying, unless steps are taken to tell others what has happened or publicly share the material. The breadth of the potential audience is increased; for example, when nasty comments are posted on a website, the audience that may see these comments is potentially very large. Finally, it is difficult to escape from cyberbullying; the victim may be sent messages to their mobile or computer, or access nasty website comments, wherever they are.

Incidence

The incidence figures for school bullying vary greatly depending on measurement criteria. For example, what frequency and time span are asked about and whether the information comes from self, peer, teacher or parent report. In the UK and similar Western industrialized countries, some 5 per cent of children might be seen as regular or severe bullies, and some 10 per cent as regular or severe victims. These are appreciable minorities of children and young people, and are of concern because of the suffering caused by bullying, and the long-term effects. Worldwide (including the UK), the incidence of traditional bullying seems to be showing some decline, perhaps due to school-based interventions; but cyberbullying has increased or at least is not decreasing (Rigby and Smith, 2011).

Roles in bullying

Victims

Many studies have examined correlates of the victim role. Victims of bullying often experience adverse effects. A meta-analysis by Hawker and Boulton (2000) found that victimization was most strongly related to depression, moderately associated for social and global self-esteem and less strongly associated with anxiety. In extreme cases, victims may commit suicide (Kim and Leventhal, 2008).

Hodges et al. (1997) found that having few friends, or friends who cannot be trusted or who are of low status; and sociometric rejection (dislike by peers), are risk factors for being a victim. Some victims come from over-protective or enmeshed families (Curtner-Smith et al., 2010). Children who are both bullies and victims (aggressive victims) may come from particularly troubled or abusive families (Schwartz et al., 1997).

Having a disability or special educational needs is another risk factor for being a victim. Children with special needs are two to three times more at risk of being bullied; they are also more at risk of taking part in bullying others (Mishna, 2003). Possible reasons for this include: particular characteristics that may make them an obvious 'target'; in mainstream settings these children are usually less well integrated socially and lack the protection against bullying which friendship gives; and those with behavioural problems may act out in an aggressive way and become 'provocative victims'.

Bullies

Personal correlates of the bullying role include temperamental factors (such as being hot-tempered: Olweus, 1993), readily attributing hostile motives and having defensive egotism (Salmivalli et al., 1999); however ringleader bullies at least may have high social intelligence and theory of mind skills, although used for anti-social ends – they can be 'skilled manipulators' (Sutton et al., 1999). At the interpersonal level, bullying children tend to be peer-rejected in infant/junior school but less so in secondary school; towards adolescence, some aggressive and bullying children can have quite high status in peer groups (Pellegrini and Bartini, 2001).

Family factors have been commonly implicated as risk factors for children who persistently bully others. They are more likely to come from families lacking warmth, in which violence is common and discipline inconsistent (Curtner-Smith et al., 2010).

Other roles in bullying

Salmivalli et al. (1996) identified a diversity of roles and stressed the importance of the wider peer group. They assessed roles of ringleader bullies (who take the initiative), follower or associate bullies (who then join in), reinforcers (who encourage the bully or laugh at the victim), defenders (who help the victim) and bystanders (who stay out of things), as well as the victims themselves. Subsequently some investigators have distinguished between bystanders (who see the bullying but do not act in any way) and outsiders (who just have not seen what is happening). Also, victims are often divided into so-called passive victims, who have not directly provoked the bullying; and provocative victims, who can be thought to have contributed to their being bullied by having acted in an annoying, provocative way to peers (sometimes labelled aggressive-victims, or bully/victims) (Pikas, 1989).

The characteristics of those children who are prepared to actively defend victims are of interest and importance. Some research finds that defenders are more empathic (Nickerson et al., 2008); however, other research suggests that empathy alone is not enough. In addition, defending is predicted by feelings of self-efficacy, and high sociometric standing, such that defenders can feel confident and empowered to defend, despite the strength and popularity of some bullying children (Caravita et al., 2009).

Coping and telling

Pupils use various coping strategies to deal with attempts to bully them. Rates of telling a teacher are less in older pupils, and boys (Naylor et al., 2001; Hunter and Boyle, 2004). A study of pupils aged 13–16 years in schools with peer support systems found the five most frequent coping strategies were to talk to someone, ignore it, stick up for yourself, avoid/stay away from bullies and make more/different friends (Smith, Talamelli et al., 2004). Over a two-year period, those who had stopped being victims more often had talked to someone about it than those who had stayed victims or become victims. Coping strategies can be complex and dependent on many factors; telling teachers can be successful but needs a consistent and effective response from teaching staff.

Attitudes about bullying in the peer group are important. Although most pupils say they do not like bullying, a significant minority do say they could join in bullying. These 'pro-bullying' or 'anti-victim' attitudes increase with age up to 14–15 years, after which they start to decline. Such anti-victim attitudes are more marked in boys than girls – and especially for boys as regards boy victims (Olweus and Endresen, 1998).

Action to assess, reduce and prevent school bullying

The awareness and knowledge generated by some two decades of research has fed into methods and programmes to assess, reduce and prevent bullying. While community and family factors are relevant, most effort has been put into school factors, and ways of working with individual pupils and school classes. These school-based actions take a variety of forms.

Government guidance

In 2011, the Department for Education (DfE) for England and Wales replaced the former Department for Children, Schools and Families (DCSF, 2007) *Safe to Learn* guidance with *Preventing and Tackling Bullying: Advice for Head Teachers, Staff and Governing Bodies* (DfE, 2011). This document states that it is the school's responsibility to decide on how to respond to bullying and that there is no single solution to bullying which will suit all schools. The DfE only provides very general guidelines on prevention and intervention. The guidance foregrounds legislation, emphasizing the statutory obligations on schools with regard to behaviour, which establish clear responsibilities to respond to bullying. The Education and Inspections Act (2006) states that schools must have measures to encourage good behaviour and prevent all forms of bullying among pupils, which should be included in the school's behaviour policy and communicated to all pupils, staff and parents. The act also extends the head teacher's remit to regulate pupil conduct outside the school. Other laws cited include the Equality Act (2010), which can be used for discrimination and prejudice-based bullying. Criminal law can be invoked for incidents involving harassment or threatening behaviour and cyberbullying. The police should be involved if schools feel a criminal offence has been committed. In January 2012, a new OFSTED (schools inspection) framework was introduced which includes behaviour and safety, and schools will have to demonstrate the impact of their anti-bullying work.

Reporting, recording and auditing for bullying

Many schools use various forms of reporting systems and some kind of incident report form. These range from traditional paper-based systems to computer programmes (e.g. SIMS, SHARP, SERCO). Reporting systems need to be non-stigmatizing and need to protect vulnerable pupils. An efficient centralized recording system can monitor behaviour, target pupils for additional support (e.g. peer support) and provide evidence for the effectiveness of a school's anti-bullying work. Schools with effective reporting and recording systems often identify vulnerable pupils at intake using information provided by their feeder primary schools.

In addition, researchers have developed several methods to get incidence figures. A widely used approach has been to use pupil self-report questionnaires, usually anonymous; this method is most suitable for large surveys, for example surveying a whole school. Although a school may devise its own questionnaire, there are a lot of pitfalls in questionnaire design so it may be best using an established version. Some examples are available from the Anti-Bullying Alliance website (www.abatoolsfor-schools.org.uk/default.aspx). Besides incidence, questionnaires can give information on where bullying happens, what pupils have done about it, etc. However if it is anonymous, individual bullies or victims cannot be identified.

Peer nominations provide an alternative pupil-based approach. Here pupils are asked to nominate classmates for involvement in roles such as bully, or victim. This is probably best done by someone from outside the school so that pupils can respond in confidence. Two common instruments are by Slee and Rigby (1993), and the Salmivalli Participant Role Scale (Salmivalli et al., 1996). Multiple informants can provide good reliability in identifying bullies or victims, but this method is time consuming, and ethical issues are raised by asking pupils to identify others in this way.

School-based interventions

Some school-based interventions are targeted at the whole school, or class; some at the behaviour of those doing the bullying; some at those who are victims; some at bystanders or likely defenders. We have broadly divided these strategies into:

- proactive strategies which can be used as a whole school approach and are designed to make bullying less likely to happen
- peer support, which uses pupils themselves to prevent and respond to bullying
- reactive strategies, which are ways of dealing with bullying incidents once they have occurred.

Much of the evidence on the use and perceived effectiveness of these strategies comes from a national survey of schools in England, carried out in 2010; this also furnishes some case-study examples cited below (Thompson and Smith, 2011).

Proactive strategies
Whole-school policy on bullying

Since 1999, schools in England and Wales have been legally required to have some form of anti-bullying policy. A whole school policy should define bullying comprehensively, state the responsibilities of all concerned in the school and clearly explain what actions will be taken to reduce bullying and deal with incidents when they occur. School policies vary in scope (Smith, Kupferberg et al., 2012), but provide a framework for the school's response involving the whole school community: pupils, teachers, learning mentors, school support staff, governors and parents/carers. There is only modest evidence so far that having a good policy translates into lower rates of school bullying or violence.

Research Example: Exploring Anti-Bullying Policies

Research suggests that school anti-bullying policies may lack coverage in important areas. In this study, Smith et al. (2012) analysed 217 school anti-bullying policies, from 169 primary schools and 48 secondary schools in one county. A 34-item scoring scheme was devised to assess policy (see copy on companion website). Overall schools had about half of these items in their policies. Most included a definition of bullying including reference to physical, verbal, material and relational forms, and clarifying the difference from other kinds of aggressive behaviour; and statements about improving school climate; how sanctions will depend on type or severity of incident; and contact with parents when bullying incidents occur. But many schools did not mention other important aspects, and there was low coverage of cyberbullying, homophobic bullying, bullying based on disabilities, or faith; teacher–pupil bullying; responsibilities beyond those of teaching staff; following up of incidents; and specific preventative measures such as playground work, peer support, inclusiveness issues and bullying to and from school. Findings were compared with an analysis of 142 schools from the same county, six years earlier, showing that there had been some improvement; but the range of scores across schools remained very large (from 2/34 to 28/34).

Reference

Smith, P. K., Kupferberg, A., Mora-Merchan, J. A., Samara, M., Bosley, S. and Osborn, R. (2012), 'A content analysis of school anti-bullying policies: A follow-up after six years.' *Educational Psychology in Practice*, 28: 61–84.

Adult modelling of behaviour

Adult modelling of positive relationships and communication is used by most English schools. School staff must lead by example and effectively practise what they preach, as pupils need the emotional intelligence of good role models. In one case study school, staff attitudes had changed during a campaign to address homophobic language; staff who used to laugh, now challenged it, and the campaign was seen as a success (Thompson and Smith, 2011).

School councils

School councils involve pupils – usually elected representatives – who meet regularly with members of school staff to discuss and decide on policy issues, which can include anti-bullying work. School councils not only provide opportunities for pupil feedback but also for schools to listen to them. Specialized forms of school councils include anti-bullying committees which can be effective in providing feedback about anti-bullying work from a pupil forum. Pupil recommendations and feedback must be acknowledged and acted upon, otherwise it becomes 'tokenistic' (Thompson and Smith, 2011).

Systems that support parent/carer involvement

Involving parents and carers in anti-bullying work has been a priority in government guidance. Parental involvement in anti-bullying work can be facilitated by regular newsletters, consultation on policies or after-school clubs to support parents of at-risk children. When a school is responding to bullying incidents, parents can be directly involved either through informal meetings or restorative conferences. Many schools have specific staff to liaise with parents (home-school workers; parent support advisors). Some schools find it difficult to engage parents at all, with, for example, special e-safety presentations poorly attended (Thompson and Smith, 2011).

Improving the school grounds

Most direct forms of bullying happen in the school grounds, so effective strategies for behaviour outside the school building are important. These can include improving school grounds, school grounds policies and training lunchtime supervisors. These are rated higher in primary schools; secondary schools are more likely to have installed CCTV, which not only records and provides evidence of bullying, but can also act as a deterrent. Peer support schemes are also used to supervise breaktime activities and organize lunchtime clubs to support lonely or vulnerable pupils (Thompson and Smith, 2011).

Curricular materials/approaches

Classroom activities can be used to tackle issues associated with bullying, progressively and in an age, gender and culturally appropriate way. Such curricular approaches can raise awareness of bullying and the school's anti-bullying policy, and develop skills, empathy and assertiveness in confronting bullying. These can include more passive activities such as literature, audio-visual materials and videos; or more active forms such as group work and the use of computer-based virtual environments where pupils can act out roles and see the consequences.

These can have positive effects, but only temporarily if curriculum work is not backed up by continuing anti-bullying work and policy (Smith and Sharp, 1994). OFSTED (2003a) reported schools with the most successful approaches to bullying canvassed and took full account of pupils' views and they dedicated curriculum and tutorial time to discussing relationships and matters like bullying. Curriculum work was most effective when delivered through creative, interactive lessons but skilled staff were essential to effective delivery (Thompson and Smith, 2011).

An evaluation of two e-safety films used by secondary schools, Childnet International's *Let's Fight It Together* about cyberbullying for KS3 and Child Exploitation and Online Protection's (CEOP) *Exposed* about sexting (i.e. sending sexually explicit images and texts using mobile phones) for KS4 were part of a DAPHNE III project on cyberbullying. Both films and resources were rated as good by the pupils and staff (Thompson et al., in press) (http://bullyingandcyber.koinema.com/en/).

Quality circles

Quality circles (QCs) are problem-solving groups of pupils formed for regular classroom sessions. Subjects can include bullying. There is a set of procedures to follow about group formation; data gathering and presentation of outcomes. Paul et al. (2010 and in press) reported on the use of QCs in a UK secondary school in the context of understanding and reducing bullying and cyberbullying. QCs were an effective means of gathering information on bullying and cyberbullying in school. The use of the QCs was an engaging process for pupils, and encouraged young people to provide a realistic perspective on the bullying problems occurring in school. Pupils suggested a range of solutions to these problems, and the information gained was useful to staff in understanding how bullying was changing over time (e.g. new forms of cyberbullying); and gave some suggestions for intervention.

PSHE: Personal, Social, Health and Economic education

PSHE provides school staff with a clear opportunity to work on bullying, particularly within the sections on citizenship, emotional health and well-being and safety. PSHE can develop awareness of different types of bullying and the consequences of bullying; promote confidence and assertiveness in challenging and coping with bullying; and develop strategies for conflict resolution. PSHE is a main way of delivering anti-bullying work to the whole school through the curriculum but the subject needs skilled, enthusiastic staff to deliver it effectively (Thompson and Smith, 2011).

SEAL: Social and Emotional Aspects of Learning

The SEAL resource is a whole-school approach to developing social and emotional skills, to promote positive behaviour, attendance, learning and well-being. The Secondary SEAL programme was launched as a pilot in 2005. It included a Year 7 learning and teaching resource, with four themes: A place to learn (setting the context for learning); Learning to be together (social skills and empathy); Keep on learning (motivation); and Learning about me (understanding and managing feelings). An evaluation by Humphrey et al. (2010) reported that the secondary SEAL curriculum lacked structure and consistency in delivery and that schools needed greater guidance about maximizing the impact of the resource. Staff were compromised by lack of time and resources; parents/carers were not sufficiently involved in the development and delivery and the SEAL resource needed on-going 'rigorous' evaluation before being 'rolled out' to schools. The evaluation did not specifically address the support provided for pupils who bully, or any individual level improvements in their behaviour.

Assertiveness training

Through regular in-class or after school sessions, pupils (e.g. victims or those at risk) can learn specific strategies for dealing with difficult situations – such as attempts to bully them – in assertive rather than passive or aggressive ways. They can talk about their experiences, and learn and practise effective responses. Various skills/techniques are taught, such as 'broken record' or 'fogging'. Although expensive and time-consuming, training has been shown to help victims develop useful strategies and it works best with periodic refresher sessions (Smith and Sharp, 1994).

Peer support schemes

Peer support uses the knowledge, skills and experience of young people themselves in a planned and structured way to prevent and reduce bullying. Selected pupils are trained to be *peer supporters*, to deal with interpersonal conflicts, social exclusion and bullying in proactive and non-violent ways. Peer support schemes can also be used reactively, to respond to bullying incidents and support all involved. In the secondary sector, peer supporters, usually from older year groups, can be used to support younger pupils at transition and can also provide one-to-one mentoring/counselling for bullied pupils in a designated room. Schemes include peer mentoring; peer listening/counselling and peer mediation with some schools using buddy schemes at the Year 7 transition.

Particular types of peer support schemes and evaluations of their effectiveness are presented in the next sections.

Circles of friends/Circles of support /Supportive friends

Volunteer pupils are trained to befriend and support other pupils who are identified as isolated or rejected by their peers and hence vulnerable to bullying. Training involves increasing empathic skills, developing a flexible and creative method to form positive relationships with peers and ingenuity in devising practical strategies to support victims. Circles of friends are used for isolated and bullied pupils, helping to build relationships, improve disruptive behaviour and integrate newcomers. However, the strategy is time-consuming, needing close adult monitoring and input to be effective (Thompson and Smith, 2011). OFSTED (2003b) reported significant effects with pupils feeling less isolated in the knowledge that some peers would not remain passive if they were intimidated or troubled.

Befriending/buddy schemes

In befriending or buddy schemes, peer supporters are trained to offer support and friendship to pupils in everyday situations. Although more popular in the primary than secondary sector, buddy schemes were used at transition to help the youngest Year 7 pupils adjust to a new school. Buddies regularly attended registration in form or tutor time for the first term, with their attendance gradually reducing over the year as Year 7s grew in confidence. Buddy schemes also provided a drop-in service at a pre-designated time and place. In one school, a bus buddy scheme was being piloted to provide support for younger pupils on public transport (Smith and Watson, 2004; Thompson and Smith, 2011).

Peer mentoring

Peer mentoring schemes are a common form of peer support in the secondary sector. They aim to create a supportive relationship between two pupils, combining practical advice and encouragement about issues such as bullying. Peer mentors are contactable via a 'bully box', the school intranet or referral by member of staff. In some secondary schools, older pupil mentors can help train younger ones (OFSTED, 2003a). Mentoring is most effective when agreed ways of working are clear and there is good staff supervision and support of the mentors (Cowie and Wallace, 2000; Smith and Watson, 2004).

Peer mediation

Peer mediation is a problem-solving process, which encourages pupils to define the problem; identify and agree key issues, discuss and brainstorm possible options; negotiate a plan of action and agreement and follow up and evaluate outcomes. Pupil mediators can be trained in conflict-resolution skills, including restorative approaches. Secondary school pupils thought that their peer mediation scheme worked better if the peer mediators came from an older age group and the bullied and bullying pupils were seen separately (Thompson and Smith, 2011).

Bystander (defender) training

This targets the group dynamics of bullying. Defenders intervene to stop the bullying or comfort pupils who experience bullying. Rigby and Johnson (2006) showed a video depicting bullying in the presence of bystanders to late primary and early secondary school pupils in Australia: 43 per cent indicated that they were likely to help the victim. Girls reported more defending behaviour than boys.

CyberMentors

A UK charity, Beatbullying launched a new form of virtual peer support called CyberMentors in 2009. Pupils are trained in 2-day workshops. Staff are briefed separately by the Beatbullying trainers. Cybermentors and mentees log on and mentor on demand. The website, moderated by Beatbullying staff, has a software filter to protect the identity of mentors and mentees and screen online dialogue. Cybermentors can refer mentees on to senior cybermentors and counsellors for further support if necessary. The CyberMentor scheme has been evaluated by Banerjee et al. (2010); Thompson and Smith (2011) and more recently as part of a DAPHNE III project on cyberbullying (http://bullyingandcyber.koinema.com/en/).

The training is rated highly by pupils, although some staff wanted more feedback and continuing support after the initial training session for pupils. Of those cybermentors and cybermentees completing an online questionnaire, most were female, aged 11–18 years. Cybermentors and mentees who reported cyberbullying incidents said that most lasted several weeks; involved social networking sites; and that the victims knew the perpetrators, who were about the same age. The Beatbullying website was rated as easy to use and safe, and cybermentors as easy to contact and talk to.

Other forms of peer support used in secondary schools

BeatBullying's sports mentors are an effective way of keeping younger pupils involved in constructive activities at break times. If sports mentors are also trained in basic conflict resolution, this gives them additional skills for dealing with minor incidents and fallouts.

Lunchtime clubs are a non-stigmatizing way to access peer support and can provide a safe haven for vulnerable pupils at breaktimes. Less exposing and off-putting for pupils, clubs provide the opportunity for pupils to discuss any problems in their own time.

General evaluation of peer support schemes

Cowie and Smith (2010) argued that as a means of reducing bullying, peer support schemes could operate through a general improvement in school climate, through helping individual pupils who use the scheme to stop being victimized, and by reducing general rates of bullying throughout the school. There is good evidence for effects on school climate: schools using well-managed peer support schemes are seen as being more caring and concerned about pupil well-being, and the schemes are known and supported by pupils and staff. In addition, peer supporters themselves generally benefit from the experience (Houlston and Smith, 2009). There is evidence from individual cases for effects on victimized students: some pupils, who use peer support schemes for reasons of being bullied, do report being helped. However there is only equivocal evidence regarding reductions in rates of bullying: most of the relevant studies do not report significant changes in general levels of bullying behaviour as a result of implementing a peer support scheme. Crucial issues include the selection and training of peer supporters; the gender balance in recruitment (there are often more girl than boy volunteers, particularly in the secondary sector); adequate and continuing supervision by an accessible member of staff; effective promotion of the scheme; and sufficient take-up of the scheme by users so that peer supporters feel positive in their role (Cowie and Smith, 2010).

Research Example: The Use of Peer Support Schemes in English Schools

This study reported findings from a survey of the way peer support was being used in English primary and secondary schools. Regional strata samples of schools were selected from an online database. Questionnaire data was obtained from 240 schools (130 primary and 110 secondary), of which 186 had peer support schemes. An adjusted estimation (which corrects for non-response error) suggested that 62 per cent of schools were using a structured peer support scheme. The mean number of pupils trained as peer supporters ranged from 2 to 280 but averaged around 32; in secondary schools, these were mostly from Key Stage 4 (Years 10 and 11) and pupils in sixth form, with typically more girls than boys being trained as peer supporters. In secondary schools, the most popular types of peer support schemes were mentoring and befriending, followed by mediation and counselling. The most commonly mentioned objectives for recipients of peer support were to provide support, help or guidance for school transition and for bullying or conflict resolution problems.

Reference

Houlston, C., Smith, P. K. and Jessel, J. (2009), 'Investigating the extent and use of peer support initiatives in English schools'. *Educational Psychology,* 29: 325–44.

Reactive strategies

Reactive strategies deal with bullying situations when they have arisen. They range from more punitive or sanction-based approaches, through restorative practices, to more indirect and non-punitive approaches. In the UK, the DfE recommends that bullying should always incur some form of sanction, and that schools should apply disciplinary measures to pupils who bully in order to show clearly that their behaviour is wrong (DfE, 2011). However, many professionals prefer less direct approaches, at least for less severe cases of bullying. A school's philosophy on this should be evident in their anti-bullying policy.

Direct sanctions

Direct sanctions are a collective term describing a range of punishments, which may vary in severity and be used on a graded scale if bullying persists. They can range through reprimands/serious talks from the head teacher; meetings involving parents or carers; temporary removal from class; withdrawal of privileges and rewards; disciplinary measures such as detentions; punishment such as litter-picking/school clean-ups; through to temporary or permanent exclusion. Direct sanctions are expected to impress on the perpetrator that what he/she has done is unacceptable and to promote understanding of the limits of acceptable behaviour; to give an opportunity for pupils who bully to face up to the harm they have caused and learn from it; to deter him/her from repeating that behaviour; to signal to other pupils that the behaviour is unacceptable and deter them from doing it; and to demonstrate publicly that school rules and policies are to be taken seriously.

Milder sanctions can be implemented by all school staff but only the head and deputy head teachers can temporarily and permanently exclude pupils. Despite only half of anti-bullying leads (the person responsible for coordinating anti-bullying strategies) in local authorities in England recommending the use of direct sanctions to respond to a bullying incident, the vast majority of schools (92%) used them, more than any other strategy (Thompson and Smith, 2011). However, only 62 per cent of schools reported that the bullying stopped as a result. In secondary schools, direct sanctions were the preferred strategy for physical bullying, bullying through damaging belongings, race-related bullying, homophobic bullying and cyberbullying.

Direct sanctions work best as a clear set of consequences expressed in the anti-bullying policy and mostly used within the framework of other strategies (e.g. restorative approaches). Some secondary schools now use a 'seclusion' or 'isolation' room as a form of internal exclusion for problematic behaviour, including bullying. Referral to a Pupil Referral Unit is the most serious form of sanction and it is important to provide a re-integration process for excluded pupils returning to school.

> ## Case Study: Direct Sanctions Used with Other Strategies for Physical Bullying – an Interview with a Bullying Pupil (Thompson and Smith, 2011)
>
> K overheard a girl talking in a slightly negative way about K's sister, who had recently joined the school. K attacked this girl on the stairs. K had had other fights with girls, who were usually younger, mostly Year 7 and one in Year 8. The attacks were witnessed by 'most of Year 8'. This had been going on for some time and was serious because it involved physical violence. A teacher witnessed her attacking other girls and took K to the head teacher. She was interviewed by the anti-bullying lead and the behaviour and attendance officer and was excluded for three days. On her return, K had to see the anti-bullying lead twice a week for a couple of months to talk about bullying, her feelings and the feelings of the people she had bullied. This changed her – she used to bully girls all the time but now she had stopped. K was put on an anger management course. She regularly filled out diagnostic questionnaires to monitor her progress and discussed her behaviour at length with the anti-bullying lead, who helped her to see the perspective of the victims. K had apologized to the bullied girl and now they 'got on really well'. She had not really understood what bullying was before. She thought the school did a 'good job of stopping people bullying other people'.
>
> ## Questions
>
> 1. What were examples of good practice in this case study?
> 2. What alternative or additional actions might be taken?

School Tribunals/Bully Courts

A School Tribunals or Bully Court is an elected court of pupils which meets after an alleged incident has occurred; all concerned are interviewed, including witnesses and the Tribunal or Bully Court decides what punishment (if any) is appropriate. A school staff member chairs the court. It is not popular with teachers and rarely used. Some schools have adapted their school council as a tribunal (Thompson and Smith, 2011).

Restorative Approaches

Restorative Approaches emphasize a restoration of good relationships, rather than retribution. They cover a hierarchy of flexible responses, ranging from informal conversations through to formal facilitated meetings or conferences. In a short or 'mini' conference, an informal meeting is held between the pupils involved, led by a trained member of staff, in which incidents and harm caused are examined, and the offender(s) are asked to discuss possible means of reparation. In a full restorative conference, a formal, structured meeting takes place involving pupils, along with their parents/carers, friends and school representatives, who are brought together to discuss and resolve an incident. Prior to this large meeting, the staff member leading the conference holds individual interviews with the participants to ensure a full conference is appropriate, and that everyone is completely prepared for it.

The underlying principle is to resolve conflict and repair harm by focusing on the perpetrator, who is made aware of the victim's feelings, encouraged to acknowledge the impact of what they have done and given an opportunity to make reparation; those who have suffered have the opportunity to have their harm or loss acknowledged and amends made (Restorative Justice Consortium, 2005).

Restorative approaches are being increasingly used in schools for all types of anti-social/inappropriate behaviour, including bullying. Over two-thirds of schools report using restorative approaches, second only to direct sanctions (Thompson and Smith, 2011). Effective use of restorative justice depends on pupils being able to talk about feelings and relationship issues. A good 'seedbed' for this is problem-solving circles/circle time. Although used more in the primary sector, circle time experiences can facilitate simple restorative approaches such as restorative reminders, restorative discussions and restorative thinking plans and could be used with Year 7s.

Some evaluations have reported successful outcomes of restorative practices in schools. In the UK, a national evaluation found that 92 per cent of conferences were resolved successfully, and three months later, 96 per cent of agreements remained intact (Youth Justice Board, 2004). Most school staff reported that their school had benefited, although no general improvements in pupil attitudes were found at a whole-school level. Other evaluations acknowledge that while restorative approaches may offer a more positive approach to repairing harm, they may become 'a form of social control', as much of the language is derived from the criminal justice system (e.g. offender, perpetrator and victim) (Cremin, 2010).

Sherman and Strang (2007) recommend that to be effective, restorative practice needs to be adopted as a whole-school approach fully supported by senior management, and with adequate training in restorative techniques for staff. Without this, tensions can arise with prevailing sanction-based practices. Thompson and Smith (2011) collected 285 bullying incident forms from 35 case study schools, which showed that those schools using restorative approaches with whole staff training and the consistent application of restorative strategies were more successful at stopping bullying (79%) than less consistent (64%) and non-restorative schools (58%). Direct sanctions were still used if pupils 'refuse to restore'.

Case Study: Restorative Approaches Used for Cyberbullying – an Extract Taken from a Bullying Incident Record Sheet (Thompson and Smith, 2011)

'Two year 9 boys, who were fully aware that a year 7 had special needs (autism), got him to kneel down in a crowd of onlookers and told him to call them "king" and "emperor" whilst bowing. They filmed him. Others also called things for him to say. He was apparently engaged in this, unaware of how cruel their actions were. Three weeks later they uploaded it to Facebook where it was seen by the year 7s boy's class, who began to mimic him and demand they worship them too. The boy was devastated by peer bullying and by the realisation about true nature of earlier encounter'.

The school initially responded by 'excluding the year 9 boys. A restorative conference was held on the boys' return and included the mother of victim, both bullies and their mothers. The intention was not only to ensure they understood the real harm of what they had done and to ensure that it would not be repeated, but also to reassure victim's parent that her son would be safe from them. Additionally, there was support from peers and support from Achievement Support Centre staff in school. Work was also done with boy's own class and those who had mimicked him'.

The school's use of a restorative conference 'reassured the bullied boy, so that he could come to school again. He had been so upset that he wouldn't come to school, take his coat off, put his hood down, and raise his head from table level'.

'The restorative conference was key to educating the boys about the real harm that had been done but was also critical in reassuring victim and parent that school could be made safe'.

Questions

1. How essential were restorative approaches in this case study?
2. How well can restorative approaches be combined with other strategies (taking this case study as one example)?

The Pikas Method or Method of Shared Concern

The Shared Concern, or Pikas Method, was developed in Sweden by Pikas (1989, 2002), as a non-punitive counselling-based approach for school bullying. It uses a combination of individual and group meetings, structured around five consecutive phases: individual talks with suspected bullies; individual talk with the victim; preparatory group meeting; summit meeting; and follow-up of the results. This approach is expected to sensitize bullying children to the harm they are doing to the victim (enabled by a lack of hostile blaming attitude on the part of the interviewer), encourage positive behaviours to the victim and also encourage provocative victims to change their behaviour in positive ways.

An Australian evaluation found that the method was 'well endorsed' by practitioners using it; 'highly successful' in improving the situation for bullied pupils and 'generally helpful' in improving the attitudes and behaviour of bullying pupils. Further research was needed to identify which cases were most suited to the application of Shared Concern (Rigby and Griffiths, 2010).

Thompson and Smith (2011) found that only 5 per cent of schools in England (mostly primary) used the Pikas method, with little staff training to support delivery. It was seen as an 'educative process' for those involved. However many schools had no knowledge of the method or confused it with information gathering after a bullying incident.

Support Group Method (Seven Steps approach)

The Support Group Method (formerly called the No Blame approach) was developed by Robinson and Maines (2007). It is a non-punitive approach which aims to change problem behaviours through a mixture of peer pressure to elicit a pro-social response, and self-realization of the harm and suffering caused to the victim. There are seven steps: the facilitator talks individually to the bullied pupil; a group meeting of six to eight pupils is then set up, some suggested by the victim but without his/her presence; the facilitator explains to the group that the victim has a problem, but does not discuss the incidents that have taken place; the facilitator assures the group no punishment will be given, but instead all participants must take joint responsibility to make the victim feel happy and safe; each group member gives their own ideas on how the victim can be helped; the facilitator ends the meeting, with the group given responsibility for improving the victim's safety and well-being; individual meetings are held with group members one week after the meeting to establish how successful the intervention has been.

The Support Group Method works on the premise of lasting change rather than retribution, and is expected to develop emotional awareness, peer support and social skills, and empathy of pupils involved. Young (1998), in a slight adaptation of the method, reported that of 51 support group sessions studied, 80 per cent resulted in immediate success and 14 per cent a delayed success; with the remaining 6 per cent having only limited success. An evaluation by Smith et al. (2007) is described in the Research Example below. Thompson and Smith (2011) found that 10 per cent of schools used the Support Group Method. The strategy was used most for relational and verbal bullying. It was seen as encouraging pupils to take responsibility for their actions through empathy with the bullied pupil. Some schools use it because it is non-confrontational and avoids 'punishment', with others refusing to use it as it avoids directly assigning blame or responsibility.

Research Example: Evaluating the Support Group Method

The Support Group Method (SGM) is used as an anti-bullying intervention in schools, but the avoidance of direct sanctions for perpetrators of bullying has aroused some controversy. This study surveyed the use of and support for the Support Group Method in Local Authorities and schools; and obtained ratings of satisfaction with its use; sources of evidence for such ratings; and comments on how it is used in practice. Questionnaires were sent to Local Authorities and schools in England, and were available on a website; useful replies were obtained from 57 Local Authorities and 59 schools. Some two-thirds of LAs were supportive of the SGM in general terms, although fewer said they had sufficient evidence to judge effectiveness. The modal rating when given was 'satisfactory'. Most schools had used SGM for one to five years, often across the whole school. Two-thirds received direct training in the method. Over one-half of schools gave a rating of effectiveness, based on teachers, pupils and parents; the modal rating was 'very satisfactory'. Responses and open-ended comments revealed that details of use varied considerably and that some schools had substantially modified the method. Some confusion about the ways of implementing SGM was evident, which might explain some hostile comments reported elsewhere. Issues of parental involvement, and backup availability of sanctions, were commonly mentioned.

Reference

Smith, P. K., Howard, S. and Thompson, F. (2007). 'A survey of use of the Support Group Method in England, and some evaluation from schools and Local Authorities'. *Pastoral Care in Education*, 25: 4–13.

Analyses of intervention programmes

In some countries, large-scale intervention programmes have taken place. Here, many elements of proactive, peer support or reactive strategies are combined, and used over a large number of schools, with the outcomes evaluated using some kind of pre/post-test design. The first large-scale school-based intervention campaign was carried out at a nationwide level in Norway in 1983. Olweus (1993) monitored this campaign in primary and junior high schools in Bergen; the nationwide intervention was supplemented by further support and advice from his research group – the beginnings of his Olweus Bullying Prevention Programme. He found that from 1983 to 1985, reported bullying fell by 50 per cent, for both boys and girls. This encouraging finding has been widely reported and has inspired much subsequent work. More recent work in Norway includes the ZERO programme directed by Roland (2011). Recent work by Olweus (Olweus and Limber, 2010) finds reductions in the range of 21–50 per cent in grades 5 to 7.

The largest intervention programme in the UK was the DfE Sheffield project, from 1991–4 (Smith and Sharp, 1994). The project worked with 23 schools over 4 terms. Each school developed a whole school policy and chose from a range of other interventions. There was a 17 per cent reduction in being bullied for primary schools and small reductions (around 3–5%) in 5 of the 7 secondary schools. In addition there was a strong positive correlation between amount of effort (as assessed by both research team and pupils) and outcomes achieved.

Other interventions; meta-analyses

Other wide-scale interventions have taken place in many countries (Smith et al., 2004). In general, most interventions have some positive impact but with more modest effects than the 50 per cent reduction found in Olweus' work in Bergen. One that does report this level of success is a project in Andalusia (Ortega, del Rey and Mora-Merchan, 2004), where a broad-based intervention was sustained over a four-year period. A new intervention campaign in Finland, KiVa, recently rolled out on a national basis, includes both virtual learning environments in the classroom, and the use of pro-social, high-status peers as defenders. Reductions in bullying are substantial (c.40%), with indications that both more disciplinary methods, and non-punitive approaches, can be helpful (Kärnä et al., 2011).

A meta-analysis of 44 school-based intervention programmes internationally (Ttofi and Farrington, 2011) found that on average, these reduced bullying by around 20–23 per cent and victimization by around 17–20 per cent. Ttofi and Farrington (2011) identified various programme components as important (or less important) contributors to success. However some of their conclusions (such as the desirability of focusing on older rather than younger children; or not using peer support strategies) have been criticized (Smith, Salmivalli and Cowie, 2012).

We need to learn from both successes and failures in school-based interventions. They surely are necessary and vital, and results so far have been modestly encouraging. But we do also need to consider whether intervening in schools only is enough. Bullying does not only happen in schools and schools are only part of the problem and part of the solution.

Conclusion

School bullying is a pervasive problem. It now has a research history spanning the last 25 years. During this period, a considerable amount of useful knowledge has been gained and has fed into a range of intervention strategies and programmes. These have had modestly encouraging results but vary considerably. There is no one solution, but a wide range of approaches have been found to be useful, and many work well in combination. Some important advances have been made in tackling this important social problem, but much remains to be done to reduce bullying appreciably and effectively.

Summary

This chapter has explored:

- The nature of pupil–pupil bullying in schools
- Ways of assessing the extent of the problem
- A range of proactive, peer support and reactive strategies to reduce bullying
- The effectiveness of programme-based interventions

Acknowledgements

We are grateful for support from the DCSF/DfE for a grant to examine anti-bullying strategies in schools (www.education.gov.uk/publications/standard/publicationDetail/Page1/DFE-RB098), and from the DAPHNE III program for a grant to evaluate the effects of some cyberbullying interventions (http://bullyingandcyber.koinema.com/en/).

Annotated further reading

Cowie, H. and Jennifer, D. (2007), *Managing Violence in Schools: A Whole-school Approach to Best Practice*. London: Sage.

Through training guidelines, selected research findings, case studies, problem-solving activities and supportive materials, this book provides the basic skills to create a climate in which teachers and pupils work and learn together in greater harmony than before. The whole-school community approach involves as many members of the whole-school community as possible, including, teachers, school management, non-teaching staff members, parents, governors, the local community, external organizations and representatives from the wider society as a whole.

Rigby, K. (2010), *Bullying Interventions in Schools: Six Basic Approaches*. Camberwell: ACER.

Ken Rigby has written several very readable books on bullying; this one compares six main reactive strategies for tackling bullying in schools. These are the traditional disciplinary approach; strengthening the victim; mediation; restorative practice; the support group method; and the method of shared concern. The strengths and difficulties of each approach, and relevant evidence, are considered.

Smith, P. K., Pepler, D. J. and Rigby, K. (eds) (2004), *Bullying in Schools: How Successful Can Interventions Be?* Cambridge: Cambridge University Press.

This is a more in-depth account of the implementation and effects of anti-bullying programmes in eleven different countries. Thirteen different programmes are considered, in terms of the background to the work, the planned intervention, how it worked in practice and what was achieved.

Useful websites

www.education.gov.uk/publications/standard/publicationDetail/Page1/DFE-00062–2011

This government website lists publications, including the statutory obligations on schools with regard to clear responsibilities to respond to bullying. This specific document replaces the previous advice (*Safe To Learn: Embedding Anti-bullying Work in Schools*). It outlines the Government's approach to bullying, legal obligations and the powers schools have to tackle bullying and the principles which underpin the most effective anti-bullying strategies in schools. It also lists further resources through which school staff can access specialist information on the specific issues that they face.

www.antibullyingalliance.org.uk

Founded in 2002 by NSPCC and National Children's Bureau, the Anti-Bullying Alliance (ABA) brings together over 130 organizations into one network. It aims to develop a consensus around how to stop and prevent bullying, to influence policy, and to work to develop and disseminate best practice, in partnership with a range of organizations across England. The website has many useful links and resources, and includes plans for the annual anti-bullying week.

www.beatbullying.org

Beatbullying is a leading bullying prevention charity in the UK. Beatbullying works with children and young people across the UK to stop bullying. It aims to empower people to understand, recognize, and say no to bullying, violence and harassment by giving them the tools to transform their lives and the lives of their peers. Programmes include CyberMentors and MiniMentors, which have peer mentoring and peer activism at their heart.

References

Banerjee, R., Robinson, C. and Smalley, D. (2010), *Evaluation of the Beatbullying Peer Mentoring Programme*. Report for Beatbullying. University of Sussex.

Caravita, S., DiBlasio, P. and Salmivalli, C. (2009), 'Unique and interactive effects of empathy and social status on involvement in bullying'. *Social Development*, 18: 140–63.

Childline (2008), *Every School Should Have One: How Peer Support Schemes Make Schools Better*. London: NSPCC.

Cowie, H. and Smith, P. K. (2010), 'Peer support as a means of improving school safety and reducing bullying and violence'. In B. Doll, W. Pfohl and J. Yoon (eds), *Handbook of Prevention Research*. New York: Routledge, pp. 177–93.

Cowie, H. and Wallace, P. (2000), *Peer Support in Action – from Bystanding to Standing By*. London: Sage.

Cremin, H. (2010), 'RJ into schools: Does it go? Some theoretical and practical considerations'. ESRC funded seminar series: Restorative Approaches in schools.

Curtner-Smith, M. E., Smith, P. K. and Porter, M. (2010), 'Family level intervention with bullies and victims'. In E. Vernberg and B. Biggs (eds), *Preventing and Treating Bullying and Victimization*. Oxford: Oxford University Press, pp. 177–93.

DCSF (2007), *Safe to Learn: Embedding Anti-bullying Work in Schools*. Available online at www.antibullyingalliance.org.uk/tackling_bullying_behaviour/in_schools/law,_policy_and_guidance/safe_to_learn.aspx

DfE (2011), *Preventing and Tackling Bullying: Advice for Head Teachers, Staff and Governing Bodies*. Available online at www.education.gov.uk/publications ref: DFE-00062–2011.

Duncan, N. (1999), *Sexual Bullying: Gender Conflict in Pupil Culture*. London: Routledge.

Education and Inspections Act (2006). UK: The Stationery Office.

Equality Act (2010). UK: The Stationery Office.

Greene, M. B. (2006), 'Bullying in schools: A plea for measure of human rights'. *Journal of Social Issues*, 62: 63–79.

Hawker, D. S. J. and Boulton, M. J. (2000), 'Twenty years research on peer victimization and psychosocial maladjustment: A meta-analytic review of cross-sectional studies'. *Journal of Child Psychiatry and Psychiatry*, 41: 441–55.

Hodges, E. V. E., Malone, M. J. and Perry, D. G. (1997), 'Individual risk and social risk as interacting determinants of victimisation in the peer group'. *Developmental Psychology*, 33: 1032–9.

Houlston, C. and Smith, P. K. (2009), 'The impact of a peer counselling scheme to address bullying in an all-girl London secondary school: A short-term longitudinal study'. *British Journal of Educational Psychology*, 79: 69–86.

Houlston, C., Smith, P. K. and Jessel, J. (2009), 'Investigating the extent and use of peer support initiatives in English schools'. *Educational Psychology*, 29: 325–44.

Humphrey, N., Lendrum, A. and Wigelsworth, M. (2010), *Social and Emotional Aspects of Learning (SEAL) Programme in Secondary Schools: National Evaluation*. DFE-RB049.

Hunt, R. and Jensen, J. (2007), *The School Report: The Experiences of Young Gay People in Britain's Schools*. London: Stonewall.

Hunter, S. C. and Boyle, J. M. E. (2004), 'Appraisal and coping strategy use of victims of school bullying'. *British Journal of Educational Psychology*, 74: 83–107.

Hunter, S. C., Boyle, J. M. E. and Warden, D. (2007), 'Perceptions and correlates of peer-victimisation and bullying'. *British Journal of Educational Psychology*, 77: 797–810.

Jimerson, S. R., Swearer, S. and Espelage, D. L. (eds) (2010), *Handbook of Bullying in Schools*. New York and London: Routledge.

Kärnä, A., Voeten, M., Little, T., Poskiparta, E., Kaljonen, A. and Salmivalli, C. (2011), 'A large scale evaluation of the KiVa antibullying program: Grades 4–6'. *Child Development*, 82: 311–30.

Kim, Y-S. and Leventhal, B. (2008), 'Bullying and suicide: A review'. *International Journal of Adolescent Mental Health*, 20: 133–54.

Mishna, F. (2003), 'Learning disabilities and bullying: Double jeopardy'. *Journal of Learning Disabilities*, 36: 336–47.

Monks, C. and Coyne, I. (eds) (2011), *Bullying in Different Contexts*. Cambridge: Cambridge University Press.

Monks, C. and Smith, P. K. (2006), 'Definitions of 'bullying': Age differences in understanding of the term, and the role of experience'. *British Journal of Developmental Psychology*, 24: 801–21.

Naylor, P., Cowie, H. and del Rey, R. (2001), 'Coping strategies of secondary school children in response to being bullied'. *Child Psychology and Psychiatry Review*, 6: 114–20.

Nickerson, A. B., Mele, D. and Princiotta, D. (2008), 'Attachment and empathy as predictors of roles as defenders or outsiders in bullying interactions'. *Journal of School Psychology*, 46: 687–703.

OFSTED (2003a), *Bullying: Effective Action in Secondary Schools*. London: OFSTED.

— (2003b), *A Study of Children and Young People who Present Challenging Behaviour*. London: OFSTED.

Olweus, D. (1993), *Bullying at School: What We Know and What We Can Do*. Oxford: Blackwell.

Olweus, D. and Endresen, I. M. (1998), 'The importance of sex-of-stimulus object: Age trends and sex differences in empathic responsiveness'. *Social Development*, 3: 370–88.

Olweus, D. and Limber, S. (2010), 'The Olweus Bullying Prevention Programme: Implementation and evaluation over two decades', in S. R. Jimerson, S. Swearer and D. L. Espelage (eds), *Handbook of Bullying in Schools*. New York and London: Routledge, pp. 377–401.

Ortega, R., del Rey, R. and Mora-Merchan, J. (2004), 'SAVE model: An anti-bullying intervention in Spain', in P. K. Smith, D. Pepler and K. Rigby (eds), *Bullying in Schools: How Successful Can Interventions Be?* Cambridge: Cambridge University Press, pp. 167–85.

Patchin, J. W. and Hinduja, S. (2010), 'Trends in online social networking: Adolescent use of MySpace over time'. *New Media and Society*, 12: 197–216. doi:10.1177/1461444809341857.

Paul, S., Smith, P. K. and Blumberg, H. H. (2010), 'Addressing cyberbullying in school using the quality circle approach'. *Australian Journal of Guidance and Counselling*, 20, 157–68. doi: 10.1375/ajgc.20.2.157.

— (in press), 'Revisiting cyberbullying in schools using the quality circle approach'. *School Psychology International*.

Pellegrini, A. D. and Bartini, M. (2001), 'Dominance in early adolescent boys: Affiliative and aggressive dimensions and possible functions'. *Merrill-Palmer Quarterly*, 47, 142–63.

Pikas, A. (1989), 'A pure conception of mobbing gives the best for treatment'. *School Psychology International*, 10: 95–104.

— (2002), 'New developments of the Shared Concern Method'. *School Psychology International*, 23: 307–26.

Restorative Justice Consortium (2005), *Statement of Restorative Justice Principles: As Applied in a School Setting*. London: Restorative Justice Consortium. Available online at www.restorativejustice.org.uk.

Rigby, K. (2002), *New Perspectives on Bullying*. London and Philadelphia: Jessica Kingsley.

Rigby, K. and Griffiths, C. (2010), *Applying the Method of Shared Concern in Australian Schools: An Evaluative Study*. Canberra: Department of Education, Employment and Workplace Relations (DEEWR). Available online at www.deewr.gov.au/schooling/nationalsafeschools/pages/research.aspx

Rigby, K. and Johnson, B. (2006), 'Expressed readiness of Australian schoolchildren to act as bystanders in support of children who are being bullied'. *Educational Psychology*, 26: 425–40.

Rigby, K. and Smith, P. K. (2011), 'Is school bullying really on the rise?' *Social Psychology of Education*, 14: 441–55.

Robinson, B. and Maines, G. (2007), *Bullying: A Complete Guide to the Support Group Method*. London: Sage.

Roland, E. (2011), 'The broken curve: Norwegian manifesto against bullying'. *International Journal of Behavioural Development*, 35: 383–8.

Salmivalli, C., Kaukiainen, A., Kaistaniemi, L. and Lagerspetz, K. (1999), 'Self-evaluated self-esteem, peer-evaluated self-esteem, and defensive egotism as predictors of adolescents' participation in bullying situations'. *Personality and Social Psychology Bulletin*, 25: 1268–78.

Salmivalli, C., Lagerspetz, K., Björkqvist, K., Österman, K. and Kaukiainen, A. (1996), 'Bullying as a group process: Participant roles and their relations to social status within the group'. *Aggressive Behavior*, 22: 1–15.

Schwartz, D., Dodge, K. A., Pettit, G. S. and Bates, J. E. (1997), 'The early socialization of aggressive victims of bullying'. *Child Development*, 68: 665–75.

Sherman, L. W. and Strang, H. (2007), *Restorative Justice: The Evidence*. London: The Smith Institute.

Slee, P. T. and Rigby, K. (1993), 'Australian schoolchildren's self-appraisal of interpersonal relations: The bullying experience'. *Child Psychiatry and Human Development*, 23: 272–83.

Smith, P. K. (2012), 'Cyberbullying and cyber aggression'. in S. R. Jimerson, A. B. Nickerson, M. J. Mayer and M. J. Furlong (eds), *Handbook of School Violence and School Safety: International Research and Practice*. New York: Routledge, pp. 93–103.

Smith, P. K. and Sharp, S. (eds) (1994), *School Bullying: Insights and Perspectives*. London: Routledge.

Smith, P. K. and Watson, D. (2004), *Evaluation of the CHIPS (ChildLine in Partnership with Schools) Programme. Research report RR570*. London: DfES.

Smith, P. K., Howard, S. and Thompson, F. (2007), 'A survey of use of the Support Group Method in England, and some evaluation from schools and Local Authorities'. *Pastoral Care in Education*, 25: 4–13.

Smith, P. K., Pepler, D. J. and Rigby, K. (eds) (2004), *Bullying in Schools: How Successful Can Interventions Be?* Cambridge: Cambridge University Press.

Smith, P. K., Salmivalli, C. and Cowie, H. (2012), 'Effectiveness of school-based programs to reduce bullying: A commentary'. *Journal of Experimental Criminology* (in press).

Smith, P. K., Talamelli, L., Cowie, H., Naylor, P. and Chauhan, P. (2004), 'Profiles of non-victims, escaped victims, continuing victims and new victims of school bullying'. *British Journal of Educational Psychology*, 74: 565–81.

Smith, P. K., Kupferberg, A., Mora-Merchan, J. A., Samara, M., Bosley, S. and Osborn, R. (2012), 'A content analysis of school anti-bullying policies: A follow-up after six years'. *Educational Psychology in Practice*, 28: 61–84.

Smith, P. K., Mahdavi, J., Carvalho, M., Fisher, S., Russell, S. and Tippett, N. (2008), 'Cyberbullying: Its nature and impact in secondary school pupils'. *Journal of Child Psychology and Psychiatry*, 49: 376–85.

Smith, P. K., Morita, Y., Junger-Tas, J., Olweus, D., Catalano, R. and Slee, P. (1999), *The Nature of School Bullying: A Cross-National Perspective*. London and New York: Routledge.

Sutton, J., Smith, P. K. and Swettenham, J. (1999), 'Social cognition and bullying: Social inadequacy or skilled manipulation?' *British Journal of Developmental Psychology*, 17: 435–50.

Thompson, F. and Smith, P. K. (2011), *The Use and Effectiveness of Anti-bullying Strategies in Schools*. DFE-RR098. London: DfE.

Thompson, F., Robinson, S. and Smith, P. K. (in press). 'An evaluation of some cyberbullying interventions in England'. In M. L. Genta, A. Brighi and A. Guarini (eds), *Cyberbullismo: Ricerche e Strategie di Intervento* [*Cyberbullying: Research and Intervention Strategies*]. Milano: Franco Angeli.

Tippett, N., Houlston, C. and Smith, P. K. (2011), *Prevention and Response to Identity-Based Bullying among Local Authorities in England, Scotland and Wales*. Equality and Human Rights Commission. Research Report 64.

Tokunaga, R. S. (2010), 'Following you home from school: A critical review and synthesis of research on cyberbullying victimization'. *Computers in Human Behavior*, 26: 277–87.

Ttofi, M. M. and Farrington, D. P. (2011), 'Effectiveness of school-based programs to reduce bullying: A systematic and meta-analytic review'. *Journal of Experimental Criminology*, 7: 27–56.

Young, S. (1998), 'The Support Group approach to bullying in schools'. *Educational Psychology in Practice*, 14: 32–9.

Youth Justice Board (2004), *National Evaluation of the Restorative Justice in Schools Programme*. Youth Justice Board Publication, Number D61.

4

Children and Young People Affected by Domestic Violence and Abuse: The Role of Schools in Promoting Safety, Well-Being and Protection

Christine Harrison and Ravi Thiara

Chapter Outline

Introduction

Over the last decade it has been recognized that witnessing domestic violence and abuse is a major source of harm for children and young people, which can have a serious impact on their health, development and well-being (Mullender et al., 2002; Holt et al., 2008). Although it is difficult to determine accurately how many children in the UK this involves, it is likely substantially to exceed the 750,000 a year estimated by the Department of Health (2002), since it is known to be an under-reported form of gender violence (Smith et al., 2011). Awareness has also increased about the level of domestic violence that is experienced by young people in their earliest intimate relationships (teenage relationship violence) (Barter et al., 2009). The majority of children affected can be regarded as children and young people in need (as defined by Section 17 of the Children Act 1989) or children in special circumstances (as described in Standard 5, the National Service Framework for Children, Young People and Maternity Services, Department of Health, 2007). Often in the past they have been referred to as hidden or forgotten victims of domestic violence (Unicef, 2005), who may never come to the attention of child welfare, or criminal justice agencies. Nearly all of those affected, however, will be attending schools and having contact with education professionals.

School can be a haven for children and young people affected by domestic violence in different ways. The routine of going to school, gaining a sense of achievement, having positive relationships with peers, and adults, can be a source of resilience and self-esteem (Johnson, 2008). Schools can also provide a safe and non-stigmatizing source of information, and help and support (to mothers as well as children and young people). For children and young people living with the most extreme and damaging effects of domestic violence, teachers and pastoral tutors who know them well are uniquely placed to recognize this, and to intervene to offer appropriate and timely services. Finally, school communities are in a position to develop and provide interventions that promote the safety and recovery of children who are affected. Importantly, these interventions include whole-school anti-violence strategies integrated within the curriculum and Personal Social Health and Economic education (PSHE), classroom strategies through which teachers can support children and specialist services for individual and groups of children provided within the school.

While education professionals are able to promote the well-being of children affected by domestic violence, they need also to be aware that children's (and women's) safety needs may be such that child protection procedures have to be discussed or initiated. The relationship between domestic violence and child protection is complex, and relies on effective inter-professional working between education professionals, child protection leads in schools and other professionals involved with children, including social workers (Department for Children, Schools and Families, 2010).

Critical studies of childhood centralize an understanding of children and young people as an economically and socially powerless social group that may experience multiple and intersecting discrimination (Wyness, 2012). Where the experience of domestic violence and abuse is concerned, these theoretical insights prompt us, when considering the impact on children of living with domestic violence and abuse, to recognize:

- the importance of seeking their perspectives
- the impact on them of other aspects of discrimination and oppression (such as racism)
- the need to involve children and young people as active participants.

This book about pastoral care concentrates on young people aged between 11–16 years, a critical period in developmental terms (Meece and Daniels, 2007; Maholmes and Lomonaco, 2010). Where this chapter about domestic violence and abuse is concerned, it is important to remember that they may be affected not only by what happens within this stage of their life, but also by what may have happened earlier in their lives: domestic violence has cumulative effects which are more serious if exposure commenced at a young age and has been frequent, enduring and severe (Rossman, 2001).

The chapter draws on relevant national and international research to address the following questions:

- What is known about the extent and nature of domestic violence?
- What is the impact on children and young people of domestic violence, including post-separation violence?
- What is needed to support the resilience and recovery of children and their mothers?
- What whole-school, classroom or individual strategies can be developed to support children and promote their safety and well-being?

Research about the nature and extent of domestic violence

Consistent with the weight of research findings, this chapter adopts the following definition of domestic violence and abuse: 'Domestic violence typically involves a pattern of physical, sexual and emotional abuse and intimidation, which escalates in frequency and severity over time. It can be understood as the misuse of power and exercise of control (Pence and Paymar, 1996) by one partner over another in an intimate relationship, usually by a man over a woman, occasionally by a woman over a man and also occurring amongst same-sex couples' (Humphreys and Mullender, 1998, p. 6). Gendered terminology is used in this chapter to reflect this dominant pattern of domestic violence, and to acknowledge that women comprise by far the majority of victims or survivors of domestic violence. It is appreciated that women can perpetrate domestic violence, and that this also occurs in same-sex relationships, raising the same issues of safety for children and adult survivors (Donovan, et al., 2006; McCarry et al., 2008). In these instances, the impact on children is likely to be the same, and should neither be underestimated nor minimized.

The nature of domestic violence

Much can be understood about the harmful impact of domestic violence and abuse on children and young people by reviewing its nature and form. As indicated above, domestic violence includes physical, sexual, psychological or financial violence inflicted within an intimate or family-type relationship. Numerous research studies have shown how domestic violence is rarely confined to a single form of abuse, but rather it involves the imposition of multiple and overlapping forms of violence intended to maintain the perpetrator's power and control over their female partner (Department of Health, 2005). Figure 4.1 below illustrates these different forms of violence and highlights how domestic violence can permeate every aspect of a child's life and well-being. Domestic violence isolates women and children from sources of help and support, and results in homes dominated by fear and apprehension (Hague et al., 2003). An examination of interrelationships between different aspects of

Physical - pushing, shoving, punching, biting, scratching, pinching, slapping, shaking, suffocating, strangling, 'fun' fights, choking, cutting, burning, genital mutilation and 'honour' violence

Psychological and emotional - isolating, name calling, constant criticism, belittling, accusing, undermining, contradicting, swearing, hurting pets, underining parenting threatening the children

Sexual - rape, demeaning sexual practices, forced sexual contact or acts with others, pimping, pornography, ignoring religious prohibitions, unsafe sex, forced marriage

Financial - stopping a woman from working, witholding money, gambling, taking money from women, not paying child maintenance, financial irresponsibility

Figure 4.1 Adapted from: Department of Health (2005) *Responding to Domestic Abuse: A Handbook for Health Professionals.* London: Stationery Office

domestic violence also demonstrates that, rather than being impulsive or indicative of a loss of control related to anger, alcohol or drug misuse, premeditation and deliberation are often involved.

Children's own accounts of living with domestic violence also reveal the interrelated nature of domestic violence and abuse, as in one child's description that domestic violence is:

> When your dad shouts, makes everyone frightened and hurts your mum.
> (Mullender et al., 2002, p. 36)

The extent of domestic violence

Although under-reported, domestic violence and abuse is one of the most frequently reported serious criminal offences, representing 18 per cent of violent crime in England and Wales, and one twentieth of all crime (Smith et al., 2011). As already indicated, domestic violence is pre-eminently a gender-based crime, and research suggests that one in four women will experience domestic violence during her lifetime

(Hester et al., 2000). Not only has it been established that domestic violence usually involves multiple forms of violence, but also it is known to escalate in severity and frequency over time (Department of Health, 2005). Each year, there are 13 million incidents or threats of physical violence against women from partners or former partners, 76 per cent of which are repeat incidents (Flatley et al., 2010). This form of gender violence is more likely than other violent crimes to result in injury; the more severe the physical violence that occurs, the more likely that sexual violence will also be inflicted by perpetrators (Richards, 2004; McFarlane and Malecha, 2005). In 2009/10, 54 per cent of women murder victims in England and Wales were killed by a partner or former partner (Smith et al., 2011), and in almost half these cases there was a history of previous violence. When there is escalating violence, sexual violence is a significant risk marker for domestic homicide, a phenomenon also noted in Australia, Canada and the US (Richards, 2003; Sully and Greenaway, 2005; Braaf, 2008).

A range of factors limits women's access to safety and support, for themselves and their children. Consequently, women endure on average 35 assaults before they are able to make a report to the police (Yearnshaw, 1997), although there are recent indications of women's greater willingness to report (Hester and Westmarland, 2005). More than this, however, will be endured by women from Black and minority ethnic groups, including refugees and asylum seekers, who face even more formidable barriers to accessing services and securing safety for themselves and for their children (Thiara and Breslin, 2006; Patel and Siddiqui, 2010; Thiara and Gill, 2012).

Research about the impact of domestic violence on children and young people

Given evidence about the extent and nature of male violence towards female partners and ex-partners, it is not surprising that this constitutes a major source of adversity and harm for children and young people who are direct or indirect witnesses. Although it is difficult to estimate how many children's health, development and well-being are affected, the numbers are likely to be substantial (Hester et al., 2000; Worral et al., 2008; Radford et al., 2011a). Possibly one in three children and young people will be exposed to some degree during their childhood or young adulthood (Cawson, 2002), and a recent NSPCC study estimated that 18 per cent of 11- to 17-year-olds had been exposed to domestic violence and abuse (Radford et al., 2011a). Despite their mothers' efforts to shield them, even children and young people who have not directly witnessed domestic violence may be aware that it is happening and will be affected by this (Gorin, 2004; Radford et al., 2011b). In between 75 per cent and 90 per cent of families where men have been violent to women, children have been in the room or in the room next door when this happened (Mullender, 2004):

> It used to be behind closed doors. But I used to know and I would see the bruises that she had before that. (12-year-old girl, Mullender et al., 2002, p. 93)

When exploring harm caused to children, it is important also to consider the impact of domestic violence on women's health, including their mental health, on women's parenting and on their relationships with their children (Radford and Hester, 2006; Lapierre, 2010). Mothers remain the most important route to safety and recovery for children and young people, and their most important source of support (Hogan and O'Reilly, 2007); attempts to promote mothers' safety are likely to benefit their children (Humphreys et al., 2006).

Children can be negatively affected in many ways by exposure to domestic violence and abuse. They can see or hear violence. They can get caught up in violence. They can suffer because they live in a violent atmosphere and their mother is constantly frightened. They may be exposed to perpetual criticism of their mother, or suffer as a result of economic deprivation and social isolation that is frequently an aspect of domestic violence. They may experience frequent moves of home and school and sources of support may be lost, including family relationships and friendships. As already noted, the relationship between mothers and children may be a specific target of domestic violence, and women often report being prevented from providing children with the kind of care that they want to provide (Bancroft and Silverman, 2002;

Kaye et al., 2003). Children may be manipulated by threats or induce-ments on the part of perpetrators, who are known to involve children and young people in violence, for example by encouraging them to act in an abusive way towards their mother (McGee, 2000).

Studies emphasize that children's responses to domestic violence are variable, and that age, gender, disability, stage of development and other factors will influence the consequences for them (Mullender et al., 2002). The nature of domestic violence means that most children and young people who are exposed to it will be affected, but at the same time some children appear to have greater resilience than others, and they may have more protective factors in their lives (Humphreys, 2006). It is also important to recognize that when children are also facing other forms of discrimination, such as poverty, racism or homophobia (Sokoloff and Dupont, 2005) the harmful impact of domestic violence may be exacer-bated. Such experiences may also be incorporated in the perpetrator's violence (e.g. in the form of racist abuse towards a mother or child). For Black or minority ethnic children and young people, racism (or fears of racism), and lack of cultural sensitivity, have meant that they have had difficulties in accessing services, adding to distress and harm (Thiara and Breslin, 2006; Malley-Morrison and Hines, 2007; Izzidien, 2008).

The complicated and traumatic impact of exposure to domestic vio-lence and abuse may be manifest in a range of emotional, social, psy-chological and behavioural responses (Hester et al., 2000) with both short- and longer-term implications; the greater children's exposure, the poorer their developmental outcomes will be, including those related to learning and educational development (Kitzmann et al., 2003). The literature describes the effects in terms of externalized responses, such as aggression, destructiveness, defiance and internalized responses, such as anxiety, depression, fear and low self-esteem. There may also be somatic signs of distress, such as stomach aches and headaches, and both externalized and internalized responses may result in difficulties in social interactions with adults and peers, including difficulties at school (Kitzmann et al., 2003; Martinez-Torteya et al., 2009).

Many children, including those exposed to severe or persistent violence, show signs of post-traumatic stress disorder (PTSD) (Jarvis et al., 2005; Graham-Bermann and Seng, 2005). Children affected in this way may display more intense forms of the above internalized and externalized behaviours, and also have to deal with intrusive recall of events, 'flashbacks', avoidant or numbed responses, hyper-vigilance, inability to concentrate, watchfulness and disturbed sleep.

These are all adult and often professional views of children's experiences. When children's own experiences have been explored, they have revealed a tumultuous, confusing range of feelings that include fear, anger, sadness, terror, loss, torn loyalty, responsibility, helplessness, despair, worry and guilt (Mullender et al., 2002; Holt et al., 2008; Hogan and O'Reilly, 2007). These often result in profound feelings of shame and powerlessness (Mullender et al., 2002).

Thinking in terms of a developmental trajectory

Many children and young people exposed to domestic violence will have experienced this throughout their childhoods. Exploring the effects of domestic violence and abuse in terms of a developmental trajectory not only highlights the impact of domestic violence within a particular stage of development, but also reveals the cumulative effects of violence over a whole or substantial part of childhood and adolescence (Margolin and Gordis, 2000).

It is estimated that for 30 per cent of women who experience domestic violence, this commenced during pregnancy, and that 40–50 per cent of women who experience domestic violence are abused while pregnant (Taft, 2002; Thiara and Gill, 2012). Domestic violence during pregnancy has been described as a dual attack on the mother and the foetus (Kelly, 1994; Mezey and Bewley, 1997), as it increases the risk of foetal injury and complications during delivery, and of miscarriage and pre-term birth (Bacchus et al., 2002). It also begins the process of undermining the mother, and distorting the relationship between a mother and her child.

Like the unborn child, it is mistaken to assume that babies and young children are unaffected by exposure to domestic violence. They may lack cognitive understanding of events, but are known to react to the stress and tension caused by domestic violence with elevated levels of distress and disturbed sleep, and there are concerns about their neurological and cognitive development (Rossman, 2001) and, in extreme circumstances, failure to thrive (Bair-Merritt et al., 2006). Toddlers may have frequent stomach aches and headaches, worry about being separated from their mum, fear the dark and have nightmares. They may regress in their development and behaviour, or there may be evidence of developmental delay in speech and language.

Women frequently report being attacked while holding babies (Christian et al., 1997), or of being frightened to respond to crying babies (Taft, 2002). Significantly, research has shown that perpetrators' tactics of abuse frequently involve deliberately undermining mothering (Thiara et al., 2006; Lapierre, 2010). This can impact on women's ability to look after children, especially if they become socially isolated, or use drugs and alcohol as a survival strategy (Humphreys et al., 2006; Radford and Hester, 2006).

During the middle years of childhood, children may increasingly demonstrate their distress through their behaviour and emotional responses. This can include withdrawn reactions, wanting to fade into the background and more difficult and aggressive behaviour, as they attempt to make sense of and survive their conflicted feelings, and the consequences of domestic violence and abuse for themselves, their mothers and their siblings. Children may have been directly or indirectly exposed to sexual, physical and emotional violence for several years. Their relationship with their mother may be further compromised as children start to question whether she really is bad, or incompetent. Mortal fear may be experienced when children see that their mother cannot protect herself. If she cannot protect herself, how can she protect them?

> It used to happen all the time when he was around. I used to shut myself up in my room and listen to my music to block it all out. (Girl, Thiara and Gill, 2012, p. 43)

Children and young people's self-confidence and self-esteem may increasingly be eroded, and difficulties in relationships with peers and adults exacerbated. Some of these worrying effects may be overlooked, and others can be misconstrued, for example, as Attention Deficit Hyperactivity Disorder (ADHD).

> She was doing so badly at school. The teachers would call me all the time, she was not listening, she wasn't settled, it has impacted on her a lot . . . to see knives, to see fights every minute. (Girl, Thiara and Gill, 2012, p. 42)

There are parallels between the experiences of women and those of their children. Women who have endured escalating domestic violence and abuse find that their coping abilities are severely diminished. They struggle to parent increasingly distressed children, as 'depression saps their energy and self-esteem, while the numbing aspects of trauma may cut them off from being emotionally available to their children' (Humphreys and Thiara, 2002, p. 55).

At the same time, during this period, children often describe changing understandings of what has been happening, as they move from uncertainty to gradual realization:

> He always used to say that she hit him first and she started it. But she didn't. (12-year-old girl, Mullender et al., 2002, p. 168)

A focus on young people

Adolescents who have lived with domestic violence for several years frequently experience intense feelings of responsibility, guilt, anger and a sense of despair and powerlessness over their lives. They may try to escape their difficult circumstances in different ways. Some strive for educational attainment, and a group of children and young people affected by domestic violence appear to find solace in their academic achievements (Mullender et al., 2002). Others develop survival strategies through the use of drugs and alcohol, and have an exceptionally blasé approach to risky activities. Alternatively, they may experience high levels of anxiety and depression, and turn their feelings of powerlessness in on themselves.

> I used to feel I was bleeding inside. (15-year-old girl, Mullender et al., 2002, p. 110)

The intensity of young people's difficulties and their behavioural responses may bring them into confrontational situations in schools and, if underlying contributory factors are not obvious, they are liable to be labelled as problematic. Isolated and disaffected, they are over-represented in those who are excluded from school, the young homeless and those at risk of involvement in offending (Hester et al., 2000; Holt et al., 2008).

As they get older, young people are more likely actively to intervene when domestic violence or abuse is perpetrated against their mothers, to protect her or their siblings (Mullender et al., 2002). Often this involves shouting, but interviews with women show how worried they are about young people physically intervening, as this young man did:

> I was punching him and my mum was crying. (Thiara and Gill, 2012, p. 44)

While there are undoubted dangers in such interventions, it is also the case that some young people view having intervened as a source of empowerment.

Young people's understandings can shift again during adolescence, and one insidious impact of domestic violence is that young people's strong feelings often become directed towards their mothers. Women may have stayed with violent partners because they thought it was best for their children, only later to find that their children question why they did so (Mullender et al., 2002). Occasionally, young people's anger and frustration are expressed through verbal and physical violence towards their mothers (Radford et al., 2011b).

Some research has found a gendered dimension to responses, with young men being described as more likely to display externalized responses, and young women internalized responses (Evans et al., 2008), and this has contributed to ideas about an intergenerational transmission or cycle of violence. Mullender et al. (2002) showed, however, that young people cannot simply be categorized within a gendered typology of externalized or internalized responses. Nor is there an inevitable cycle of violence: the majority of young people who have witnessed domestic violence do not repeat this in their adult lives (Laing, 2000).

Domestic violence, child abuse and other forms of victimization: Making the connections

While the impact of living with domestic violence on children and young people's development and well-being is serious enough, this may be exacerbated if they are contending with multiple or overlapping forms of maltreatment (Mullender, 2004; Radford et al., 2011a). A substantial literature confirms the interconnected nature of domestic violence and child abuse (Hume, 2003; Walby, 2004). Domestic violence towards a mother increases the likelihood of violence towards her child, and the severity and the length of time over which violence has occurred increases the risks for children. One extensive research review showed a correlation between the occurrence of domestic violence and that of child abuse of between 30 per cent and 66 per cent (Edleson, 1997).

Cawson's research in the UK also underlined the relationship between domestic violence and child abuse (Cawson, 2002), and Radford et al.'s more recent study showed that children who have experienced child maltreatment are at least twice as likely to have also witnessed domestic violence (Radford et al., 2011a). Domestic violence and abuse is known to be present in the majority of cases (75–80%) where child protection conferences are convened (Humphreys and Thiara, 2002; Thiara, 2010).

Post-separation violence

For many women and children, violence intensifies after separation (Kelly, 1999; Statistics Canada, 2005), and some women suffer persistent post-separation violence (Humphreys and Thiara, 2002) over long periods of time (Harrison, 2008; Thiara and Gill, 2012). Murders of women and children where there is a history of domestic violence frequently take place at the point of separation (Wilson and Daly, 2002; Richards, 2003; Saunders, 2004).

Children living with post-separation violence are considered among the most distressed in the population, displaying high levels of behavioural and emotional disturbance and persistent depression (Holt et al., 2008; Stanley, 2011). For these children, contact with violent men may be of little benefit and may impede their recovery (Jaffe et al., 2003). Conversely, where children have no contact with violent fathers, the harm they have sustained can be ameliorated. Children's recovery has been found to be related to that of their mother; continuing threats or contact proceedings used to protract conflict often mean that mothers are unable to recover, which has an indirect effect on children (Strategic Partners, 1998; Sturge and Glaser, 2000):

> He still follows my mum. He's always been standing outside and my mum kept telling the police but the police don't arrest him. . . . (Boy, Thiara and Gill, 2012, p. 45)

Case Study: Jack

Jack is 12 years old and you have been his tutor since he began senior school 18 months ago. He is lively and enthusiastic, and can sometimes be a handful in a classroom situation. You are aware that Jack's father has been violent towards his mother, and that Jack has directly witnessed physical attacks that have involved the police. Jack's mother has kept the school advised of the situation. She separated from Jack's father eight months ago, and has since been really concerned that Jack's father may attempt to take him out of school. Jack had no contact with his father for two months, but is now seeing him every weekend, with supervision.

You have been looking out for Jack and had hoped that things would have improved after the parental separation. However, you have noticed that his behaviour has changed. He comes in on Monday seeming withdrawn and depressed, not mixing with his usual friends. By the end of the school week he is behaving in a truculent and aggressive manner.

Questions

1. What steps do you think could be taken to support Jack?
2. How could you create a safe and confidential space for Jack?
3. Who is appropriate to provide this support in school or outside school?

Teenage relationship violence

Research from the US, Australia and the UK demonstrates that domestic violence and abuse is commonly experienced by young people in their earliest intimate relationships, to an alarming degree (referred to in international research as dating violence or teen dating violence):

> My boyfriend and I have been together for two years – he started beating me after about three months. It makes me feel so worthless. (ChildLine, 2006, p. 4)

Some studies find higher prevalence rates for young women than for adult women (Silverman et al., 2001) and show that violence can start at a remarkably young age. Teenage relationship violence takes forms similar to those outlined in Figure 4.1 above, reflecting the intention of perpetrators to impose power and control. The significance of gender is more complex than in relation to adult domestic violence, where the vast majority of perpetrators are male, and in teenage relationship violence, a higher proportion of young women are involved.

Research Example: Teenage Relationship Violence

The first extensive study of teenage relationship violence in England, Scotland and Wales was undertaken by Barter et al., 2009. A survey of 1,353 and interviews with 91 13–17-year-olds found that a quarter of young women and 18 per cent of young men who had experienced an intimate relationship reported some form of physical violence (pushing, slapping, hitting, being held down). Where repeated violence was concerned, gender differentials widened: being the subject of physical violence a few times or often was reported by almost twice as many young women as young men. Where there was more severe violence (punching, strangling, being beaten up or being hit with an object), the numbers were much fewer, but the gender differential greater still, with this being reported by 11 per cent of young women and 4 per cent of young men. When the impact of the violence was discussed, an 'overwhelming gender division emerged' (Barter et al., 2009, p. 46), and 76 per cent of young women compared to 14 per cent of young men who had experienced physical violence felt that it had negatively impacted on their well-being. Worryingly, the study found that girls were more likely than boys to remain in a relationship once violence had occurred.

Emotional violence or control was reported by 72 per cent of girls and 51 per cent of boys, which had impacted negatively on 31 per cent of girls and 6 per cent of boys. Sexual violence was less often reported, but had been experienced by 31 per cent of girls and 16 per cent of boys. Young people with a same sex partner were more likely to report physical, emotional and sexual violence. For all the above forms of violence, having an older partner increased risks for young women, for example 78 per cent of incidents of sexual violence were imposed by an older partner.

Reference

Barter, C., McCarry, M., Berridge, D. and Evans, K. (2009), *Partner Exploitation and Violence in Teenage Intimate Relationships*. London: NSPCC.

For young women from some Black and minority ethnic communities, forced marriage[1] is a recognized form of gender violence, the majority of victims of which are young women (Kazimirski et al., 2009). Guidance for schools and other agencies about forced marriage (together with female genital mutilation and 'honour' violence) was introduced in 2008 and revised in 2010 (HM Government, 2010). Concerns remain about the low level of awareness in schools, where forced marriage is still regarded by some as a 'cultural practice' (Kazimirski et al., 2009; House of Commons Home Affairs Select Committee, 2008).

Gang-related youth violence has also been shown to include violence against young women who are gang members, or involved with gang members, overlapping with relationship violence. Young women in Firmin's study were often subject to violence from other gang members, as well as boyfriends (Firmin, 2011). Dominant gang culture resulted in young women often being treated as the possession of all gang members. The incorporation of rape as a part of gang membership in the UK is increasingly being documented (Yexley, 2009). Multiple perpetrator rape may be inflicted to test young women's commitment to a gang or gang member, to deter young women from reporting other crimes, or to intimidate others with the inviolable power of the gang.

Awareness of teenage relationship violence indicates that many young people attending school may be contending with interpersonal violence that they did not anticipate, and with which they are ill-equipped to deal. They may be frightened or ashamed of disclosing abuse, and some appear quickly to become inured to violence. Other factors also prevent young people from accessing help, including, for example, that the perpetrator attends the same school or is part of a wider family or friendship network. Distress, fear and confusion may disrupt development and learning, and destabilize protective factors and sources of resilience by creating distance between young people, their parents and friends. The extent of teenage violence also raises concerns about young people's attitudes towards gender violence, and how these are shaping the expectations and behaviours of young women and young men (Harber, 2004). Research undertaken by Burman and Cartmel (2005) found that a third of young men and a sixth of young women interviewed condoned violence in intimate relationships in some circumstances, replicating findings from earlier studies (Burton et al., 1998; Mullender et al., 2002).

Case Study: Jas

Jas is a 15-year-old young woman who has been having a relationship with a 17-year-old young man who also attends her school. This started as a friendship, but has become more serious over the last six months. Jas has never been a problem in the classroom and is a good pupil. She is punctual, her attendance is exemplary and she is popular with a core group of friends. She gets on with her work

⇨

and is predicted to get reasonable grades in her GCSEs. But you have noticed some definite changes over recent weeks. At first these were subtle – she was just a little less participative and a little more preoccupied – so you readily dismissed them. These changes are now more pronounced, and include an agitation she has never displayed before and a marked lack of concentration that is reflected in a deteriorating standard of work. You have noticed that Jas's boyfriend often seems to be hanging about her classroom and she is constantly checking her phone and texts. Today she came into class with what appear to be finger bruises round her jaw and she is distressed.

Questions. If you were Jas's Form Tutor:

1. What would be your immediate response?
2. How would you approach the issues with her?
3. If Jas discloses that her boyfriend has become increasingly controlling and last night grabbed her by the jaw, what steps would you take?

Promoting children's safety and well-being – the contribution of pastoral care

Knowing that domestic violence and abuse affects so many children and young people, and that teenage relationship violence is extensive, demonstrates the need for a wide range of services to promote safety and recovery (Stafford et al., 2007; Humphreys et al., 2008; HM Government, 2011 and 2012). There is also a need for greater attention to be given to early intervention, including the challenging area of prevention (HM Government, 2012). Children and women do recover, with appropriate help and support and services that build on their strengths and coping strategies. Safety is crucial, and children and young people need to feel and be safe before they can fully benefit (Mullender, 2004). Children's complex needs can best be met by coordinated preventive and support services that are easily accessible and delivered on an inter-agency basis by statutory agencies (health, education and children's social care) and by voluntary sector agencies (specialized domestic violence intervention services and refuges).

Schools have an important part to play in recognizing children and young people who are affected by domestic violence, and in providing information and enabling them to access appropriate services (Firmin, 2011; HM Government, 2011 and 2012). Children and young people have themselves indicated that schools are where they want to access information, to learn about domestic violence and safe relationships, and to access help and support (Mullender et al., 2002; Radford et al., 2011b; HM Government, 2012).

A useful way to explore the contribution of pastoral care in schools in this regard is to consider primary, secondary and tertiary levels of intervention with children and young people (see Figure 4.2 below). This approach is combined with understandings about gender violence that recognize the relevance of societal attitudes and values (HM Government, 2012). It concentrates on work with children and young people, but it should not be forgotten that schools can also be an important place for women to access information and support.

All three levels of intervention above have been assessed as having the potential to make a contribution to tackling domestic violence and

Figure 4.2 A framework for prevention of and early intervention in relation to domestic violence and abuse (adapted from Wolfe and Jaffe, 1999)

Level	Services to children and young people	Services or interventions to address domestic violence in schools
Primary	Universal services to promote the health and well-being of all children and young people by preventing gender violence	• School-based anti-violence strategies • Campaigns to raise awareness of domestic violence
Secondary	Services to children and young people who appear to be experiencing distress and/or difficulty that could be a result of domestic violence and abuse	• School-based services to build self-esteem • Peer support programmes • Teaching and learning support – homework clubs
Tertiary	Services and interventions where harm/abuse related to domestic violence is known already to have occurred	• Intensive therapeutic interventions • Child protection enquiries

abuse by improving prevention, protection and recovery for children and young people. It is recognized, however, that many schools, local authorities and domestic violence services will be dealing with stringent resource constraints that limit the possibilities for progressive developments.

Primary prevention – promoting the health and well-being of all children and young people by preventing gender violence

Research about domestic violence and abuse provides a compelling rationale for primary prevention and universal school-based interventions aimed at raising awareness about and reducing gender violence and other forms of prejudicial violence. Approaches designed to enable children and young people to develop knowledge about non-abusive, respectful and healthy relationships and to provide support to children and young people living with the impact of domestic violence and abuse have been more extensively developed in other countries (e.g. in the US, Canada and Australia) (Ellis et al., 2006; Barter et al., 2009). Over recent years in the UK, however, there has been greater emphasis placed on the need to integrate anti-violence strategies within the school curriculum (Ellis, 2008; HM Government, 2011 and 2012; Stanley, 2011). Children and young people support this and say that they want lessons on domestic violence in schools, and where this has already happened, the majority felt that they had benefited (Hester and Westmarland, 2005; Bell and Stanley, 2006; Thiara and Ellis, 2005).

A review of prevention work in UK schools for Womankind Worldwide (undertaken in 2004) showed that provision was fragmented, underfunded and often dependent on the efforts of individuals or groups, rather than strategic investment (Ellis, 2008). A more recent evaluation of Womankind Worldwide's *Challenging Violence, Changing Lives* (a programme delivered to Key Stages 3 and 4 in 11 UK secondary schools) showed that programmes could raise awareness of violence and gender inequality, and contribute to changing attitudes and behaviours. Drawing on findings from a number of evaluations of prevention interventions (Debbonaire, 2002; Bell and Stanley, 2006;

Womankind, 2007; Ellis, 2008) the following appear important for successful outcomes:

- A whole-school approach, which aims to develop a non-violent school culture.
- Active leadership from staff, and involvement of governors, staff and parents.
- Working partnerships with specialist domestic violence services in planning and delivery.
- A multi-agency approach, with access to specialist domestic violence support services, and support to staff delivering the work.
- Community involvement and awareness-raising; media involvement; and parallel services for survivors and perpetrators.
- Skilled, well-trained staff who can deal with disclosures.
- Participative teaching styles.

Prevention is an overarching principle in the UK's *Call to End Violence against Women and Girls Action Plan* (HM Government, 2011 and 2012), which includes media-based campaigns like the 2011 campaign to challenge attitudes about teenage relationship violence. The Action Plan also anticipates that schools will participate in establishing a more comprehensive and coherent preventive approach. There is also an expectation that gender equality and violence against women will be included in the school curriculum for PSHE and Sex and Relationship Education (Home Office, 2011, p. 8). This recognition at the level of national strategy in the UK is welcome. While schools have a duty to consider how preventing violence against women and girls can be addressed, the objectives of prevention education are likely to require secure, long-term funding and resources to train and support staff to develop their skills in the teaching of PSHE, and in relation to violence against women (Ellis, 2008).

Where fully integrated prevention approaches have not yet been incorporated within the school curriculum, more limited PSHE can provide an opportunity for children and young people attending school to access information and advice about domestic violence and abuse and their personal safety (DCSF, 2010). PSHE can also effectively generate value-based discussions, particularly when participative learning methods are used. Despite strong support for making PSHE a statutory part of the school curriculum, it remains a non-statutory subject in England and Wales. Inevitably, this reinforces PSHE's lower status than other subject areas (see www.pshe-association.org.uk).

Secondary – services for children and young people who may be experiencing distress or difficulty that could be a result of domestic violence and abuse

At this level, work in schools is likely to be directed towards children where there are early, general concerns that their well-being is being negatively affected by some aspect of their lives or circumstances, without the source of this being immediately identifiable. At any one time there will be many children and young people attending schools whose development is affected by adversity of one form or another (as recognized by the concepts of 'children in need' or children in special circumstances). This could include living with the impact of poverty, racism or homophobia, neglect or abuse, being a young carer, or living with a parent who abuses alcohol or drugs, as well as being exposed to domestic violence and abuse (Burgess et al., 2011). A key point about school-based interventions at secondary level is that they can be offered even when the source of concern is not specifically identified, on the basis that many children will need additional support to bolster resilience at some point in their childhood and adolescence. Not only is this important in its own right, but it may also increase children's willingness and confidence to talk to an adult, or peer, in greater detail about their experiences, or to access more specialized interventions within or outside school (Radford et al., 2011b).

Research with children and young people affected by domestic violence and abuse shows that opportunities to build self-confidence and self-esteem through non-stigmatizing activities are highly valued (McGee, 2000; Mullender et al., 2002). These allow children to be 'taken out of themselves' and to be involved in challenging, but age-appropriate, activities that are fun (Mullender, 2004; Radford et al., 2011b).

The developmental trajectory explored above demonstrates how easily domestic violence impacts on learning and educational attainment. Providing easy access to additional educational support, such as homework clubs, is also an important secondary intervention (Radford et al., 2011b). Changes of school can be an ordeal when children have experienced domestic violence, and careful practice in relation to all school transfers and admissions can help to minimize disruption and ensure smooth transitions.

Tertiary – services and interventions where harm related to domestic violence is known already to have occurred

This more intensive level of intervention is provided to children and young people who are known to have directly or indirectly experienced domestic violence and abuse, and can include referral to specialist therapeutic workers, drop-in services and both individual counselling and group work. All of these have been positively evaluated by children and young people, and by their mothers (Mullender, 2004). While they can be provided in a number of settings (including refuges, children's centres, health centres and schools) they have been under-resourced and not readily available (Laing, 2000).

How effective and positively evaluated these are, depends on: how timely and appropriate their delivery is; how easily they can be accessed; the specialist skills of the workers involved; and how well they meet children's requirements about safety, belief, trust and confidentiality (Hester and Westmarland, 2005; Mullender, 2004). Importantly, direct work with children should not be seen as mutually exclusive from work undertaken with women; women and children may need services together and separately to deal with their experiences and to restore relationships that may have been negatively affected by violence (Humphreys et al., 2006). It is also important to be aware that children and young people may find terms such as counselling or therapy stigmatizing, although, more than anything, children and young people have indicated that they need opportunities to be able to talk about what has happened to them (McGee, 2000; Hester et al., 2000):

> Children need someone to talk to. Because if they're like me, sometimes I'm really sad and I need someone to talk to. (9-year-old girl, Mullender et al., 2002, p. 107)

Both individual and group work with children and young people can provide valued opportunities to deal with the impact of domestic violence (Debbonaire, 2002). They can afford a number of restorative benefits, summarized by Mullender (2004, p. 4):

- Permitting them to talk about what has happened.
- Ventilating pent-up feelings about the abuse they have endured and its effect on them and their families.

- Giving reassurance that it was not their fault and they were not responsible for stopping it.
- Building and restoring self-esteem.
- Safety planning for the future.

The child protection system is also part of the tertiary end of the continuum, although there should be no automatic assumption that a child protection referral will be made (Mullender, 2004; Humphreys and Stanley, 2006). In particular, there have been concerns in the past that child protection procedures initiated in the context of domestic violence have weighed heavily on mothers and children, but allowed fathers to avoid taking responsibility (Humphreys, 2006).

Pastoral care: Professional responsibilities, awareness and training

Schools and pastoral care can play a significant role in preventing, recognizing and responding to the needs of children who have been exposed to domestic violence and abuse. For all three levels of intervention, children and young people have said that they want to access services in schools. Working partnerships between domestic violence specialists and educational specialists also allow the objectives of primary, secondary and tertiary provision to be tailored and adapted to meet the diverse needs of children and young people, taking into account demographic profile, ethnicity, language and ensuring that the needs of children with a disability are met (Mullender, 2004).

To achieve this, teachers, pastoral care staff and school governors have to be aware of the impact of domestic violence and abuse and the many ways in which this can affect children and young people's behaviour and learning. Staff need to be able to approach children and young people; to talk to them in ways which protect their confidentiality and trust; to take their concerns seriously; and to identify appropriate sources of help and support both inside and external to the school (Worral et al., 2008). This is challenging on a number of counts. Children experiencing other forms of harm or trauma may display similar signs of distress and impact to those affected by domestic violence and abuse. In addition, as discussed above, for some children the level of harm and their safety needs may be such that referral to children's social care under child protection procedures is necessary.

Training and support are essential to optimize the role of schools and pastoral care teams in relation to domestic violence and abuse, and to build the confidence of teachers, specialist child protection leads in schools and governing bodies. Many local authorities have developed strong working relationships with domestic violence intervention specialists to provide this staff training on a regular basis, as well as to have a central role in the design and delivery of school-based programmes (see, for example, the Brighton and Hove Treetop Project at www. teachrelationships.org.uk).

Conclusion

Domestic violence witnessed in childhood is a serious form of adversity affecting the health, development and well-being of a substantial minority of children and young people in the UK. For some children and young people exposure may be prolonged, from before birth to young adulthood. A particularly harmful aspect of domestic violence occurs when a child's relationship with her or his mother is targeted and compromised, as is often the case. The impact of domestic violence and abuse is profound as it is rarely only one form of abuse; it generally escalates over time, exposing children and young people to extreme forms of violence, fear and conflicted feelings. It can systematically erode those aspects of children's lives that confer protection and promote resilience. The effects on physical, emotional, social development and behaviour are most severe where children have experienced prolonged violence, multiple forms of violence or where their mothers' resources have been severely depleted, and where they have endured many moves. Teenage relationship violence has similar effects on children and young people's health and well-being.

Schools can play a key role in community strategies to prevent domestic violence and provide a range of interventions to help and support children and young people, working with other voluntary and statutory agencies, and incorporating the skills of domestic violence services.

Summary

This chapter about young people affected by domestic violence and abuse has:

- Established that hundreds of thousands of children and young people in the UK are living with the impact of domestic violence and abuse.
- Explored the nature of teenage relationship violence.
- Shown that some children show great resilience, but the physical, emotional and educational development of others is negatively affected.
- Emphasized the critical role schools can play in prevention and in providing supportive interventions for children and young people to offset the impact of domestic violence and abuse.
- Shown that children and young people want school-based services, but need to feel safe, listened to and that their coping strategies and strengths are respected.

Note

1. Forced marriage is a marriage in which either or both spouses objects to the marriage and duress or coercion is involved (Kazimirski et al., 2009).

Annotated further reading

Home Office (2011), *Teenage Relationship Abuse: A Teacher's Guide to Violence and Abuse in Teenage Relationships*. London: Home Office.

This guide is designed for teachers. As well as briefly reviewing the extent and nature of teenage relationship abuse, it alerts teachers, and others in schools, to warning signs and explores what kinds of school-wide approaches can be successfully developed.

Humphreys, C., Houghton, C. and Ellis, J. (eds) (2008), *Literature Review: Better Outcomes for Children and Young People Affected by Domestic Abuse – Directions for Good Practice*. Edinburgh: Scottish Government.

This review, commissioned by the Scottish Government, has been prepared by experts in the field. It provides a synopsis of a wide range of relevant research about domestic violence and children, and includes a chapter on primary prevention and education.

Worral, A., Boylan, J. and Roberts, D. (2008), *Children and Young People's Experiences of Domestic Violence Involving Adults in a Parenting Role.* London: SCIE.

This is a clear and succinct briefing that synthesizes research from the UK, US and Australia about the impact of domestic violence. It identifies messages for service practitioners and service users, and signposts to useful websites and networks.

Useful websites

www.avaproject.org.uk

Against Violence and Abuse is an organization providing a range of services and support to agencies and professionals in the voluntary and statutory sectors. They have a Children and Young People's Project that aims to improve safety through training, lobbying, integrating prevention work into schools, developing work to support young people, promoting models of good practice and improving coordination across services working with children, young people and women who have experienced violence.

www.womensaid.org.uk

Women's Aid is a foremost charity working to end domestic violence against women and children, with over 500 domestic and sexual violence services across the UK. The website offers legal and other information for women experiencing domestic violence, a directory of resources and access to research findings. The site also has an area called the Hideout, which is a space for children and young people to help them understand about domestic abuse, and to support them to work out what to do if it is happening to them.

References

Bacchus, L., Mezey, G. and Bewley, S. (2002), 'Women's perceptions and experiences of routine enquiry for domestic violence in a maternity service'. *British Journal of Obstetrics and Gynaecology*, 109: 9–16.

Bair-Merritt, M. H., Blackstone, M. and Feudtner, C. (2006), 'Physical health outcomes of childhood exposure to intimate partner violence: A systematic review'. *Paediatrics*, 117(2): 278–90.

Bancroft, L. and Silverman, J. G. (2002), *The Batterer as Parent: Addressing the Impact of Domestic Violence on Family Dynamics*. Thousand Oaks, CA: Sage Publications.

Barter, C., McCarry, M., Berridge, D. and Evans, K. (2009), *Partner Exploitation and Violence in Teenage Intimate Relationships*. London: NSPCC.

Bell, J. and Stanley, N. (2006), 'Learning about domestic violence: Young people's responses to a healthy relationships programme'. *Sex Education*, 6(3): 237–50.

Braaf, R. (2008), 'Evaluating domestic and family violence programs and services'. *Australian Domestic and Family Violence Clearinghouse Newsletter*, 31: 5–8.

Buchanan, A., Hunt, J., Bretherton, H. and Bream, V. (2001), *Families in Conflict: Perspectives of Children and Parents in the Family Court Welfare Service*. Bristol: Policy Press.

Burgess, C., Daniel, B., Scott, J., Mulley, K., Derbyshire, D. and Downie, M. (2011), *Child Neglect in 2011*. London: Action for Children.

Burman, M. and Cartmel, F. (2005), *Young People's Attitudes to Gender Violence*. Edinburgh: NHS Scotland.

Burton, S., Kitzinger, J., Kelly, L. and Regan, L. (1998), *Young People's Attitudes Towards Violence, Sex and Relationships*. Edinburgh: Zero Tolerance Charitable Trust.

Cawson, P. (2002), *Child Maltreatment in the Family: The Experience of a National Sample of Young People*. London: NSPCC.

ChildLine (2006), *ChildLine Casenotes: What Children and Young People Tell ChildLine about Physical Violence*. London: NSPCC. Available online at www.nspcc.org.uk/Inform/publications/casenotes/clcasenotesphysicalabuse_wdf48114.pdf.

Christian, C. W., Scribano, P., Seidl, T. and Pinto-Martin, J. A. (1997), 'Paediatric injury resulting from family violence'. *Paediatrics*, 99(2): 81–4.

Debbonaire, T. (2002), *Building Healthy Relationships and Safer Communities: Report of Westminster Domestic Violence Forum Schools Domestic Violence Prevention Project*. Bristol: DVT.

Department for Children Schools and Families (2010), *Violence Against Women and Girls Advisory Group: Final Report and Recommendation*. London: Department for Children Schools and Families.

Department of Health (2002), *Secure Futures for Women: Making a Difference*. London: Department of Health.

— (2005), *Responding to Domestic Abuse: A Handbook for Health Professionals*. London: The Stationery Office.

— (2007), *National Service Framework for Children, Young People and Maternity Services*. London: Department of Health.

Donovan, C., Hester, M., Holmes, J. and McCarry, M. (2006), *Comparing Domestic Violence in Same Sex and Heterosexual Relationships*. Bristol/Sunderland: Universities of Bristol and Sunderland.

Edleson, J. L. (1997), *The Overlap Between Child Maltreatment and Woman Battering*. Available online at www.vaw.umn.edu.

Ellis, J. (2008), 'Primary prevention of domestic abuse through education', in C. Humphreys, C. Houghton and J. Ellis (eds), *Literature Review: Better Outcomes for Children and Young*

People Affected by Domestic Abuse – Directions for Good Practice. Edinburgh: Scottish Government.

Ellis, J., Stanley, N. and Bell, J. (2006), 'Prevention programmes for children and young people', in C. Humphreys and N. Stanley (eds), *Child Protection and Domestic Violence. Directions for Good Practice*. London: Jessica Kingsley.

Evans, S. E., Davies, C. and DiLillo, D. (2008), 'Exposure to domestic violence: A meta-analysis of child and adolescent outcomes'. *Aggression and Violent Behaviour*, 13: 131–40.

Firmin, C. (2011), *This is it . . . This is My Life*. London: Race on the Agenda (ROTA).

Flatley, J., Kershaw, C., Smith, K., Chaplin, R. and Moon, D. (2010), *Crime in England and Wales 2009/10. Home Office Statistical Bulletin 12/10*. London: Home Office.

Gorin, S. (2004), *Understanding What Children Say about Living With Domestic Violence, Parental Substance Misuse and Parental Mental Health Issues*. York: Joseph Rowntree Foundation.

Graham-Bermann, S. and Seng, J. (2005), 'Violence exposure and traumatic stress symptoms as additional predictors of health problems in high-risk children'. *Journal of Paediatrics*, 146(3): 309–10.

Hague, G., Mullender, A. and Aris, R. (2003), *Is Anyone Listening? Accountability and Women Survivors of Domestic Violence*. London: Routledge.

Harber, C. (2004), *Schooling as Violence. How Schools Harm Pupils and Societies*. London: Routledge Farmer.

Harrison, C. (2008), 'Implacably hostile or appropriately protective? Women managing child contact in the context of domestic violence'. *Violence Against Women*, 14(4): 381–405.

Hester, M. and Westmarland, N. (2005), *Home Office Research Study 290 Tackling Domestic Violence: Effective Interventions and Approaches*. London: Home Office.

Hester, M., Pearson, C. and Harwin, N. (2000), *Making an Impact – Children and Domestic Violence: A Reader*. London: Jessica Kingsley.

HM Government (2010 edition), *The Right to Choose: Multi-Agency Statutory Guidance for Dealing with Forced Marriage*. London: Foreign and Commonwealth Office (Forced Marriage Unit).

— (2011), *Call to End Violence Against Women and Girls: Action Plan*. London: Cabinet Office.

— (2012), *Call to End Violence Against Women and Girls. Taking Action – The Next Chapter*. London: The Cabinet Office.

Hogan, F. and O'Reilly M. (2007), *Listening to Children: Children's Stories of Domestic Violence*. Dublin: Office of the Minister of Children.

Holt, S., Buckley, H. and Whelan, S. (2008), 'The impact of exposure to domestic violence on children and young people'. *Child Abuse and Neglect*, 32(8): 797–810.

Home Office (2011), *Teenage Relationship Abuse: A Teacher's Guide to Violence and Abuse in Teenage Relationships*. London: Home Office.

House of Commons Home Affairs Select Committee (2008), *Domestic Violence, Forced Marriage and Honour-Based Violence*. London: The Stationery Office.

Hume, M. (2003), 'The Relationship between Child Sexual Abuse, Domestic Violence and Separating Families'. Paper presented at conference Child Sexual Abuse: Justice Response or Alternative Resolution? Australian Institute of Criminology, Adelaide, 1–2 May 2004. Available online at www.aic.gov.au/conferences/2003-abuse/hume.pdf.

Humphreys, C. (2006), *Domestic Violence and Child Abuse Research and Practice Briefing*. Totnes: Research in Practice.

Humphreys, C. and Mullender, A. (1998), *Children and Domestic Violence*. Totnes: Research in Practice.

Humphreys, C. and Stanley, N. (2006), *Domestic Violence and Child Protection: Directions for Good Practice*. London: Jessica Kingsley.

Humphreys, C. and Thiara, R. (2002), *Routes to Safety: Protection Issues Facing Abused Women and Children and the Role of Outreach Services*. Bristol: Women's Aid Federation of England.

Humphreys, C., Houghton, C. and Ellis, J. (eds) (2008), *Literature Review: Better Outcomes for Children and Young People Affected by Domestic Abuse – Directions for Good Practice*. Edinburgh: Scottish Government.

Humphreys, C., Mullender, A., Thiara, R. and Skamballis, A. (2006), 'Talking to my mum: Developing communication between mothers and children in the aftermath of domestic violence'. *British Journal of Social Work*, 6(1): 53–63.

Izzidien, S. (2008), *I Can't tell People What is Happening at Home: Domestic Violence within South Asian Communities – The Specific Needs of Women, Children and Young People*. London: NSPCC.

Jaffe, P. G., Lemon, N. K. D. and Poisson, S. E. (2003), *Child Custody and Domestic Violence: A Call for Safety and Accountability*. Thousand Oaks, CA: Sage Publications.

Jarvis, K. C., Gordon, E. E. and Novaco, R. W. (2005), 'Psychological distress of children and mothers in domestic violence emergency shelters'. *Journal of Family Violence*, 20(6): 398–402.

Johnson, B. (2008), 'Teacher-student relationships which promote resilience at school: A micro-level analysis of student's views'. *British Journal of Guidance and Counselling*, 36(4): 385–98.

Kaye, M., Stubbs, J. and Tolmie, J. (2003), *Negotiating Child Residence and Contact Arrangements Against a Background of Domestic Violence*. Nathan, Australia: Socio-legal Centre, Griffiths University.

Kazimirski, A., Keogh, P., Kumari, V., Smith, R., Gowland, S., Purson, S. with Khanum, N. (2009), *Forced Marriage – Prevalence and Service Response: DCSF Research Report No. 128*. London: DCSF.

Kelly, L. (1994), 'The Interconnectedness of Domestic Violence and Child Abuse: Challenges for Research Policy and Practice', in M. Mullender and R. Morley, R (eds), *Children Living with Domestic Violence*. London: Whiting and Birch.

— (1999), *Domestic Violence Matters*. London: HMSO.

Kitzmann, K. M., Gaylord, N. K., Holt, A. R. and Kenny, E. D. (2003), 'Child witnesses to domestic violence: A meta-analytic review'. *Journal of Consulting Clinical Psychology*, 71: 339–52.

Laing, L. (2000), *Issues Paper No 2: Children, Young People and Domestic Violence*. Sydney: Australian Clearing House.

Lapierre, S. (2010), 'More responsibilities less control: Understanding the challenges and difficulties in mothering in the context of domestic violence'. *British Journal of Social Work*, 40: 1434–51.

Maholmes, V. and Lomonaco, C. G. (2010), *Applied Research in Child and Adolescent Development: A Practical Guide*. Hove: Psychology Press.

Malley-Morrison, K. and Hines, D. A. (2007), 'Attending to the role of race/ethnicity in family violence research'. *Journal of Interpersonal Violence*, 22 (8): 943–72.

Margolin, G. and Gordis, E. B. (2000), 'The effects of family and community violence on children'. *Annual Review of Psychology*, 445–79.

Martinez-Torteya, C., Bogat, A., von Eye, A. and Levondosky, A. (2009), 'Resilience among children exposed to domestic violence'. *Child Development*, 80: 562–77.

McCarry, M., Hester, M. and Donovan, C. (2008), 'Researching same sex domestic violence'. *Sociological Research Online*, 13(1)8. Available online at http://socresonline.org.uk/13/1/8.html.

McFarlane, J. and Melecha, A. (2005), *Sexual Assault among Intimates: Frequency, Consequences and Treatments*. National Institute of Justice. Available online at www.ncjrs.gov/pdffiles1/nij/grants/211678.pdf.

McGee, C. (2000), *Childhood Experiences of Domestic Violence*. London: Jessica Kingsley Publishers.

Meece, J. and Daniels, D. H. (2007), *Child and Adolescent Development for Educators*. Lexington, US: McGraw-Hill.

Mezey, G. and Bewley, S. (1997), 'Domestic violence and pregnancy'. *British Journal of Obstetrics and Gynaecology*, 104: 528–31.

Mullender, A. (2004), *Tackling Domestic Violence: Providing Support for Children Who Have Witnessed Domestic Violence*. London: Home Office.

Mullender, A., Hague, G., Imam, U., Kelly, L., Malos, E. and Regan, L. (2002), *Children's Perspectives on Domestic Violence*. London: Sage.

Patel, P. and Siddiqui, H. (2010), 'Shrinking Secular Spaces : Asian Women at the Intersection of Race, Religion and Gender', in R. K. Thiara and A. K. Gill (eds), *Violence Against Women in South Asian Communities*. London: Jessica Kingsley.

Pence, E. and Paymar, M. (1996), *Education Groups for Men who Batter: The Duluth Model*. New York: Springer Publishing Company.

Radford, L. and Hester, M. (2006), *Mothering Through Domestic Violence*. London: Jessica Kingsley Press.

Radford, L., Aitken, R., Miller, P., Ellis, J., Roberts, J. and Firkin, A. (2011b), *Meeting the Needs of Children Living with Domestic Violence in London*. London: NSPCC.

Radford, L., Corral, S., Bradley, C., Fisher, H., Bassett, C., Howat, N. and Collishaw, S. (2011a), *Child Abuse and Neglect in the UK Today*. London: NSPCC.

Richards, L. (2003), *Findings from the Multi-Agency Domestic Violence Murder Reviews in London*. London: Metropolitan Police.

— (2004), *Getting Away with it: A Strategic Overview of Domestic Violence, Sexual Assault and 'Serious Incident' Analysis*. London: Metropolitan Police Authority.

Rossman, B. B. (2001), 'Longer Term Effects of Children's Exposure to Domestic Violence', in S. A. Graham-Bermann and J. L. Edleson (eds), *Domestic Violence in the Lives of Children: The Future of Research, Intervention, and Social Policy*. Washington, DC: American Psychological Association.

Saunders, H. (2004), *Twenty-Nine Child Homicides: Lessons Still to be Learnt about Domestic Violence and Child Protection*. Bristol: Women's Aid Federation of England.

Silverman, J. G., Raj, A., Mucci, L. A. and Hathaway, J. E. (2001), 'Dating violence against adolescent girls and associated substance use, unhealthy weight control, sexual risk behaviour, pregnancy, and suicidality'. *Journal of the American Medical Association*, 286(5): 572–9.

Smith, K., Coleman, K., Eder, S. and Hall, P. (2011), *Homicides, Firearm Offences and Intimate Violence 2010/2011. Home Office Statistical Bulletin 02/12*. London: Home Office.

Sokoloff, N. J. and Dupont, I. (2005), 'Domestic violence at the intersections of race, class and gender'. *Violence Against Women*, 11(1): 38–64.

Stafford, A., Stead, J. and Grimes, M. (2007), *The Support Needs of Children and Young People Who Have to Move Home Because of Domestic Abuse*. Edinburgh: Scottish Women's Aid.

Stanley, N. (2011), *Children Experiencing Domestic Violence*. Totnes: Research in Practice.

Statistics Canada (2005), *Family Violence in Canada: A Statistical Profile*. Ottawa: Canadian Centre for Justice Statistics.

Strategic Partners (1998), *Contact Services in Australia – Research and Evaluation Project*. Canberra, Australia: Legal and Family Services, Attorney General's Department.

Sturge, C. and Glaser, D. (2000), *Contact and Domestic Violence: The Experts' Court Report*. London: Family Law.

Sully P. and Greenaway K., (2005) 'Tackling domestic homicide'. *Policing Today*, 11(1): 25–6.

Taft, A. (2002), *Violence Against Women in Pregnancy and after Childbirth: Current Knowledge and Issues in Healthcare Responses*. Australian Domestic and Family Violence Clearinghouse Issues Paper 6. Sydney, Australia: UNSW.

Thiara, R. (2010), 'Continuing control, child contact and post separation violence', in R. K. Thiara and A. K. Gill (eds), *Violence Against Women in South Asian Communities*. London: Jessica Kingsley.

Thiara, R. and Breslin, R. (2006), 'Message is loud and clear: A look at domestic violence among families from ethnic minorities'. *Community Care*, 2 November: 32–3.

Thiara, R. K. and Ellis, J. (2005), *London-Wide Schools' Domestic Violence Prevention Project: An Evaluation. Final Report*. London: Westminster Domestic Violence Forum.

Thiara, R. K. and Gill, A. (2012), *Domestic Violence, Child Contact and Post-Separation Violence: Issues for South Asian and African-Caribbean Women and Children*. London: NSPCC.

Thiara, R. K., Humphreys, C. Skamballis, A. and Mullender, A. (2006), *Talking to My Mum: Developing Communication between Mothers and Children in the Aftermath of Domestic Violence, Final Report*. London: Big Lottery Fund.

Unicef (2005), *Behind Closed Doors: The Impact of Domestic Violence on Children*. New York: Unicef/Body Shop/Stop Violence in the Home.

Walby, S. (2004), *The Cost of Domestic Violence*. London: Women and Equality Unit.

Wilson, M. and Daly, M. (2002), *Homicide*. New York: Aldine de Gruyter.

Wolfe, D. A. and Jaffe, P. G. (1999), 'Emerging strategies for the prevention of domestic violence'. *Futures of Children*, 9(3): 133–44.

Womankind (2007), *Preventing Violence, Promoting Equality: A Whole-School Approach*. London: Womankind.

Worral, A., Boylan, J. and Roberts, D. (2008), *Children's and Young People's Experiences of Domestic Violence Involving Adults in a Parenting Role*. London: Social Care Institute of Excellence.

Wyness, M. (2012), 'The Social Construction of Childhood: Sociological Approaches to the Study of Children and Childhood', in R. Adams (ed.), *Working with Children and Families*. Basingstoke: Palgrave.

Yearnshaw, S. (1997), 'Police Protection', in S. Bewley, J. Friend and G. Mezey (eds), *Violence Against Women*. London: Royal College of Obstetricians and Gynaecologists.

Yexley, M. (2009), *Multi-Perpetrator Rape and Youth Violence*. London: Metropolitan Police Authority. Available online at www.mpa.gov.uk/committees/sop/2009/091105/07/.

Separation and Divorce: School Responses

Paula Hall and Noel Purdy

Introduction

One of the most sensitive and commonly overlooked areas of pastoral care in schools is the impact on children and young people of the separation and divorce of their parents. In this opening section we look first at the changing nature of the modern family in the UK and beyond. We then examine trends in divorce and consider the contested debate over its consequences on children.

The family context in which children and young people are raised has evolved over the past half-century, but the pattern in the UK is one of continuity *and* change. On the one hand most children still live in a traditional family unit in one household with two parents, and yet on the other hand a wider diversity of complex family structures has emerged, which includes a significant rise in the number of lone parent families, step-families, cohabiting couples, same sex families and families where grown-up children are living at home for longer (Social

Issues Research Centre [SIRC], 2008). The structures are more transient than ever before with children more likely to experience a number of different family models through their childhood. The modern family thus tends to include fewer consanguineous family members (as birth rates have fallen) but is more likely to comprise new and often complex networks of non-consanguineous family members (e.g. step-siblings, step-parents).

Nonetheless, it would be rash to claim, as does Halsey (2000, p. 7), that 'the family as an institution is in trouble' or that we must urgently find solutions to 'a problem of widespread disorder' and 'collapsed community'. For instance, statistics collated by the Office for National Statistics (2012) indicate that, although there has been a 7.2 per cent fall in the number of married couple families in England and Wales from 2001 to 2011, they are still the norm, representing 67.2 per cent of the total number of families. Over the same period, the number of opposite sex cohabiting couple families has risen from 12.5 per cent to 16.0 per cent, and the number of lone parent families from 14.8 per cent to 16.1 per cent. Due to the introduction of new legislation in 2004 there are now also 59,000 civil partner families in England and Wales (0.3% of the total number of families), 5,000 of which have dependent children.

Divorce rates have also risen overall over time. Figures for England and Wales (Office for National Statistics, 2012) show that in 1860 there were just 103 divorces; in 1910 this had risen to 596; by 1960 the figure was 23,868; and most recently in 2010 there were 119,589 couples who divorced in England and Wales after an average of just 11.4 years of marriage. The reasons for the rise in the number of divorces are myriad but some observers have attributed the changes to the rise in secularization, a greater social acceptance of divorce, the increasing economic independence of women and rising expectations for personal fulfilment from marriage (Cherlin, 1992; Popenoe, 1993; Furstenberg, 1994).

Although there has been an overall rise in the number of divorces over the past 150 years throughout the Western world, over the past decade the numbers have actually begun to fall in many countries. For instance, in England and Wales the total of 119,589 couples who divorced in 2010 represents a fall of 14.9 per cent since 2000. A similar pattern can be found in the US where the number of divorces fell by 7.6 per cent from 2000 to 2010 (CDC, 2012) and in Scotland where there was a fall of 6.7 per cent from 2000–1 to 2009–10 (Scottish Government, 2012). Over the same time period (2000–10), however, there was a very slight rise (0.7%) in the number of divorces in Australia (Australian Bureau of Statistics, 2012) and a more significant rise (10.6%) in the number of divorces granted in Northern Ireland (NISRA, 2011).

The number of divorces is related to the number of marriages which take place, and so it is perhaps inevitable that there has been a decline in the number of divorces in the UK given that the number of marriages is also in decline. For instance the number of marriages celebrated in England and Wales fell by 3.3 per cent from 249,227 in 2001 to 241,100 in 2010 (the number of marriages in England and Wales in 2009 was the lowest since 1895). This is a picture which is mirrored in the US (CDC, 2009). It is impossible to predict the likelihood of marriages ending in divorce since it involves an impossible projection. However statistics for England and Wales reveal that 22 per cent of marriages in 1970 had ended in divorce by the 15th wedding anniversary, whereas 33 per cent of marriages in 1995 had ended in divorce after the same period of time. Accuracy allows us to say only that for couples who married in England and Wales in 1995, the likelihood of their marriage ending in divorce by the year 2010 was one in three (Office for National Statistics, 2012).

Remarriages for divorced couples are also increasingly common (and are more likely to end in divorce again): for instance in England and Wales in 2009, 24 per cent of the men and 22.8 per cent of the women who got married were previously divorced (at least once). Consequently, it is claimed that step-families are the fastest growing family type in the UK (Tufnell, 2012).

Of particular interest here is the fact that in 2010 in England and Wales, the 119,589 divorcing families included a total of 158, 957 children (54,593 aged 16 or over and 104,364 under 16). In Australia in 2010 there were over 46,000 children impacted by the divorce of their parents (Australian Bureau of Statistics, 2012). In the US it is estimated that more than 1 million children experience parental divorce each year (Amato, 2000).

In relation to the consequences of parental separation and divorce on children, there has been much polemical debate in recent years. Some have argued for instance that the demise of the nuclear two-parent family and the rise of fatherless lone parent families is the main cause of many current social problems (Popenoe, 1993; Blankenhorn, 1995; Glenn, 1996; Nock, 2002). It has been argued, for instance, that society is experiencing 'end-of-the-line' family decline and that children need stable nuclear family structures in order to become successful adults (Popenoe, 1993, p. 540). Blankenhorn (1995, p. 1) goes further and notes that in the US fatherlessness, the result of the breakdown of marriage as a stable institution, 'is the most harmful demographic trend of this generation' and is 'the engine driving our most urgent social problems, from crime to adolescent pregnancy to child sexual abuse to domestic violence against women'. Nock (2002) argues further that the damaged social institution of marriage must urgently be 'revitalized' for the twenty-first century.

By contrast other scholars have refuted what they see as a false nostalgia for an idealized bygone age when the nuclear family predominated (Skolnick, 1991; Coontz, 1992; Stacey, 1996). It is argued that more harm is caused, not by the loss of the parent through a separation, but by the preceding period of emotional hostility in the home (Allison and Furstenberg, 1989; Cherlin, 1991; Stacey, 1993). Stacey (1993, p. 547) concurs and acknowledges profound transformations in the nature of the modern family but bemoans the inexcusable 'scapegoating of unconventional families' and the championing of the 'ideology of the family', advocating instead the formation of a social environment 'in which diverse family forms can sustain themselves with dignity and mutual respect'.

The impact of separation and divorce on children and young people

One of the most common misconceptions about the impact of divorce is that it is a discrete event to which children can and will finally adjust, whereas a body of research evidence over the past three decades and beyond clearly suggests that the impact of divorce on children can still be felt many years later (Wallerstein and Kelly, 1979; Furstenberg and Cherlin, 1991; Amato, 2000; Wallerstein et al., 2002; Marquardt, 2005).

In their review of over 200 research studies, Rodgers and Pryor (1998) concluded that the children of separated families are more likely to:

- Grow up in households with lower incomes, poorer housing and greater hardship.
- Achieve less in socio-economic terms when they become adult than children from intact families.
- Develop behavioural problems including withdrawn behaviour, aggression, delinquency and other anti-social behaviour.
- Perform less well at school and gain fewer educational qualifications.
- Be admitted to hospital following accidents, to have reported health problems and visit their GP more often.
- Leave school and home early.
- Become sexually active at an early age, become pregnant, give birth outside marriage and form cohabiting relationships.
- Report depressive symptoms, smoke, drink and take drugs during adolescence and adulthood.

There are several initial emotional reactions following parental separation that are common to children and young people of all ages. The first of these is *shock*. Research suggests that many children had no idea at all that their parents' relationship was breaking down. For instance, Wallerstein and Kelly (1979) found that news of their parents' separation often came as a 'bolt of lightning' (p. 11) to the children and that 'fully one-third of the children had only a brief awareness of their parents' unhappiness prior to the divorce decision' (p. 38). In addition, 'Four-fifths of the youngest children studied were not provided with either an adequate explanation or assurance of continued care. In effect, they awoke one morning to find one parent gone' (p. 39). Thus, many children only learn about the separation when it is a 'fait accompli' and even then are likely to receive only a 'fuzzy account' of what is going on (Furstenberg and Cherlin, 1991, p. 24). Some children may be aware that the marriage was not happy, but few question that it will continue. Even where there has been significant parental conflict, children are more likely to look forward to the day when their parents amicably resolve their differences, than consider the possibility of divorce.

The second reaction that is common to all children is *fear*. Children of any age can feel profoundly vulnerable and alone. The family structure that has been depended on has collapsed and their immediate response will be either consciously or unconsciously to worry about what this means for them and who will take care of them (Wallerstein and Kelly, 1979). Most children also worry about their parents (both the one who is leaving and the one who remains). These feelings of anxiety will be exacerbated if a parent is showing overt signs of distress. Many children also feel a huge sense of rejection when parents separate. Even older children who can rationalize that 'Dad left mum, not me' can struggle not to take at least some of the departure personally. An embittered mother who tells their child that 'Daddy left them' will of course aggravate these feelings.

Third, the strong sense of fairness that children and young people feel, often leaves them struggling with *divided loyalties* (Marquardt, 2005). Even when family relationships are strained, children love both parents and want to be loved back. But if one is more obviously hurting than the other, or one is being openly blamed, then they may feel that they should take sides to redress the balance. By taking sides, however, they also know that they may risk hurting the other parent. This leaves many children feeling torn in two by their conflicting need to show their love and support for both parents equally.

Guilt is a fourth reaction common to children of all ages, although most common among the very young (Wallerstein and Kelly, 1979). Young children are, by nature, egocentric. As they focus their psychological attention on their individual growth and survival, there is a tendency to assume that life revolves round them. This means that as well as worrying about the impact the separation will have on them, they will also wonder if they were in some way responsible.

Fifth, many children feel an intense *isolation* as a result of divorce. Even though it is estimated that one in four children will see their parents divorce before they reach the age of 16, it is still an event that is rarely discussed in the classroom or in the playground. And while parents are engrossed in their own individual and powerful emotions of loss and anger, children are often left to cope alone, caught between two worlds (Marquardt, 2005). Wallerstein and Kelly (1979, p. 49) found that the loneliness of the child at this time is profound, and noted that '. . . the only youngsters not particularly lonely were those well-functioning adolescents whose capacity to rely upon peers for diversion and support was quite good, and who enjoyed the father's continued interest.'

Research Example: The Moral and Spiritual Impact of Divorce on Children

'Is there really any such thing as a good divorce?' To answer this question, Marquardt (2005) reports the findings of a study across the US of children of divorce, in which she interviewed 71 college graduates between the ages of 18 and 35, and surveyed 1,500 randomly selected young adults, half of whom had experienced their parents' divorce before the age of 14 and half of whom grew up in intact families. The highly original focus of this study was the impact of divorce on children's moral and spiritual lives, an area which has rarely been considered in international research.

Marquardt argues that children of divorced families are 'travellers' between two worlds, the worlds of their parents. During the marriage, it is the parents' job to make sense of their different values and opinions and to reach a consensus. Following a divorce Marquardt maintains that this task of making sense of the two worlds passes to the child, but there is no support given as they try to work out who they are and what they believe, often pitted between two quite contrasting sets of values. She argues that for children of divorce 'if we were to survive, we had to become early moral forgers' (p. 81), forging their own values and cutting through the contradictions between their parents' differing ways of living, and alone. Children of divorce are thus more likely to develop their own moral values independently of their parents, and at least three times more likely to say that they do not share the same moral values as their parents, especially their fathers.

In terms of personal faith, Marquardt found that young people from divorced families were more likely to agree that institutional religion was not relevant to them, more likely to claim that they could find ultimate truth without help from a religion, and much less likely to attend church now, compared to children from intact families. They were much less likely to say that their parents had encouraged them to practise a religious faith and also much less likely to attend religious services regularly as a child. Poignantly, of those young adults who attended a church at the time of their parents' divorce, two-thirds said that no one – neither clergy nor members of the congregation – reached out to them during this difficult period in their lives.

Marquardt's study is important in that it shows enduring moral and spiritual consequences of divorce, even in the lives of adults who are relatively successful (as College graduates). For Marquardt there is therefore no such thing as a good divorce.

Reference

Marquardt, E. (2005), *Between Two Worlds – the Inner Lives of Children of Divorce*. New York: Three Rivers Press.

Age-specific reactions

In addition to the emotions that are felt by children of all ages, there are some common reactions that are specific to each age group. Setting these age bands is of course arbitrary as all children develop at different rates.

Ages 11–12

This is the age when children are beginning the psychological task of establishing their individual identity and, consequently, it can be particularly difficult to manage change. When so much is changing on the inside, it is especially important that the outside world remains constant. Hence children in this age group can find the disintegration of the family structure particularly threatening to their sense of emotional stability. Viewing the world in black and white is still a tendency for this group and can be accompanied by a growing range of strongly held beliefs and principles. Consequently this group is especially vulnerable to being caught up in a blame game and may quickly choose to blame one parent rather than manage the difficult balance of maintaining ambivalence. It is common for one parent to be saddled with all the responsibility for the breakdown, and feelings of anger towards that parent may be intense. Where parents are using children as weapons, this group will unfortunately rise to the challenge as taking sides may feel much safer than 'sitting on the fence' (Wallerstein and Kelly, 1979).

Children in this age group are also beginning to play with adult roles and they may use these roles as a way of caring for their parent. They are more likely than any other age group to become 'mummy's little helper' and/or to try to take on the role of 'little husband or wife'. Taking on these inappropriate levels of responsibility can help to ease their feelings of powerlessness and some parents mistake this as evidence that their children are coping well. In terms of behaviour, anger may leak out in behaviours and some may withdraw more to confide in friends or throw themselves into an expanding social life. Some revert back to more childlike behaviours and may seek attention and affection through a host of somatic illnesses such as headaches and stomach aches. They may also start engaging in more risk-taking behaviour such as stealing or playing up at school as a way of drawing attention to their needs for stability and control (Hall, 2007).

Ages 13–16

During adolescence changes in mood and behaviour are often the norm. This group are at the age where they can begin to easily articulate their feelings if they wish to, but some will choose to act out their feelings in increasingly rebellious ways. Beneath the natural rebellion that marks the transition into adulthood, many teenagers also have a strong moral streak. Paired with a growing awareness of relationships, this means that this age group may demonstrate righteous indignation at any behaviour by parents that is deemed inappropriate. The right to make decisions that affect the young person's life may also be challenged if they perceive their parents as having made a mess of their own. Any signs of hypocrisy will also be challenged such as a parent who suggests that 'putting your family first' should be a priority or one who previously claimed 'they would always be there for them' and then leaves.

Fitting in with peers is also a priority with this age group and hence anything that may cause embarrassment or impact on their social life will be stressful. Any evidence or hint of sexual infidelity or a parent's sexual problems will be especially challenging to young people of this age. Knowing that a parent is about to be single closes the generation gap and can leave them feeling anxious about whether or not they are still in charge.

Some adolescents will demonstrate their feelings by acting out in rebellious ways. There may be an increase in risk-taking in the areas of alcohol, drug use and self-harming and more sexual risks may be taken. Rebellion may be extended to school as a way of getting back at parents, especially those who have maintained education as a type of moral duty.

In most cases, adolescents will inevitably miss out on the stable family structure which is so essential in their development of greater independence and maturity, as parents are preoccupied with their own needs or are not available or able to concentrate their efforts on the adolescent's problems. This can be combined with looser family structures, controls and discipline, which can make adolescents particularly vulnerable to 'the temptations of the adolescent world' (Wallerstein and Kelly, 1979, p. 83).

In summary, it is clear that there is no 'best' age for children to experience parental separation, and that, although sometimes different, there are problems to be faced at any age. Research has shown that the older a child is, the more awareness they have of the complexities of families and relationships and therefore the more understanding they may have. Generally speaking older children also have a wider network of people they can turn to for support and comfort. With growing awareness and wisdom, however, comes less time to change and adapt. Marquardt (2005, p. 189) recounts how, as children of divorce, 'We grew up too soon' while Wallerstein and Kelly (1979, p. 83) note that the adolescents in their study 'felt that the time available to them for growing up had been drastically foreshortened. They felt hurried and pressed to achieve quickly the independence which is usually achieved over several years'.

Hall (2007) identifies five different roles which children and young people can adopt in their reactions to parental separation:

The Silent Child – on hearing that their parents are splitting up, some children will withdraw into silence (especially teenage children). For some the quietness is simply a way of getting time alone to process what has happened while others may prefer to talk to friends rather than family. Some will have learned to use silence as a weapon and may withdraw into silence as a way of demonstrating their anger at what has occurred.

The Angry Child – anger may be overt and demonstrated through shouting, abusive comments and slamming of doors or it may be more subtle with moodiness (common in teenage years). There may be disobedience and oppositional behaviour, and adults across the board may face rebellion. For some, being angry and 'naughty' has always been a way in which they have gained attention. As this may be a time when there is little attention available at home, the behaviour may be heightened.

The Clingy Child – a significant sense of insecurity is likely to hit most children soon after the news has been broken. In young children this is acted out in 'clingy' behaviour, while for older children and young people there may be a very real fear of being separated from their parents. Some will become particularly attached to the departing parent, fearing that they will not return, while others will 'cling' to the parent who is staying at home, feeling they are the last bedrock of security. This 'clinginess' can extend to teachers or favoured classroom assistants or pastoral carers who may be seen as more reliable and responsible than parents.

The Fragile Child – this is a child, similar to the clingy child, who has perhaps usually been fairly healthy, independent and self-reliant but who may begin to complain of a host of minor ailments from headaches and rashes to stomach aches, and sometimes extending to more serious phantom health concerns. They may become scared and nervous of doing anything new or alone and may become more anxious about school work and friendship groups than before. This behaviour often masks a deeper anxiety that they are not going to cope and a fear that their needs may be overlooked.

The Perfect Child – some children will respond to the anxiety of family breakdown by becoming 'perfect'. Rather than overtly demonstrating any negative emotion, they will suppress difficult feelings and behave in a way that will please both parents. This may be an attempt to alleviate unspoken feelings of guilt, or to ensure the on-going love and attention of both parents. When one parent is showing obvious signs of distress it may be an attempt to cheer them up and show their devotion. Or in some cases it is a way of trying to make home life so perfect that their parents might change their mind and want to stay together after all.

What influences reaction

Several studies have considered the importance of different factors which influence how well a child copes with their parents' separation or divorce (Wallerstein and Kelly, 1979; Furstenberg and Cherlin, 1991; Rodgers and Pryor, 1998; Amato, 2000; Marquardt, 2005). In addition to consideration of the child's age and individual roles (as discussed above), research has highlighted the importance of the following moderating factors following the separation:

   i.   the ability of the resident parent to function effectively as a parent (related to their own psychological well-being)
  ii.   continued, healthy relationships with the resident parent (most often the mother)
 iii.   continued, healthy relationships with the non-resident parent (most often the father)
 iv.   the economic sufficiency and stability of the resident parent
  v.   a low level of conflict between the separated parents
 vi.   strong friendships with peers

vii.   interest, love and support from other family members (e.g. grandparents)

viii. support from others (e.g. neighbours, ministers)

ix.   the use of active coping skills

x.   having access to therapeutic interventions

xi.   the degree to which the school was able to offer support and understanding (see section below).

Divorce is for life

Whatever age a child is when their parents separate, their parents will (most likely) be separated for life. Many still view divorce as a discrete event that children 'get over', or a temporary crisis whose effects wear off soon after the break-up, rather than as something that will affect them for the rest of their lives. For instance, when they are planning their 16th or 18th birthday party, their parents will still be separated. When they are graduating or getting married, their parents will still be apart. When their children are being christened or they are arranging visits over Christmas, their parents will not be in the same home. Even when children and young people have come to terms with the shock of separation, and they have worked through the painful feelings of loss, anger, embarrassment, divided loyalties and rejection, there will still be numerous frustrations and tensions created by juggling their lives between separated parents. If those parents continue to be at war with each other, or if new partners create a greater divide, then those complications will be magnified. Twenty-five years after the beginning of their longitudinal study, Wallerstein et al. (2002) interviewed adults whose parents divorced when they were children, and found a pattern of significant and enduring effects:

> It's feeling sad, lonely, and angry during childhood. It's travelling on planes alone when you're seven to visit your parent. It's having no choice about how you spend your time and feeling like a second-class citizen compared with your friends in intact families who have some say about how they spend their weekends and their holidays. It's wondering whether you will have any financial help for college from your college-educated father, given that he has no legal obligation to pay. It's worrying about your mum and dad for years – will her new boyfriend stick around, will his new wife welcome you into her home? It's reaching adulthood with acute anxiety. Will you ever find a faithful woman to love you? Will you find a man you

can trust? Or will your relationships fail just like your parents' did? And most tellingly, it's asking if you can protect your own child from having these same experiences in growing up. (p. 4)

Case Study: Jenny

Jenny is 14 and has started playing up at school. Until now she had always been a model pupil but since the Easter break her behaviour has significantly deteriorated. Jenny's parents separated five years ago and she and her younger sister, Helen, live with their mum and step-dad, John. She remembers her mum leaving when she was nine because she had fallen in love with another man. A few weeks later she and John got a house and Jenny and her sister Helen moved in. Her dad was upset that they left but he reassured them that everything would be alright. They saw their dad regularly and really liked their mum's new boyfriend and loved being bridesmaids when she and John got married a year later. Up until recently, it had seemed that the divorce and remarriage had very little impact on Jenny and she had adapted very well. This all began to change six months ago when a story line on the TV soap *Hollyoaks* was about a woman having an affair. The explicit scenes and the anger the character generated among her on-screen family touched a nerve with Jenny that she didn't know was there. For the first time, she realized that her mum must have been having an affair with John for some time before she decided to leave her dad, and also that if it hadn't been for John, her family would probably still be together. She asked her mum to tell her what had happened but she refused, saying it was all 'water under the bridge now'. So she asked her dad who confirmed that John had been a friend of her mum's from work and that the affair had been going on for years. Jenny was outraged and inconsolable. She was disgusted by what her mum and John had done and angry that her dad had seemed to just give in to it. These adults were not the people she thought they were and she felt stupid for ever having trusted them. As far as she was concerned, she'd been lied to and deceived and her parents were hypocrites for pretending to have such a 'normal' life.

Questions

1. Why have Jenny's feelings towards John and her mum changed?
2. How might she be feeling towards other adults in authority, such as teachers at school?

School responses to separation and divorce

In this section we consider the range of possible responses which a school can provide to help support a child whose parents have separated and/or divorced. These responses fall into two broad but overlapping categories: whole-school responses and individual teacher responses.

Whole-school responses

A supportive pastoral ethos

The bedrock of support for a child whose parents have separated is a school whose pastoral ethos is supportive. Much has been written about the nature of school ethos. For instance, Donnelly (2000, p. 134), defines it as 'a fashionable but nebulous term often employed by organisational theorists, educationists and theologists to describe the distinctive range of values and beliefs, which define the philosophy or atmosphere of an organisation'. Donnelly identifies a range of different perspectives on school ethos, ranging from those who see it embodied purely in a series of policy documents to those who argue instead that ethos is something much more informal which concerns social interaction and is not something which can be easily documented. In relation to the pastoral ethos of a school, it is clear that there is truth in both perspectives, so that a pastoral ethos in relation to the support of a child whose parents have separated must be captured in a policy or set of procedures (thus ensuring a common understanding and consistency of implementation) but must also be lived out in the daily interactions between and among members of staff (teaching and non-teaching), pupils and parents. A supportive pastoral ethos thus comprises both the tangible (written statements of policy and procedure) and also the intangible (positive, supportive, inclusive relationships). A strong pastoral ethos, developed and refined over time, ensures that the structures are in place to support children in the event of a parental separation.

Improving communication

The policy context within the UK has, since the Plowden Report (DES, 1967), emphasized the role of parents as 'partners' in their children's education. It has been reported that there is a clear link between family input and pupil outcomes, even after all other factors such as social disadvantage and maternal education have been taken out of the equation (Desforges and Abouchaar, 2003). More recently *Every Parent Matters* (DfES, 2007, p. 1) has suggested that 'Parents and the home environment they create are the single most important factor in shaping their children's well-being, achievements and prospects'. In 2003 the government's *Excellence and Enjoyment* (DfES, 2003) made three proposals in order to maximize parental involvement: providing parents with information; giving parents a voice; and encouraging parental partnerships with schools. When a family unit dissolves in the event of a separation or divorce, the nature of the partnership envisaged by the government becomes markedly more difficult and complex.

The first and most fundamental challenge faced by schools is that very often they are (at least initially) not made aware of the parental separation, and when they are, it is often 'through the grapevine' or as a result of a homework or behavioural problem involving a pupil whose parents have separated. Wallerstein and Kelly (1979) found in their US study that school teachers were frequently unaware that a child's parents were divorcing. They note that some of the parents had deliberately not informed the school for fear of their child being labelled as a child of divorce, while others felt that teachers could not be trusted with such intimate information. More common however was the parents' failure to recognize that their separation could impact at all on their child's behaviour and performance at school, or a failure to realize that the school's ability to support the child might be enhanced by background knowledge to the problem.

The consequence of such a breakdown in communication is that the child receives less support than they might and, as Wallerstein and Kelly conclude, 'It is ironic that at a time in our society when parents increasingly hold the schools responsible for their child's well-being, these same parents fail to provide some of the important tools for the teachers' effective functioning' (1979, p. 266). Similar findings emerge from a smaller UK study: Holland (2000) found that 79 per cent of his secondary school sample found out about a parental separation 'through the grapevine' (e.g. other pupils, staff) rather than being informed by the parents themselves. Even when the information was known by the school, unlike other forms of loss such as family bereavement, head teachers did not see it as appropriate to disseminate this kind of information to the whole staff, once more hindering a compassionate school response and the provision of effective support across the secondary school, where a pupil could be taught by ten or more members of staff.

Consequently, the first response is that schools must improve their lines of communication with parents, making it clear that it is entirely appropriate and indeed essential that the school be informed of a major change in family circumstances such as a family separation or divorce. Moreover it is important that parents are made aware of the need to inform schools as a matter of urgency, rather than waiting first for a problem to arise. In addition, it is crucial that schools communicate the necessary information confidentially to all the teachers who teach the particular child, including substitute teachers, so that teachers have a level of understanding of the potential consequences of the separation for the child's learning.

The final area of communication which is often overlooked is communication with *both* parents following the separation. Too often schools neglect to keep the non-resident parent (most often the father) informed of their child's progress, failing to invite them to parent/teacher interviews and overlooking the need to send them a copy of a school report. As a result, non-resident parents are further marginalized from their child's education. As Daly (2009) notes, the school must make a commitment (however inconvenient) to joint parental communication to protect a parent's individual right to participate in their child's education, and this should form an important element of the school policy.

A school policy on separation and divorce

Few schools have a written policy in this regard. However the development of such a policy ensures that there is clarity across the entire school community about the roles of parents and the school in seeking to facilitate the pastoral care of a pupil whose parents have separated. Any school policy on separation/divorce should emphasize the prioritization of the well-being and learning of the child through the separation, and the need to maintain clear lines of communication between both parents and the school. A school should at the very least inform its parents through the policy of their willingness to communicate with both resident and non-resident parents and to offer separate parent–teacher meetings if desired, and also of their openness to discuss their child's support and progress at any time in light of the separation. Parents should also be reminded of their responsibility to keep the school informed of the contact details of both parents, the desired addresses for correspondence and any changes of contact details or custody arrangements. As with any policy, its success depends largely on the degree to which it has been produced collaboratively (and thus has ownership), and the extent to which it has been read, understood and applied consistently by all parties.

Case Study: A Member of a School Pastoral Care Team Relates the Story of How Her School is Working to Support Two Siblings Impacted by Divorce

'We are currently working with one family where the parents split up about a year ago. There are two children: a girl (Sophie) now in sixth form and a boy (James) in year 9. At the time of the split only Sophie was at the school and the impact on her was immense. She had been very hard-working and involved in school life, but after the separation her self-confidence fell to zero and her school work deteriorated badly. We informed all of her teachers by email (with her mother's permission) just to give them an understanding of the situation and to encourage them to look out for any signs that Sophie was struggling. I also met regularly with Sophie on an informal basis just to check how she was doing and if there was anything we could do to support her. Was she falling behind with her coursework? Could I speak to the teacher and ask them to show some consideration? I also offered her support from the external counselling service and after about six months she took up the offer and found it really helpful. Things seemed to have settled until about six months ago when the dad announced that he was moving in with his girlfriend and they were living close by. This unsettled Sophie again. For her younger brother, James, the dad's decision to move in with his girlfriend has been even worse. James is very close to his dad and blames his mum for the split. He has frequent rows with her and has begun to miss school. We have offered counselling to James but he has not taken up the offer yet. The counselling service is good, but it's only one session a week. For the rest of the time it is still up to the pastoral care team in the school to support Sophie and James. Last year Sophie did her GCSEs and did quite well. Now, though, we are supporting Sophie and

⇨

James through their adjustment to this latest phase of change following the initial separation. Parents think that children handle divorce well – that isn't usually the case. The fall-out is often enormous and it lasts for years. We are working with children like Sophie and James day in, day out.'

Questions

1. What support did the school offer to Sophie and James?
2. Is there anything else the school could do to help?

Teacher responses

The role of the classroom teacher and its limitations

It is important that children of divorce should know that their relationship with each class teacher is secure and intact, especially at a time when other relationships in their lives have changed. It is the responsibility of all teachers to be supportive of such pupils and their attitude should therefore be compassionate, yet professional at all times. Frieman (1993) found that primary school children want their teachers to know about their family situation and want to talk about their feelings and be listened to. For secondary school pupils, the situation is more complex. Some of these older children will readily talk to a trusted teacher (e.g. their Form Tutor), but others will be more reticent out of a sense of embarrassment or shame or may struggle to entrust any adult with such sensitive information. Where a pupil does want to talk, in the first instance, teachers must be prepared to listen, but should be ready to refer pupils to their Form Tutor or Head of Year to follow through with a plan of support.

It is thus important that the classroom teacher recognizes the necessary limitations of their role in supporting pupils through experiences of parental separation. It must be remembered that a classroom teacher's involvement has as its aim not the resolution of the parental difficulties nor the unnecessary prying into a highly sensitive family situation, but simply to promote the well-being of the child through showing understanding of the situation, and ensuring that any appropriate support is provided to facilitate the child's ability and readiness to learn in the classroom. Teachers should therefore resist any tendency or temptation to discuss the particular details of the separation or to take sides in any dispute. Teachers should also be wary of assuming the role of surrogate parent in order to offer support and compassion to a struggling and potentially 'clingy' pupil. Where a teacher with pastoral responsibility (e.g. a Head of Year) does meet with the parent(s) of a pupil, the focus should remain on how to ensure that the pupil's sense of well-being and academic progress are supported and maintained through a period which may involve practical adjustments such as moving house and moving between parents' houses, but also significant emotional stress with a range of possible behavioural consequences (as detailed above). It is crucial that schools respond quickly in order to prevent the situation escalating. As Miller et al. (1999) explain, parents are more likely to be cooperative if they see that their child's behaviours are in their early stages and that the school is investing time and effort in ensuring that the situation does not deteriorate further.

Schools now often have arrangements for professional counselling to be provided to pupils on a referral basis. Such counselling should be used, with pupil and parental consent, for those pupils whose emotional needs cannot be adequately met through the ordinary pastoral structures of the school.

Divorce in the curriculum

Many schools are now pro-actively teaching pupils at Key Stages 3 and 4 about relationships and divorce and this is clearly to be welcomed. Such teaching forms part of the non-statutory programme of study for Personal Well-Being within The National Curriculum's Personal, Social, Health and Economic Education (England and Wales). At Key Stage 3 for instance, the non-statutory programme of study suggests that pupils should learn about 'the features of positive and stable relationships, how to deal with a breakdown in a relationship and the effects of loss and bereavement' (QCA, 2007a, p. 249). At Key Stage 4 the content is more explicit and suggests teaching pupils about 'the impact of separation, divorce and bereavement on families and the need to adapt to changing circumstances' (QCA, 2007b, p. 259). While these are valuable suggestions, the likelihood of these topics being taught effectively in schools is hampered, first, by their non-statutory status within the National Curriculum, and, second, by the lack of high-quality resources available for teachers to deliver lessons on this complex subject.

Pupil behaviour

Within the individual classroom, it is essential that a teacher has an understanding of the possible impact of parental separation on a pupil's readiness to learn, but also that the classroom environment itself remains one of safety, stability and predictability. This is especially important for a pupil whose home life has just fallen apart and where the normal pattern of daily life may have been thrown into chaos. For such children, coming into an environment where there is certainty and established routines offers a welcome sense of continuity and stability.

Teachers should also ensure that there is a continued consistency in their management of behaviour in the classroom. Children who have undergone any emotional trauma still need to know that traditional boundaries exist in relation to school discipline and that failure to adhere to the behavioural expectations has consequences, which should be fair and consistent. When teachers are made aware of a child's family situation, they are more likely to respond appropriately to any behavioural consequences in class and to understand the true cause of the outburst. Children should be held accountable for their behaviour as before but can be supported to realize what behaviours are acceptable and unacceptable in the classroom context.

On occasion, and depending on the particular emotional needs of a pupil, it may be valuable to allow a pupil who is particularly upset the opportunity to access a quiet space, either within the classroom or in another recognized room within the school. In such a situation, it is important that such a facility is agreed in advance so that the pupil and teacher are aware of the relevant procedures and that issues surrounding the pupil's safety and protection have been carefully considered.

Academic expectations

Teachers should also maintain high academic expectations of children experiencing parental separation. At such times, children often have a sense of abandonment and accompanying low self-esteem. Lowering academic expectations (while perhaps out of the best of intentions) only serves to confirm a view of themselves as worthless, a self-image often created through the emotional turmoil of the separation. As Cole et al. (2005, p. 54) argue, 'Ideally it is best to let the student know that, despite the travails of his or her life, your expectation is that the student will continue to meet the high standards set for all the children, and that the school will help to make that possible.' Nonetheless, teachers may need to assist pupils in managing the practical challenges of moving between parents' homes and in ensuring that they have all their books for the next day at school. It would also not be unreasonable for a classroom teacher to show some additional consideration (within reason) in respect of homework or coursework deadlines.

Promoting integration

Given the vulnerability of pupils in the aftermath of parental separation, it is important that teachers are vigilant towards the potential for such pupils to become isolated and withdrawn. This may be due to their own anxiety, low self-esteem and fear which might make them unwilling to interact normally with their peers. Conversely, pupils who have become aggressive as a response to their disrupted home life may have isolated themselves from their normal circle of friends. In either case teachers must create opportunities (through paired or group work) for pupils to interact and collaborate, thus helping to maintain healthy relationships. Where it is clear that these relationships have broken down, teachers should act quickly to ensure that any bullying is dealt with effectively in accordance with the agreed school procedures.

Non-academic strategies

Another way of supporting a child's emotional well-being at a time of parental separation is to ensure that the child is still able to participate fully in a range of extra-curricular activities. Participation in such activities helps children to sense a consistency of routine against a changing family context, allows the child to maintain healthy relationships with peers outside the more rigid confines of the classroom and gives the child a further opportunity to experience affirmation and praise at a time when self-esteem is often lowered and confidence has been dented. Involving a child of divorce in non-academic extra-curricular activities is therefore one of the most effective ways for a teacher to help them. Sporting activities in particular are advantageous in that they also allow an outlet for built-up frustration.

Conclusion

This chapter has highlighted the enduring impact of parental separation and divorce on children and young people and has suggested numerous ways in which schools can begin to address this important issue which affects so many pupils every year. However this chapter also makes it clear that the need is not simply to manage a temporary emotional crisis in the lives of the children at the time of the parental separation, and to await the restoration of normality immediately thereafter. Instead, it has been argued in this chapter that many children and young people will continue to struggle with the impact of divorce for many months and years after the initial separation. There is thus an onus on schools to provide understanding and support not just in the short term, but also in the medium and long term too. Consequently schools must work to acknowledge the magnitude of the impact on children and young people, to remove the stigma which can stand in the way of effective school responses and to offer appropriate support whenever necessary during a pupil's school career, using the existing internal pastoral care system of the school and/or drawing on external support. However, schools and individual teachers must also be equipped with the confidence, skills and resources to be able to tackle the subject of divorce within the curriculum, raising awareness and developing children's coping skills so that they will be better able to deal with the impact of this pervasive issue, should the need arise.

Summary

This chapter has explored:

- The nature of modern family life and the incidence of divorce
- The impact of separation and divorce on children and young people
- School responses to separation and divorce.

Annotated further reading

Hall, P. (2007), *Help Your Child Cope with Divorce*. London: Vermilion.
   This is a sensitive, accessible guide for parents including clear advice and guidance on how to minimize the impact of divorce on children.

This book includes an explanation of the age-specific issues faced by children, professional comments and stories and quotes from children, and practical checklists and case studies.

Marquardt, E. (2005), *Between Two Worlds – the Inner Lives of Children of Divorce*. New York: Three Rivers Press.

This is an account of a pioneering US study conducted with Norval Glenn surveying 1,500 young adults from both divorced and non-divorced families. Marquardt, herself a child of divorce, provides a report of the study which is interwoven with her own experiences and numerous stories of children's experiences of divorce as they try to make sense of living between two worlds.

Useful websites

www.divorceaid.co.uk

This is a useful website where leading independent experts from the legal and therapy professions offer advice, support and information on all aspects concerning divorce, including legal and financial advice for parents. There are also sections for children and young people.

www.relate.org.uk

Relate is the UK's largest provider of relationship support, helping over 150,000 people of all ages, backgrounds and sexual orientations every year. The website provides details of Relate's services to adults, young people and also workshops and courses for schools. Counselling and support are offered to young people in a variety of locations (including many schools) and also via skype, email and telephone.

References

Allison, P. D. and Furstenberg, F. F. (1989), 'How marriage dissolution affects children: Variations by age and sex'. *Developmental Psychology*, 25: 540–9.

Amato, P. R. (2000), 'The consequences of divorce for adults and children'. *Journal of Marriage and the Family*, 62: 1269–87.

Australian Bureau of Statistics (2012), *Marriages and Divorces, Australia, 2010*. Available online at www.abs.gov.au/AUSSTATS/abs@.nsf/DetailsPage/3310.02010?OpenDocument.

Blankenhorn, D. (1995), *Fatherless America: Confronting Our Most Urgent Social Problem*. New York: Basic Books.

Center for Disease Control and Prevention (2009), *Births, Marriages, Divorces, and Deaths: Provisional Data for 2009*. Available online at www.cdc.gov/.

— (2012), *National Marriage and Divorce Rate Trends*. Available online at www.cdc.gov/nchs/nvss/marriage_divorce_tables.htm.

Cherlin, A. J. (1991), 'Longitudinal studies of effects of divorce on children in Great Britain and the United States'. *Science*, 252(5011): 1386–9.

— (1992), *Marriage, Divorce, Remarriage*. Cambridge, MA: Harvard University Press.

Cole, S., Greenwald O'Brien, J., Gadd, M. G., Ristuccia, J., Wallace, L. and Gregory, M. (2005), *Helping Traumatised Children Learn*. Boston: Massachusetts Advocates for Children.

Coontz, S. (1992), *The Way We Never Were: American Families and the Nostalgia Trap*. New York: Basic Books.

Daly, C. (2009), 'In the eye of a divorce storm: Examining the modern challenge for Irish schools educating children of divorced and separated families'. *Irish Educational Studies*, 28(3), 351–65.

Department of Education and Science (1967), *Children and their Primary Schools (Plowden Report)*. London: HMSO.

Department for Education and Skills (DfES) (2003), *Excellence and Enjoyment: A Strategy for Primary Schools*. London: DfES.

— (2007), *Every Parent Matters: Creating Opportunity, Releasing Potential, Achieving Excellence*. London: DfES.

Desforges, C. and Abouchaar, A. (2003), *The Impact of Parental Involvement, Parental Support and Family Education on Pupil Achievement and Adjustment: A Literature Review*, Research Report RR433. London: DfES.

Donnelly, C. (2000), 'In pursuit of school ethos'. *British Journal of Educational Studies*, 48:2, 134–54.

Frieman, B. B. (1993), 'Separation and divorce: What children want their teachers to know: Meeting the emotional needs of preschool and primary school children'. *Young Children*, 48: 58–63.

Furstenberg, F. F. (1994), 'History and current status of divorce in the United States'. *The Future of Children*, 4: 29–43.

Furstenberg, F. F. and Cherlin, A. J. (1991), *Divided Families: What Happens to Children When Parents Part*. Cambridge, MA: Harvard University Press.

Glenn, N. (1996), 'Values, Attitudes and the State of American Marriage', in D. Popenoe, J. Elshtain and D. Blankenhorn (eds), *Promises to Keep: Decline and Renewal of Marriage in America*. Lanham, MD: Rowman and Littlefield.

Hall, P. (2007), *Help Your Child Cope with Divorce*. London: Vermilion.

Halsey, A. H. (2000), 'Introduction', in A. H. Halsey and J. Webb (eds), *Twentieth Century Social Trends*. London: MacMillan.

Holland, J. (2000), 'Secondary schools and pupil loss by parental bereavement and parental relationship separations'. *Pastoral Care in Education*, 18:4, 33–9.

Marquardt, E. (2005), *Between Two Worlds – the Inner Lives of Children of Divorce*. New York: Three Rivers Press.

Miller, P. A., Ryan, P. and Morrison, W. (1999), 'Practical strategies for helping children of divorce in today's classroom'. *Childhood Education*, 75: 5, 285–9.

Nock, S. (2002), 'The Social Costs of De-Institutionalizing Marriage', in L. J. Waite, A. J. Hawkins, L. D. Wardle and D. O. Coolidge (eds), *Revitalizing the Institution of Marriage for the Twenty-First Century: An Agenda for Strengthening Marriage*. Westport, CT: Greenwood Press.

Northern Ireland Statistics and Research Agency [NISRA] (2011), *Statistical Bulletin: Marriages, Divorces and Civil Partnerships in Northern Ireland (2010)*. Available online at www.nisra.gov.uk/.

Office for National Statistics (2012), *Marriages, Cohabitations, Civil Partnerships and Divorces*. Available online at www.ons.gov.uk.

Popenoe, D. (1993), 'American family decline, 1960–1990: A review and appraisal'. *Journal of Marriage and Family*, 55(3): 527–52.

Qualifications and Curriculum Authority (2007a), *PSHEE Personal Well-Being Programme of Study (non-statutory) for Key Stage 3*. Available online at www.qca.org.uk/curriculum.

— (2007b), *PSHEE Personal Well-Being Programme of Study (non-statutory) for Key Stage 4*. Available online at www.qca.org.uk/curriculum.

Rodgers, B. and Pryor, J. (1998), *Divorce and Separation: The Outcomes for Children*. York: Joseph Rowntree Foundation.

Scottish Government (2012), *Divorces and Dissolutions 2009–2010*. Available online at www.scotland.gov.uk.

Skolnick, A. (1991), *Embattled Paradise: The American Family in an Age of Uncertainty*. New York: Basic Books.

Social Issues Research Centre [SIRC] (2008), *Childhood and Family Life: Socio-demographic Changes*. Oxford: SIRC.

Stacey, J. (1993), 'Good riddance to the family: A response to David Popenoe'. *Journal of Marriage and the Family*, 55(3): 545–7.

— (1996), *In the Name of the Family: Rethinking Family Values in the Postmodern Age*. Boston: Beacon Press.

Tufnell, C. (2012), *A New Family – the Fun and Hard Work of Building a Stepfamily*. Available online at www.careforthefamily.org.uk.

Wallerstein, J. S. and Kelly, J. B. (1979), *Surviving the Break-up*. New York: Basic Books.

Wallerstein, J., Lewis, J. and Blakeslee, S. (2002), *The Unexpected Legacy of Divorce*. London: Fusion Press.

Bereavement: Challenges and Opportunities for Schools

Mary F. Lappin

6

Chapter Outline

Introduction

It is generally accepted that bereavement, particularly the death of someone of personal significance can have a profound impact on the lives of individuals, families and communities. Significant loss (whether through separation, divorce, emigration, imprisonment or illness) brings with it grief reactions, adversity and the need for adjustment and adaptation, yet in death we are faced with irreversibility and a finality that can seem harsh and impenetrable. It is well known that bereavement brings a complexity of emotional and cognitive responses, which will be highlighted in this chapter, but the significance of the loss and the reactions to it must be considered from the perspective of the grieving child or young person if there is to be genuine understanding, and if support and guidance are to be effective.

One can be bereft and grieve in a myriad of ways as a result of a range of losses, often related to, or resulting from the death of someone close. While the field of psychology has for some years promoted the management and normalization of grief, where the bereaved master their adversity and cope with resulting losses, it is only in more recent times that education has embraced not just therapeutic interventions but also the importance of learning about loss and grief through educational programmes and curricula.

A voice of caution may warn against an overemphasis on a therapeutic dimension within schools, with a potential blurring of the psychological/counselling realm, and the promotion of scholarly knowledge, understanding and skills within the world of education. This is an understandable source of anxiety, for a fusion of worlds, whereby boundaries are ambiguous, can be emotionally dangerous and educationally ineffective. Nevertheless, educators do recognize that the impact of home events and circumstances can create a temporary or long-term barrier to learning, which must be addressed through additional support mechanisms.

The importance of meeting children's additional educational needs has been enshrined in policies and legislation in recent years in different jurisdictions. For instance, in Scotland, the Education (Additional Support for Learning) (Scotland) Act 2004 provides the legal framework underpinning the support systems for children and young people, and is based on the concept of 'additional support needs'. This concept refers to any child or young person who, for whatever reason, requires additional support for learning. Some possible causes of these additional support needs are listed in the summary guidance (Scottish Executive, 2004, p. 2):

> Additional support needs can arise from any factor which causes a barrier to learning, whether that factor relates to social, emotional, cognitive, linguistic, disability, or family and care circumstances. For instance, additional support may be required for a child or young person who is being bullied; has behavioural difficulties; has learning difficulties; is a parent; has a sensory or mobility impairment; is at risk; or is bereaved.

The *Supporting Children's Learning Code of Practice* (Scottish Government, 2010, §14) recognizes that additional support needs can often be met within the school community, but that there are also occasions when some children and young people will 'require additional support from agencies from outwith education services if they are to make progress'. Here it is recognized that there can be a vital role for 'counselling provided by a voluntary agency for a child who has been bereaved and needs support to help her overcome difficulties in school' (Scottish Government, 2010, §14).

Grief models and theories

There are many theories and models of grief but this chapter will focus on those with the greatest significance to the field of education. The theories of John Bowlby on attachment have played a significant role in the understanding of grief responses, particularly in children and young people. His research (e.g. Bowlby, 1960, 1980) established that children are capable of grieving and recognized that absence from a loved one has an impact on well-being. It is against a landscape of family, neighbourhood and school that the child lives out a loss experience and resulting changes. Adversity of any kind brings with it challenges in adjustment and adaptation for adult and child alike. While it is unusual for a child to experience prolonged upset and distress, there are emotional reactions and behaviours that are not dissimilar to those of adults such as anxiety, deep sadness, insecurity, anger and vulnerability. In many ways grief is an instinctive and intuitive response to separation from someone or something significant. Reassuringly, research informs us that most children, with adequate care, support and information, will do well and make progress emotionally, cognitively and educationally (Haine et al., 2008). Nevertheless, we do a disservice to our children and young people if we do not give cognizance to the on-going longing and prolonged grief that can be experienced after the initial grief responses (see Waisanen, 2004).

There are common grief reactions to any experience of significant loss. While society generally recognizes that bereavement is a time of adversity, it is not the only source of grief. Other life changes can leave one bereft, such as divorce, separation, immigration or imprisonment. Death is nevertheless unique in its inevitability, universality and finality.

Freud is considered a main influence in the field of loss and bereavement, yet it is important to highlight that his often quoted *Mourning and Melancholia* (Freud, 1917) was an exploration of the differences between grief and depression. Anyone who has experienced the death of a significant other recognizes that a tendency towards, or feelings related to, depression are common. It is not unusual for the bereft to feel at least a dip in a sense of well-being or self-esteem and, at most, a depressive burden that one cannot lose. Clearly, one's sense of balance and equilibrium is disturbed.

The work of Kübler-Ross proposes a process paradigm. Her notable text *On Death and Dying* (Kübler-Ross, 1970) is still influential in grief counselling and hospice work. Kübler-Ross suggests a 'five stages of grief model', incorporating denial, anger, bargaining, depression and acceptance whereby the bereft navigate through their grief experience. This grief stage model helps in the understanding of and adaptation to personal loss through death. The term *stages of grief* is perhaps unfortunate as bereavement is not as tidy as the term would suggest. However it does Kübler-Ross a disservice to suggest that she promoted a reductionist view of the grief experience as a predictable series of responses encountered in linear fashion, and from which the individual inevitably emerges with a final resolution and adaptation. A bereaved person may experience unfavorable emotions and a sense of movement from one adverse reaction to another, but to intimate that there is a predictable set of responses overlooks the reality that human beings grieve in unique and, at times, unexpected ways. Schuchter and Zisook (2000, p. 23) warn against a literal acceptance of a stage paradigm and advise that there may be 'overlapping, fluid phases that vary from person to person' comprising an initial period of shock, a period of upset and social withdrawal, and finally a 'culminating period of restitution'. Schuchter and Zisook (2000, p. 25) suggest further that 'some aspects of grief work may never end for a significant proportion of otherwise normal bereaved individuals'.

It may be tempting to posit a point of closure or end point in grieving, yet often there is no such discernible end point. Instead the bereaved are engaged in an ongoing renegotiation of meaning over time. Bereavement is a complex and painful phenomenon often replacing a person's security and stability with vulnerability, deep sadness, anxiety and pain. Grief, emotional responses and adversity must also be seen in relative and not in absolute terms. Those in grief have a perspective very different from those in the supportive role, and a grief model is a reminder of this reality. The research of Kübler-Ross involved careful listening to and observations of the dying who in turn are able to teach observers about the experienced reality of grief. Through her observations Kübler-Ross recognized common traits, reactions and patterns in the wrestle with grief and loss.

The seminal work of Bowlby (e.g. 1960, 1980) and Murray Parkes (1972) stresses that grief is a process with a pattern of emotional responses such as disbelief, anger, numbness, loneliness and physical sensations such as tightness in the chest, nausea, loss of appetite and insomnia. In fact Bruce (2002) defines grief as a 'natural, inevitable neuropsycho-biological response to any kind of significant loss' (p. 28), a useful and all-embracing definition which suggests a multifaceted impact, even if it risks pathologizing grief and insinuates a curative focus. Viewing grief as an illness can be unhelpful. For instance, Silverman (2000, p. 24) states that 'when grief is characterized in the language of medicine, it is described in terms of symptoms people manifest, as if they suffer from a "condition"'. She goes on to suggest that the common feelings and physical sensations experienced by the bereaved can be communicated as something 'wrong' and warns against a simplistic view that simply 'getting feelings out' can cure or relieve the symptoms. Clearly, the grief process is much more complex, for the reality of people's lives, their dispositions and personalities, and the attachments they form are intricate and multifarious. Loss brings change, adaptation and transition where relationships can shift; economic status can be enhanced or diminished; and roles and responsibilities can become more fluid. One thing is however certain: a return to life as it was before is unattainable. Undoubtedly it is a time of stress, but meaningful learning and growth can take place in the discovery of how to effectively manage such stress and adversity.

By contrast Neimeyer's (1997, 1998, 2001) theories of grief correspond to a constructivist view of learning whereby the learner makes meaning or constructs new ideas based upon experience and knowledge. Neimeyer (1997, 1998, 2001) would challenge some central assumptions within mainstream bereavement theories, such as the suggestion that the end point of grief is 'the letting go' of the attachment to the deceased, or that grief involves the working through of grief reactions and the relinquishment of attachment ties. Traditional grief theories have assumed that successful grieving requires withdrawal of psychic energy from the loved one. Contemporary grief theories recognize, however, that roles often adapt in maintaining a continuing bond with the deceased. Within some grief theories a central emphasis on emotion and a focus on the element of catharsis in the grieving process are inadequate and must be supplemented with a greater attention to the cognitive and meaning-making process of grief. A desire to place emphasis on meaning is understandable, for the finding of a logical or coherent reasoning can bring comprehension and enlighten the way forward. Indeed experience is meaningful and allows for growth when comprehension is granted. The death of an elderly, sick relative, notwithstanding the pain of loss, can 'make sense' for the life has been long and the body is not functioning so well. The unexpected death of a young person or the unanticipated death of a parent is harder to reconcile. A complete understanding of why a loved one dies at a particular time and not another, why a significant person meets an untimely and unexpected death, or what happens after death is however more difficult, although many do find meaning and make sense of these complex questions through a personal religious faith.

Murray Parkes (1972) and Bowlby (1960, 1980) recognized that the bereaved not only move through grief stages but also weave in and around, revisiting a stage and its emotional and cognitive impact. New and enhanced understandings of grief models continue to be offered in the field of thanatology (the study of death and dying, from the Greek word *thanatos* meaning death). Stroebe, Stroebe and Hanson (1999) recognize the experience of grief as a dynamic process, which allows for both the expression of feelings as well as the need to control feelings. Understanding and working through the impact of grief and its adaptation process are thus important rudiments of grief work and adjustment to loss. The internal and external landscape experience dynamic change and at times resistance, and hopefully adaptation and integration. Klass and Walter (2001) are not alone in disputing the notion that those grieving will at some point leave behind or break the 'emotional bonds' with the deceased. Instead they support a 'continued bond model' whereby those grieving can maintain a relationship with the deceased and integrate them into life, while allowing an openness to new relationships.

Another highly influential model within grief counselling and research is that of William Worden. Worden (1996) advocates a task model whereby the bereaved work through their loss experience and reach reconciliation and adjustment. The four tasks of mourning (Worden, 1996) are: to accept the reality of the loss; to work through the pain of grief; to adjust to an environment in which the deceased is missing; and to emotionally relocate the deceased and move on with life. These tasks are not followed in a linear or specific order, but rather recognize the cyclical and often unpredictable nature of grief. In other words one can weave in and out of the tasks as required. The Grief and Loss Education programme, *Seasons for Growth*, adopts Worden's four tasks as its core content and structure, building in opportunities for young people to work through an acceptance of their loss, recognize the adversity and painful emotions that can arise as part of their 'loss story' and look at effective coping strategies and how to reinvest emotional energy without severing a continued relationship with the deceased. Interestingly, and understandably, given the need for structure and progression, *Seasons for Growth*, with Worden's theory at its core, generally explores the tasks in a linear framework with due activities, sharing and learning at each task. The structure of the learning begins with acceptance of the reality of loss and ends with reinvestment of emotional energy. At the heart of the learning and exploration learners recognize and understand that grief reactions are revisited and experienced in different ways and at varying times of life. A metaphor of the seasons is particularly helpful in recognition of this concept. Graham and Anderson (2002, p. 2) note that *Seasons for Growth* draws on the metaphor of seasons for 'seasons of the year provide a rich symbolic framework in which to explore issues of change and loss'. Essentially, parallels are made between the seasons of the year and the experience of grief. For instance, like seasonal changes, grief is an inevitable part of life, and just as each season requires adjustment if we are to meet its challenges, so too grief and loss require adjustment and strategies to cope with resulting challenges.

Clearly a task model suggests that the bereaved need to actively engage and work with the emotional turbulence and resulting losses that bereavement can bring, ideally reaching some form of acceptance.

Themes of similarity and diversity are evident in grief and loss work; grief counsellers, self-help books, bereavement theory and research regularly tell us that each bereaved person is unique and will deal with loss and grief in a unique way. This point is often stressed and can be a source of consolation and encouragement, granting the bereaved permission to react and respond to their pain and adversity in their own way and in their own time. On the other hand there are common grief reactions suggesting a shared experience. While we look for advice and guidance on how to deal with death, especially when it is unanticipated and untimely, it must be remembered that there are no easy formulae or solutions to this most challenging aspect of human experience. Within grief and loss education there is an emphasis on recognizing and naming emotional reactions, understanding cognitive responses and highlighting healthy and effective coping strategies. A resilience model is often promoted in the resolution of grief reactions, aimed at supporting children and young people to navigate through life's adversities with a healthy sense of self, knowing where and whom to ask for support.

Learning about loss and grief

Training in Grief and Loss Education programmes is becoming increasingly sought after in UK schools with a view to addressing the well-being and educational needs of pupils who have experienced significant loss through death or family break-up. Essentially all those who actively work with the bereaved young person are seeking to support the griever in readjusting to an environment whereby the deceased is no longer physically present. Understandably educating pupils about and supporting them through their grief experience within a task model paradigm sits comfortably in an educational framework, for pupils can engage in cognitive endeavour, develop emotional literacy and move towards enhanced confidence. Grief and Loss Education programmes often aim at equipping children and young people (through a peer support framework) with the knowledge, skills and dispositions to cope with their experiences of loss and grief. Often programmes do not aim to assist only the bereaved, but also support young people through a range of loss experiences, including family change through separation and divorce. Arguably, learning about death and bereavement need not be restricted

to those pupils who have encountered the death of someone significant since loss, change and death are concepts worthy of exploration
and reflection for all pupils. Thanatology is promoted in parts of North
America with an emphasis on incorporating knowledge about death
in a general school and college curriculum. Within the UK, death is
explored to a certain extent within such subjects as Religious Education,
Personal, Social, Health and Economic (PSHE) education, Citizenship,
Science and Nature Studies. Engagement with the subject is determined
by teacher confidence and disposition, quality of resources and curriculum emphasis. Grief and Loss Education expands the opportunity for
engagement with an emphasis on learning about the impact of loss, the
promotion of resilience and the fostering of a capacity for dealing with
change and adversity, particularly that which can come about as a result
of any significant loss.

In learning about death, naturally the teacher must be considerate
of the developmental stage of pupils. Clearly the young child has a very
different grasp of the finality, universality and inevitability of death
from the adolescent. Children grow in their awareness and understanding of the abstract – the work of Piaget (1932), Kohlberg (1981) and
Fowler (1995) is testament to this. Bereavement websites, charities and
academic texts often provide an overview of a developmental understanding of death, but it is important to recognize that developmental
theories paint with a broad brush. They serve in classifying broad elements of children's growth and yet they are imperfect instruments, since
it is now widely acknowledged that children do not develop according
to firm timelines or stages. In Table 6.1 for instance we see that children younger than 2 years old have no concept of death, although can

Table 6.1 Children's developing concept of death

0–2 years	No concept of death: the experienced is that of separation.
2–5 years	Death is temporary, reversible like sleep. Dead people have feelings and bodily functions. Some people may not die.
5–9 years	Moving towards irreversibility of death and the beginnings of an appreciation of the universality of death (except perhaps themselves).
10+ years	Awareness of long-term consequences of death. Personal awareness. Reflections on fate, injustice/justice.

display symptoms of separation. As they get older, there is an understanding of death but not of its irreversibility; it is not uncommon for young children to expect those who have died to return at some point or to 'come back from heaven in time for dinner'. Throughout the primary school years they move towards an appreciation of irreversibility and that death is universal, but often exclude themselves in this equation. Approaching the age of 10 and through adolescence there is a recognition that death can come unexpectedly and at times this seems unfair and unjust. For instance, the mother of young children who becomes ill and subsequently dies or the young person who dies as the result of a road accident gives cause for reflection on the part that fate may have to play, the unpredictability of death and the adversity experienced by those who are bereft.

Reactions and responses to grief are generally experienced in four ways: cognitively, emotionally, physically and behaviourally. There is hesitation in stating that these responses are normal, for this suggests a qualitative judgement. Instead the emphasis is placed on common grief reactions (see Table 6.2)

The table presents some common reactions, though it is by no means exhaustive. It is common for any child to exhibit behaviours that suggest a regression to an earlier stage, most frequently to a memorable or perceived time of security. All stages share feelings of insecurity and vulnerability with some anxiety about a remaining family member, parent or carer leaving or dying. It is not uncommon for a physical reaction to a death of someone significant to manifest itself in low level, unidentifiable pains and a general feeling of being unwell, hence the child who complains of vague feelings of stomach ache, headache or nausea. Parents, health visitors and GPs look for signs of failure to thrive in the on-going assessment of infant development and growth, with attendance to weight gain, sleep routines, preverbal responses and any delayed development naturally becoming a source of concern, additional care and monitoring. Furthermore, a parent of very young children who is not coping with bereavement may have an additional struggle in trying to maintain the care and presence required for a baby or toddler and so will need intervention and support in fulfilling the duties and tasks of parenthood. Likewise the adolescent who is withdrawing from family and peers or the young person who seeks to protect their parent from

Table 6.2 Common responses in young people to death (adapted from Worden, 1996)

Birth to 2 years	3 to 5 years	5 to 8 years	9 to 12 years	Adolescence
Failure to thrive, feeding, sleeping, digestive disturbances, excessive crying, irritability, stranger anxiety, searching for missing loved one	Regression to earlier stage (bedwetting, tantrums), food refusal, waking at night, irritability, pre-occupied during play involving re-enacting a parent leaving, being dead, fearful of losing other parent/carer, aggressive towards others or passive and withdrawn, not always able to express/explore feelings of loss	Denial, sadness, episodic crying, increased anxiety, restlessness, over activity, school problems, physical illness, more accident prone, feelings of rejection, low self-esteem, magical thinking, acting out being angry, naughty, taking on role of 'little man/woman', guilt feelings that somehow it was child's fault	Eating/sleeping difficulties, anger, difficulties at school, changes in social behaviour, inconsolable grief, ask many detailed questions about everything that has occurred, may take on unrealistic responsibilities, fearful that remaining parent/ care will die/leave child, physical illnesses in response to stress – head and stomach, asthma, infections	Withdrawal from family and peers, school problems, increased absenteeism, confusion about identity, grieving secretly, denial, uncontrollable anger, violence towards parent, mood swings, feelings of uncertainty about the role of the adolescent in family, pseudo-maturity, feelings of guilt or resentment, worry that they are to blame, sense of abandonment

seeing any painful grief responses requires careful consideration and care from family, friends and teachers.

Additionally there can be responses that are related to the spiritual realm, where questions are posed about the existence of God, faith in the afterlife and one's identity, purpose and destiny. For instance Adams et al. (2008) present some interesting findings and insights into the spiritual experiences of children, including the field of death and dying, and an exploration of key issues in the spiritual dimension of childhood. Adams et al. (2008, p. 40) claim that 'every adult will at some point be faced with children's questions about death, and it is essential that they hear what is being said and asked. Be honest with yourself: is it you who has difficulties talking about death? If so, why? Remember that children will need your emotional support in this area, however difficult you find the topic to discuss.'

Research Example: Bereavement and School Attainment

In this small-scale study, Abdelnoor and Hollins (2004) examine the GCSE results of children throughout England who had experienced the death of a parent. The findings highlight that 'childhood bereavement appears to be a robust factor in underachievement' (p. 43). While recognizing that achievement is multi-dimensional (related to, for instance, parental support, teacher expectation, social behaviour and expectations), the study found that young people who had experienced the death of a parent scored on average half a grade below their control group in GCSE examinations. The findings also indicated that young people who had experienced parental bereavement under the age of 5 or at the age of 12 years seemed 'particularly affected' in their examination results. In terms of anxiety levels, the study showed a three or four point difference between parentally bereaved young people and their controls, with fears, worries and difficulties sleeping representing the most common anxiety responses. Abdelnoor and Hollins recognize that 'the small sample size means that results must be treated speculatively pending further research' (p. 51). Furthermore, the sample was self-selected and all (73) children were from white UK families. Nevertheless, the study does offer some pointers for discussion and an important theme for further research.

Reference

Abdelnoor, A. and Hollins, S. (2004), 'The effect of childhood bereavement on secondary school performance'. *Educational Psychology in Practice*, 20(1): 43–54.

Supporting the bereaved young person

What do we know about the needs of grieving children and adolescents? Primarily, the needs of grieving young people are multifaceted and there are well-documented analyses of the requirements of grieving children and young people. The adolescent is often considered to be particularly at risk of adverse outcomes, most probably due to the existing tasks associated with independence and transition. Furthermore, the disruption caused by the death of someone significant and its resulting changes can pose additional challenges to adolescents already facing puberty, with its hormonal changes and challenges to the sense of self. As Raphael (1984, p. 139) notes, 'there are a great many developmental changes in adolescence which may bring their own levels of psychic upheaval. The stress of bereavement is superimposed upon these'. Raphael also highlights some of the characteristics of this stage of development and provides an informative overview of influences and considerations which may affect the experience and complexity of grief for the adolescent. It is not uncommon, for instance, to witness adolescents engaging in risk-taking behaviours such as drug misuse, driving of fast cars and early sexual encounters. Generally these can be considered coping strategies or a release from emotional turbulence and bewilderment, albeit unsafe and potentially damaging to their physical, psychological and emotional health. The educator is concerned then with the development of appropriate and healthy coping strategies, whereby release, recovery and response can be expressed, respected and encouraged. The bereaved child and adolescent can face a life that is fundamentally changed in structure, family composition and routine. For some this change is welcomed for it brings relief and release from tension and conflict, while for most others it is unwanted and unwelcome.

Teachers report young people to be more anxious, withdrawn and depressed than their peers when they experience bereavement. There can be difficulties with concentration and attention which, unsurprisingly, can result in reduced assessment grades. However for some young people it can lead to improved performance, as they seek perhaps to make the deceased parent proud of their performance or as they try to escape the reality of their loss by burying themselves in school work. It is not uncommon for the origins of school difficulties resulting from a bereavement to be forgotten by adults, especially when some time has elapsed and when school life is busy and demanding. This is understandable, yet awareness that the impact of loss can continue sometime after the initial bereavement can be helpful and assist the teacher in identifying need and providing support.

The needs of grieving young people are not difficult to list, and include careful listening, supportive gestures, opportunities to talk, companionship, distraction, understanding and care. Needless to say there can be complexities and subtle nuances in the adult response to these needs. In *Children and Grief* Worden (1996) summarizes the findings of the Child Bereavement Study which mapped out the impact of the death of a parent on children and young people between the ages of 6 and 17. He proposed that there are ten needs in a young person who has experienced a family bereavement (Adequate information; Fears/Anxieties to be addressed; Reassurance that they are not to blame; Careful listening and watching; Validation of feelings; Help with overwhelming feelings; Involvement and inclusion; Continued routine; Good models of grief; and Opportunities to remember) and these are outlined in more detail below.

It comes as no surprise that young people require adequate information as to the cause of the loss, and for the younger child this requires age-appropriate explanations, providing clarity and reassurance as to the nature and cause of the death. Children's anxieties and fears also need to be addressed, particularly those surrounding guilt, safety, care and blame. It is not uncommon for the young people to blame themselves in some way for the loss, particularly where there are gaps in information as to the cause of death or ambiguity as to why or how the death occurred. The adult response clearly requires careful listening and sensitivity to messages being given through behaviours, words, activities and actions. Validation of the complexity of emotions, and help with overwhelming feelings aid the bereaved young person in dealing with and growing through their grief. Good models of grief can be beneficial in showing how the 'adult world' expresses and responds to loss, thus giving permission to the young person to weep, question, struggle and yet also providing an example of how to continue with the functions of daily life and its routines. The young person does not require the surviving carer to be superhuman but rather to be a 'good enough' or functioning care-giver. Adults who continually hide their grief from young people, often as a form of protection, can inadvertently create the false impression that grief is a private, isolated activity to be hidden and mastered alone. This does not suggest that a continued routine is inadvisable; quite the reverse is true. For many young people the continued, predictable routine of school or college can provide a welcome sense of safety, connectedness and even 'time out' from the task of grieving.

Opportunities to remember the deceased are important. Indeed Silverman and Worden's Childhood Bereavement Study (reported in Worden, 1996) discovered that even if a surviving parent finds it painful and resists talking about their deceased partner, the bereaved children and young people still shared stories with their siblings or talked with someone outside the immediate family. Schools can play an important part in the recognition of a need to remember by appreciating a pupil's wish to share a story or memory as well as the annual cultural or religious events that can be part of a school or community life. Faith schools can also offer a framework for remembering through the rituals, prayers, symbols and religious seasons, for example the recitation of Kaddish (the Jewish mourner's prayer), Christian Church services and Catholic 'Masses for the dead' during the month of November. There are of course other rituals that can allow for concrete expression and symbolic gestures, such as gatherings and assemblies to share stories, music, poetry and important memories within a sacred and respectful space.

Case Study: An Example of a School Response [based on a true story]

Jacqueline Brown, a senior teacher in an inner-city comprehensive, explains what happened: 'One day about three years ago, one of our pupils was killed and another badly injured in a road traffic accident. The boys, Jordan and Shaun, had been crossing a road on their way to school when they were struck by a speeding motorist. On that first morning, news came to the school very quickly that two of our pupils had been involved in an accident. Later in the morning we learned that Jordan had been killed and that Shaun had suffered serious injuries and was in a stable condition in hospital.

Only weeks earlier, we had completed a critical incident and bereavement policy with guidance from our Local Education Authority. On that morning, we did not have time to look at it, but we did follow the main principles. I don't know where we would have been without it, to be honest.

On that first day we brought together the boys' friends, talked with them, listened to them, and gave them an opportunity to express their feelings through a large graffiti wall mural in the boys' tutor room. We had a "time out room" where pupils could go, if and when they found it too hard to be in class. This was staffed by a trained counsellor. Later in the week we had a memorial service in the school, and many of the pupils and staff went along to the funeral service too.

In the days and weeks which followed, there were good days and bad days for Jordan's friends, and for Shaun who came back to school after about two months. When I was a pupil myself thirty years ago, if this sort of thing had happened, my generation of teachers would have told us simply to get on with our school work. That doesn't work with today's young people. They need time out; they need to express their feelings, and we have to give them the time and space to do that safely in school.

What we have learnt from the whole thing is that not all of our teachers are willing or able to personally get alongside the bereaved pupils. That's fine. We have no problem with that, but all of our teachers do need to look out for pupils who are struggling and need to know who to contact for more support. Everyone needs to know the procedures, from the head teacher to the school caretaker. It really is a whole-school response.'

Questions

1. What do you think the school did well in this case?
2. Should all teachers be expected to work directly with bereaved pupils?
3. How important is a whole-school response to bereavement?

Potential roadblocks to communication with young people are worth highlighting if support through bereavement is desired. A controlling approach from the school of 'What you need is . . .' can be frustrating and stifling, thus providing unwanted and overbearing solutions to what is essentially an emotional need for recognition and empathy, characterized by a desire to be heard and not told. Such a moralizing approach seldom serves in the accompaniment of young people and can hinder the expression and articulation of grief. Educators often promote a pedagogy of effective questioning in the education of young people to enable independent thought, self-expression and growth in the understanding of concepts and ideas. Likewise, careful and sensitive questioning can encourage the expression of grief emotions and transmit a message of care and support to a young bereaved person. It can be a worthwhile and effective means of engagement, yet inappropriate questioning can seem intrusive rather than supportive. In such questioning the adult should not be primarily concerned with the acquisition of appropriate or correct knowledge, but should instead attempt to enter into the thought process of the children and guide them towards enhancing and worthwhile coping strategies, as well as making meaning out of a loss experience. Bereavement is not only an event that happens, but also something which we endeavour to make sense of. As discussed above, this is naturally related to a child's developmental stage.

Resilience models provide a possible explanation as to why some young people cope well with adversity while others continue to struggle. A sense of control, meaning and bonding enables a young person to cope with the tasks of grieving and adjusting to change. Control suggests a competence and capability to navigate through adversity in circumstances with a sense of self and power to change. Bonding refers to a sense of connectedness with family, friends and community and feelings of being wanted and belonging. A sense of meaning relates to one's sense of relevance and importance in the world; it is about one's capacity to accomplish and make a difference. In summary, where a young person is resilient in adversity, there is a greater likelihood of a healthy working through, and a positive outcome from loss, grief and any resulting changes.

Research Example: How Do Secondary Schools Deal with Loss?

In this small-scale study Holland (2000) interviewed senior teachers in 19 secondary schools in the North of England in relation to their experiences of dealing with two forms of loss: parental bereavement and parental separation. The results show that almost two thirds of the schools (63%) included loss education in the curriculum (most commonly in Religious Education and Personal and Social Education) and that this took place most often with pupils in years 9–11 (aged 14–16). There were significant differences in how the schools found out about parental deaths (usually directly) and parental separation ('through the grapevine' in almost four out of five cases). Interestingly, almost three-quarters of schools (74%) reported that their response would be different for a death compared to a parental separation. When asked to explain this, more than a third (37%) of teachers claimed that relationship breakdown was a cultural norm, and over a quarter (26%) argued that parents and pupils may not want school involvement in a relationship breakdown. Unlike in cases of bereavement, teachers did not consider it appropriate to announce relationship breakdowns at staff briefings, nor to place such information on a notice board. Only 11 per cent of schools sent a note to subject teachers to inform them of a parental separation.

Alarmingly, all but one of the schools (95%) reported that issues of loss were not addressed in any school policy document, although 79 per cent of the research participants thought that they should be mentioned. The study shows that there is a wide variety of school response to significant loss among pupils, and that much work remains to be done to ensure that schools respond in a less ad hoc and more considered, consistent manner to help provide appropriate support to their pupils.

Reference

Holland, J. (2000), 'Secondary schools and pupil loss by parental bereavement and parental relationship separations'. *Pastoral Care in Education*, 18(4): 33–9.

Ambiguous loss and disenfranchised grief

Interestingly, for many who have experienced the death of someone significant, there can be a strange paradox in relation to presence and absence. While death brings a physical disconnection and severance, we do not disengage from loved ones just because they are physically gone, nor in fact do we necessarily connect with others just because they are physically present. In times of distress we may tap into our memories, love and affection for loved ones who are 'kept alive' in our hearts as well as, or instead of, those around us – this can aid our ability to cope and grow. Presence and absence are interesting themes in an encounter with grief, for it is not uncommon for the bereaved to feel or sense the presence of the deceased. For instance Adams et al. (2008, pp. 63–4) describe bereaved children's dreams about death and about those close to them who have died.

Ambiguity in loss refers to those losses that are less 'tidy', less definable, such as the soldier who is missing and presumed dead, the emergence of Alzheimer's disease or the vacant, detached state of the drug addict. Ambiguous loss falls into two broad categories: the physical presence of someone who is psychologically absent (e.g. someone with an illness such as Alzheimer's disease or a person in a coma); and the psychological presence of someone who is physically absent (e.g. in such circumstances as missing bodies following natural disasters or wars).

The exploration of ambiguity in loss, creating disturbance and strain, is relatively new (Boss, 1999). Ambiguity coupled with loss can create barriers and challenges in coping with the grieving process, leading to symptoms such as depression, inner conflict and conflict within relationships. Young people in our schools can be living their daily life within a context of ambiguity and ambiguous loss, such as the relatively well-adjusted child living with mentally ill parents or parents with learning disabilities, or severe addiction issues, who longs for their parents to 'take charge', to set the boundaries and fully engage in the task of parenting. Similarly, there is the child whose parent abandons the family unit, leaving no explanation or indication as to where they can be found, or the sibling of the child who has disappeared or is chronically ill and who requires additional physical and emotional energy and care from the parent.

Doka (1989) writes extensively on the topic of disenfranchised grief, referring to the grief that individuals experience when they encounter a loss that is not or cannot be publicly acknowledged, openly mourned or socially and culturally supported. He provides insight into such loss experiences which could include the unknown lover, child or mother or the unwanted and undervalued friend at the graveside. In an insightful article on disenfranchised grief, Attig (2004) focuses on the rights and the process of grief with further reflections on Doka's claim that survivors have a 'right to grieve' (Doka, 2002, p. 5). Attig (2004, p. 198) maintains that disenfranchisement of grief must be understood as the denial of a human right:

> With this understanding of a right to grieve, we can see that disenfranchising is not simply a matter of indifference to the experiences and efforts of the bereaved. It is more actively negative and destructive as it involves denial of entitlement, interference, and even imposition of sanction. Disenfranchising messages actively discount, dismiss, disapprove, discourage, invalidate, and delegitimate the experiences and efforts of grieving. And disenfranchising behaviors interfere with the exercise of the right to grieve by withholding permission, disallowing, constraining, hindering, and even prohibiting it.

By their very nature ambiguous loss and disenfranchised grief are uniquely challenging, for the child or young person is also dealing with the lack of any official or public recognition of the loss, despite the reality of the pain of grief and the need for expression and acknowledgement. Such scenarios can potentially lead to complicated and unresolved grief. Freud (1917) referred to unresolved grief (involving a tendency to distraction and preoccupation with the deceased person) as melancholia or complicated grief. He maintained that grief was complicated because the bereaved refused to relinquish the 'love object'. Yet, as Boss (2006, p. 4) asks 'What happens when a person is faced with ambiguous loss, which by its very nature is irresolvable? What happens when it is the external situation, not the person's psyche, that makes letting go of the lost object impossible?'

In other words the 'letting go' or reinvestment of one's emotional energy can be problematic for anyone bereaved (including young people), where someone significant is gone but not yet dead. Physical absence and yet psychological presence (or indeed vice versa) is a strange and complex reality, where one lives with another 'here' and 'not here' simultaneously. The mourning is often lonely and misunderstood and with no public ritual of sympathy cards and services. Deeper reflection reveals that relationships rarely have complete and continual presence, for one can be in the company of others and yet remain cognitively, psychologically and emotionally detached. Nevertheless, ambiguous loss, which is on-going, can be viewed as traumatic because the inability to resolve the situation, and to 'move on', causes pain, distress, immobilization and confusion.

Undoubtedly some young people live in families where a carer or parent is physically present, although psychologically absent at the same time, through mental illness, Alzheimer's disease or brain injury where the memory, cognition and behaviours are severely altered. A similar situation is faced by the child or young person who experiences the death of a parent or other significant family member and simultaneously the feelings of loss of the remaining parent/family members who are preoccupied with their own loss and grief or who are struggling to function due to depression or inability to function and provide the necessary care and support. These are experiences of profound loss, yet they are not necessarily surrounded by ritual, public recognition or validation.

The challenge for those who accompany the person bereft through ambiguous loss is real and difficult, for uncertainty as to the actual presence or absence of another can, of course, create conditions for unresolved grief and a sense of being 'stuck' within the experience for years or even decades. The situation can therefore lead to unresolved grief even if there is engagement with task models (e.g. Worden, 1996) whereby one may come to an acceptance of the reality of loss, a recognition and articulation of the pain of loss and a certain adjustment to life without 'the other'. Yet a reinvestment of emotional energy and letting go of the other into another reality can be problematic, for hope hangs on a thread that the day may come when the other returns.

Although written from a therapeutic or clinical perspective, Boss (2006) offers valuable insight and extensive research into loss and trauma which is useful to the educator. Here Boss shares her realization that 'getting rid' of ambiguity is impossible (p. 10), and that our goal (from a Grief and Loss Education perspective) should be to enable people to live successful lives, even within a context of ambiguity. By 'successful lives' Boss refers to lives that are lived with sense of ownership and control as well as an awareness of, and ability to, make healthy choices, and a relatively positive self-esteem and sense of self. Boss (2006, p. 164) claims that, within ambiguous loss, 'Rarely is there acceptance, and there is never closure. Rather, the revision of attachment means shifting the relationship to take into account the ambiguity of surrounding loss'. For Boss (2006, p. 169) this requires an acceptance of 'the paradox of presence and absence'. Remaining resilient within ambiguous loss requires the ability to live comfortably with the ambiguity, and she concludes (2006, p. 48) that an 'ability to sustain this comfort relies not only on his or her tolerance for ambiguity, but on the ability to live well with the ambiguity, now and in the future'.

Conclusion

Grief and Loss Education facilitates learning about death as part of life; it seeks to engage young people in the quest for meaning and identity, particularly in times of adversity and struggle, and encourages learning with and from peers and school staff. The teacher or educational professional is discouraged from dispositions of rescuing and shielding young people from loss and grief, but is instead encouraged to accompany young people in their encounter with bereavement and all its resulting turbulence, stress and pain. Humans mourn the loss of significant others. The experience of grief can be lasting and generally adults underestimate the longing young people continue to feel, long after the initial loss. Children and young people will return to their loss over time and will need the continuing support of adults as the experience of significant loss can continue to impact through life. For instance, it is not uncommon for the bereaved children to experience an acute sense of loss when they later encounter rites of passage or transitions, such as graduation day, weddings and significant birthdays. Nevertheless, most children and young people do cope well, and some adopt a restorative approach to school, where the routine of school is a relief and 'time out' from the grieving process.

In conclusion, change, and certainly death, rarely asks our permission to enter, bringing with it potential upheaval and pain. Adjustment to an environment where a loved one is no longer physically present can be arduous and challenging. Educating children and young people in how to deal with significant loss, the myriad grief responses and reactions, strategies for coping with transitions and adapting to change can enhance resilience and promote well-being, particularly in a world where identity can be transient and change can be rapid. Some young people encounter loss through the death of a close family member, friend or teacher, and for many the encounter with death brings with it subsequent emotional pain. The significance of the loss is dependent on the depth of relationship and care felt by the bereaved. Accompanying one who is bereft is indeed an important task. Bereavement can impinge on the equilibrium and a sense of well-being for children and young people. Teachers can, however, play a privileged role in this drama, for they can provide a listening ear and gentle encouragement, and can give pupils the opportunity to learn about, and the language to articulate the reality of their experience, as well as strategies to assist in walking through the turbulence and discomfort of grief.

Summary

This chapter has

- explored some of the most common models of grief (e.g. Kübler-Ross, Worden).
- considered the place of Grief and Loss Education within the school curriculum.
- examined children and young people's developing concept of death, and also their most common reactions to a significant loss.
- detailed the particular needs of bereaved children and young people, and provided guidance in relation to supporting them within an educational context.
- described the particular challenges associated with more complex cases such as ambiguous or disenfranchised grief.

Annotated further reading

Gilbert, I. (2010), *The Little Book of Bereavement for Schools*. Carmarthen, Wales: Crown House Publishing.

As the title suggests, this is a 'little book', but one which contains a wealth of useful advice to schools. It is written by Ian Gilbert whose wife died in 2008, leaving behind a grieving husband and three children, then aged 9, 13 and 18. This book has emerged out of the personal experiences of this grieving family with children at different educational phases (primary, post-primary, post-16). It comprises 15 short chapters, each offering advice which is clear, honest and reflective, and underlines how children (even within the one family) can respond quite differently to the same loss, depending on their age but also on their individual personality.

Jackson, M. and Colwell, J. (2002), *A Teacher's Handbook of Death.* London: Jessica Kingsley Publishers.

This book is designed for teachers and those who have an interest in talking openly to children about death. Each chapter has information which would be useful as preparation for such conversations or lessons, and the aim is to remove the taboo and make such conversations normal and ordinary, while not denying the sadness of individual loss. The final chapter 'Death Across the Curriculum' makes particularly interesting reading: here the authors explore how subjects right across the curriculum can be exploited to allow opportunities to discuss death openly and honestly (e.g. the life cycle in Biology).

Worden, W. (1996), *Children and Grief: When a Parent Dies.* New York: Guilford Press.

This is a classic text and still well worth reading for an authoritative, factual insight into children and grief, based on extensive interviews and assessments of school-age children who have lost a parent to death. The findings of the Harvard Child Bereavement Study (involving 70 families with 125 children between the ages of 6 and 17) are presented and also set in the context of previous research, shedding light on both the wide range of normal variation in children's experience of grief and the mediating factors that can determine the impact of bereavement on an individual child. The final section of the book explores how bereaved children can be helped, with a useful review of intervention models and activities.

Useful websites

www.winstonswish.org.uk

This excellent website is maintained by Winston's Wish, the leading childhood bereavement charity and the largest provider of services to bereaved children, young people and their families in the UK. It has an entire section designed for young people with opportunities to interact, watch video clips, listen to podcasts and post comments on the graffiti wall. There is also a useful section for schools with a Schools Information Pack, information on developing a school policy on bereavement, lesson ideas organized by Key Stage and a case study of how one school responded to the death of the parent of one of their pupils. The online shop allows you to purchase your own memory box, candles to remember and a selection of books about serious illness and bereavement.

www.crusebereavementcare.org.uk

This is a very comprehensive website with detailed information on the grief process, practical advice on what to do when someone dies and a new and interesting section on bereavement support for service families in the Armed Forces. The site also includes a section with information to help understand bereavement from a young person's perspective, and a section for schools with guidance on how to respond to a range of situations such as the death of a pupil or staff member or death through suicide. There is a special section designed for young people by young people called RD4U with information, opportunities to share experiences and a 'lads only' area where boys can tell their stories.

References

Adams, K., Hyde, B. and Woolley, R. (2008), *The Spiritual Dimension of Childhood*. London: Jessica Kingsley Publications.

Attig, T. (2004), 'Disenfranchised grief revisited, discounting hope and love'. *Omega*, 49(3): 197–215.

Bowlby, J. (1960), 'Grief and mourning in infancy and early childhood'. *The Psychoanalytic Study of the Child*, 15: 9–52.

— (1980, 1998), *Loss (Attachment and Loss)* Volume 3. London: Pimlico.

Boss, P. (1999), *Ambiguous Loss: Learning to Live with Unresolved Grief*. Harvard, MA: Harvard University Press.

— (2006), *Loss, Trauma and Resilience: Therapeutic Work with Ambiguous Loss*. London: W.W. Norton and Company.

Bruce, C. A. (2002), 'The grief process for patient, family and physician'. *Journal of the American Oesteopathic Association*, 102(9): 28–32.

Doka, K. (ed.) (1989), *Disenfranchised Grief: Recognising Hidden Sorrow*. San Francisco, CA: Jossey Bass.

— (ed.) (2002), *Disenfranchised Grief: New Directions, Challenges, and Strategies for Practice*. Champaign, IL: Research Press.

Education (Additional Support for Learning) (Scotland) Act 2004.

Fowler J. W. (1995), *Stages of Faith: The Psychology of Human Development and the Quest for Meaning*. New York: HarperCollins.

Freud, S. (1917, 2007), 'Mourning and Melacholia', in L. G. Fiorini, T. Bokanowski and S. Lewkowicz (eds), *On Freud's Mourning and Melancholia*. London: Karnac Books.

Graham, A. P. and Anderson, S. (2002), *Seasons for Growth Companion Manual: Levels 1–3*. North Sydney, NSW: Mary MacKillop Foundation.

Haine, R. A., Ayres, T. S., Sandler, I. N. and Wolchik, S. A. (2008) 'Evidence based practices for parentally bereaved children and their families'. *Professional Psychology: Research and Practice*, 39(2): 113–21.

Klass, D. and Walter, T. (2001), 'Processes of Grieving: How Bonds are Continued', in M. Stroebe, R. Hanson, W. Stroebe and H. Schut (eds), *Handbook of Bereavement Research: Consequence, Coping and Care*. Washington, DC: American Psychological Association.

Kohlberg, L. (1981), *The Philosophy of Moral Development: Moral Stages and the Idea of Justice*. New York: HarperCollins.

Kübler-Ross, E. (1970), *On Death and Dying*. London: Routledge.

Neimeyer, R. A. (1997), 'Meaning Reconstruction and the Experience of Chronic Loss', in K. J. Doka and J. Davidson (eds), *Living with Grief when Illness is Prolonged*. Washington, DC: Taylor Francis.

— (1998), *Lessons of Loss: A Guide to Coping*. New York: McGraw-Hill.

— (2001), *Meaning Reconstruction and the Experience of Loss*. Washington, DC: American Psychological Association.

Parkes, Colin Murray (1972, 1996), *Bereavement: Studies of Grief in Adult Life*. London: Routledge.

Piaget, J. (1932), *Moral Judgment of the Child*. New York: Free Press.

Raphael, B. (1984), *The Anatomy of Bereavement: A Handbook for the Caring Professions*. London: Routledge.

Schuchter, S. R. and Zisook, S. (1993), 'The Course of Normal Grief', in M. S. Stroebe, W. Stroebe and R. O. Hanson (eds), *Handbook of Bereavement: Theory, Research and Intervention*. Cambridge: Cambridge University Press.

Scottish Executive (2004), Summary Handout on the Additional Support for Learning Act. Available online at www.scotland.gov.uk/Resource/Doc/47251/0023736.pdf.

Scottish Government (2010), *Supporting Children's Learning Code of Practice*. Available online at www.scotland.gov.uk/Resource/Doc/348208/0116022.pdf.

Silverman, P. R. (2000), *Never too Young to Know: Death in Children's Lives*. New York: Oxford University Press.

Stroebe, M. S., Stroebe, W. and R. O. Hanson (1993), *Handbook of Bereavement: Theory, Research and Intervention*. Cambridge: Cambridge University Press.

Waisanen, E. M. (2004), 'Daddy'. *Journal of Loss and Trauma*, 9(4): 291–8.

Worden, W. (1996), *Children and Grief: When a Parent Dies*. New York: Guilford Press.

Self-Harm and Suicide: Positive Pastoral Strategies for Schools

7

Jo Bell

Introduction

On average, every 8 or 9 days, a young person between the ages of 11–16 dies by suicide in the UK. In the US, on average, 1 or 2 young people between the ages of 11–16 die by suicide every day (see Tables 7.1 and 7.2). Still thousands more young people deliberately self-injure (with or without suicidal intent). Getting an accurate account of the extent of this worrying phenomenon has always been notoriously problematic (mainly due to its hidden and secretive nature) and most experts speculate that the true figures may be much higher. For

Table 7.1 Total suicides (or probable suicides) among 11–16-year-olds in the UK (1999–2010)

Year	Total suicides (or probable suicides) among 11–16-year-olds in the UK
1999	42
2000	62
2001	41
2002	51
2003	42
2004	41
2005	51
2006	40
2007	56
2008	47
2009	45
2010	34

Source: Office for National Statistics, 2012; Northern Ireland Statistics and Research Agency, 2012; National Records of Scotland, 2012.[1]

Table 7.2 Suicides among 11–16-year-olds in the US (1999–2009) (figures for 2010 not available at time of print)

Year	Total suicides among 11–16-year-olds in the US
1999	662
2000	749
2001	685
2002	649
2003	629
2004	717
2005	674
2006	641
2007	556
2008	647
2009	715

Source: National Centre for Injury Prevention and Control (Centre for Disease Control). http://webappa.cdc.gov/sasweb/ncipc/mortrate10_us.html accessed 24.04.2012. Suicide was defined using the International Classification of Diseases, tenth revision (ICD10), codes X60-X84, Y87.0, *U03

example, it has been suggested that actual suicide rates vary in estimation from four to ten times greater than the recorded rates (Smith, 2004). Some estimates suggest that at least 1 in 15 young people will self-harm at some point; some evidence suggests that rates of self-harm in the UK are higher than anywhere else in Europe, although the picture across Europe is not dissimilar (e.g. Madge et al., 2008). While it is unlikely that we will ever know the true rate of self-harm and suicidal behaviour among young people, what we do know is that self-harm and suicidal behaviour among young people is now a major public health issue in the UK and beyond. Suicide consistently ranks as one of the leading causes of death for young people between 15–19 years of age in most Westernized countries. Table 7.1 shows figures for death by suicide among young people aged between 11–16 years of age in the UK (1999–2010).

There is no single, universally agreed definition of self-harm and suicidal behaviour and the terms are often used interchangeably. Suicide refers to the process of deliberately ending one's life. While detailed and definitive definitions of suicide may vary, all necessitate a central element of motivational intent. Self-harm, in its broadest sense, describes the various things that some young people do to harm themselves in a deliberate and usually hidden way. The most common methods involve 'repeatedly cutting the skin but burning, scalding, banging or scratching one's own body, breaking bones, hair pulling and ingesting toxic substances or objects are done as well' (Mental Health Foundation and Camelot Foundation, 2006, p. 18). Individuals engaging in deliberate self-harm may, or may not, have an intention to take their own life.

Self-harm is not a classified mental health disorder although mental health problems are very often associated with self-harm, in that they coexist with each other. Nor is there any such thing as a typical person who self-harms. Most professionals agree that self-harm is a response to profound emotional pain. Young people engage in self-harm because they have no other way of coping with problems and emotional distress in their lives. The average onset, according to some estimates, is 12 years old. Episodes of self-harm can be triggered as a result of a complex combination of experiences, rather than a single event (Trainor, 2010). So while significant changes or events may act as triggers, multiple daily stressors can also accumulate to produce the analogous 'pressure cooker' effect. It is the combination of stress factors in the context of poorly developed coping strategies and support systems that most often leads to self-harm and suicidal behaviour among young people. (McDougall et al., 2010).

Research commissioned by Samaritans and carried out by the Centre for Suicide Research at the University of Oxford in 41 schools in England during 2000–1 represented the UK's first large-scale, anonymous study of self-harm among school children. The research found that more than 24,000 teenagers are admitted to hospital in the UK each year after deliberately harming themselves (Hawton et al., 2002). Most had taken drug overdoses or cut themselves. The majority were not, as is sometimes believed, trying to take their lives but were instead trying to relieve an intense emotional pain which was causing them to suffer.

The research also found that 10 per cent of teenagers aged 15 and 16 years old had deliberately self-harmed – 7 per cent in the previous year. The majority, more than 64 per cent, had cut themselves. Between 10 and 15 per cent of self-harmers harmed themselves again within a year. Moreover, young people who self-harm are far more likely than other young people to go on to die by suicide. Girls were nearly four times more likely to self-harm than boys. The most common reason given was 'to find relief from a terrible situation'.

More recent UK research by *The National Inquiry into Self-Harm among Young People* (The Mental Health Foundation and Camelot Foundation, 2006) reported a wide range of factors that could trigger self-harm. The most frequent reasons mentioned by young people were: being bullied at school, not getting on with parents, stress and worry around academic performance and examinations, parental divorce, bereavement, unwanted pregnancy, experience of abuse in earlier childhood (whether sexual, physical and/or emotional), difficulties associated with sexuality, problems to do with race, culture or religion, low self-esteem and self-confidence and feelings of being rejected in their lives.

Every year such behaviour negatively affects an enormous amount of young people, their families and communities. The psychological, emotional, social, medical and financial cost is frequently devastating (Miller, 2011). Self-harm and suicidal behaviour blights the lives of young people; it seriously affects their sense of self-worth and their relationships with families and friends. Because of the stigma surrounding it, many young people do it in secret, harbouring feelings of guilt and of shame. They are also scared and often feel unable to talk either about their self-harm or about the reasons why they are doing it. This can mean that many people who self-harm find it difficult to have close physical relationships. According to the Mental Health Foundation and Camelot Foundation (2006) if and when a young person does tell someone else about their self-harm, the whole issue is frequently taken out of their hands, and their previously secretive behaviour becomes common knowledge. They are aware that everyone is watching them closely in case they self-harm again. Most importantly, the focus very often remains on the self-harm, not the underlying causes.

Although self-harm and suicidal behaviour overlap considerably, they should be understood and responded to differently (a point which will be discussed later in this chapter). Deliberate self-harm needs to be regarded as one of a range of risk factors associated with suicide, rather than as suicidal behaviour. Indeed, the majority of people who self-harm do not go on to take their own life.

The role of schools in a whole population public health approach: Education and support

The National Suicide Prevention Strategy for England (Department of Health, 2002) recognizes that suicide rates reflect the mental health of the community as a whole. One of the main goals of the strategy is to 'promote mental well-being in the wider population'. Similarly, the suicide prevention strategy for Scotland (Scottish Executive, 2002) and the US National Strategy for Suicide Prevention (United States Department of Health and Human Services, 2003) call for a whole population public health approach.

A public health approach to intervention and prevention in schools is being increasingly viewed as an important and recommended educational practice (Doll and Cummings, 2008a, 2008b; Merrell et al., 2006;

Power, 2003; Strein et al., 2003). This view is based on the premise, and repeated research findings (e.g. Hoagwood and Johnson, 2003; Doll and Cummings, 2008a), that psychological wellness is a precondition for pupils' success. Effective approaches to mental health promotion in schools should strengthen the psychological well-being and developmental competence of all pupils and promote supportive protective environments that can nurture pupils, allowing them to overcome risk factors and challenges (Doll and Cummings, 2008a). In terms of dealing with self-harm and suicidal behaviour, this should mean that all young people attending school are increasingly receiving the appropriate information and advice, and can expect to be listened to and supported.

The suggestion that educational settings are uniquely and appropriately placed to play a key role in suicide prevention has been around from at least as early as 1910 (Berman et al., 2006). Because schools are the primary site for the education and socialization of young people, and given the substantial amount of time that young people spend in school – where teaching and learning are normative tasks – they are ideally situated to deliver education, support and primary prevention interventions across populations of young people (Mental Health Foundation and Camelot Foundation, 2006). Internationally, the US and Canada have been at the forefront of development efforts. School-based suicide prevention programmes in the US developed initially in the 1970s and increased significantly in the 1980s. More recent initiatives in the UK have featured in programmes for Personal, Social, Health and Economic education (PSHE) and have typically included increasing awareness about self-harm and suicide including risk factors and warning signs, dispelling myths and misinformation about self-harm and suicide, changing attitudes about accessing help and providing information about resources in the school and community. Some programmes also provide gatekeeper education sessions for school staff members and pupils, and teach pupils problem-solving, crisis management and support skills.

The whole school approach ethos is also consistent with the values and aims of the Government Green Paper on *Every Child Matters* and *The Children Act 2004* which focus on improving every level of professional support for children and young people perceived to be vulnerable and in need. Because school personnel have daily contact with children and adolescents, they are uniquely and ideally positioned to help and support (Miller, 2011).

Given the statistics that, on average, almost every week in the UK a young person of secondary school age dies by suicide, and thousands more engage in self-harming behaviour, schools and their teachers not only have a professional responsibility but a moral and ethical responsibility to respond appropriately as part of their pastoral care provision. Regular training, particularly information that can serve as a practical guide to intervention, for staff and personnel is vital (Miller, 2011). How self-harm and suicidal behaviour should be construed and addressed in a school curriculum; what kinds of pedagogical training would teachers need to teach on this topic; whether teachers are best placed to deliver this or whether should it be left to 'specialist' outsiders; and how schools can best support and respond to self-harm and suicidal behaviour in young people will be the focus of this chapter.

Education and awareness-raising in schools

Previously in this chapter, the scale of the problem of self-harm and suicidal behaviour in young people was outlined, along with a rationale for suggesting that schools have a significant role to play in responding to and promoting psychological wellness, awareness and appropriate help-seeking skills in young people. It has been argued that schools are ideally placed to deliver this education and that such efforts should be recognized as being at the heart of pastoral care and positive mental health promotion. In the following section, with the use of research and case-study examples, and reflective questions, a number of good practice models for education and skills training are presented.

To hear that self-harm is not a topic of conversation among school staff is common. Self-harm is never discussed. No-one wants to talk about it. Many professionals feel ill-prepared to explore these concepts; many may fear that to do so will make the young person do something drastic. Indeed perhaps the most significant and dangerous myth about self-harm and suicidal behaviour in young people is that asking questions or talking about it will increase the probability that it will occur. There is no evidence that this is the case. Such fears are common and understandable; they are often based on the same assumptions that underlie the reluctance of some schools to engage with sex-education and education about illicit drug and alcohol use. The fact is that talking about it is likely to encourage young people to come forward and seek help if they are doing it. It is not likely to encourage young people to start doing it.

There is some evidence, on the other hand, that school-based prevention programmes aimed at educating young people about issues related to self-harm and suicide can be effective in reducing suicidal behaviour and increasing help seeking in young people (e.g. Kalafat, 2003; Miller et al., 2009; Zenere and Lazarus, 1997, 2009) if delivered under the right conditions. The key issue is not *whether* we talk about it, but *how* we talk about it and teachers need to be equipped with the knowledge, skills and training to enable them to talk openly about suicide and self-harm.

Before any education programme can begin, teachers must familiarize themselves with the relevant specialist resources, services and helping agencies available in their local community and school. They need to know *whom* to inform and *whom* to refer to for support, *when* and *under what conditions* (these could include a school-based counsellor, nurse or social worker, Community Adolescent Mental Health Services (CAMHS), and other local voluntary or statutory agencies). Provision and availability will vary, but the more teachers can develop links with their relevant support services, the better prepared they will be. More discussion on the importance of finding the most appropriate referral pathway (in terms of who, when and under what conditions) follows later in this chapter.

Imparting information to pupils needs to be done sensitively and carefully. The topic of self-harm and suicide is one that is potentially disturbing to pupils, but also one that is of high interest to them. Meeting smaller groups of pupils in a classroom environment is more conducive to asking questions and discussion than a large assembly hall. Pupils should be taught that mental health problems, such as depression, that often underlie suicidal behaviour, are very common in young people and that getting help for them is analogous to getting help for a physical problem. This approach may be particularly helpful for boys who may be reluctant to identify themselves as suffering from mental health issues. Raising awareness about young suicide and providing information about resources in the school and community has the collateral benefit of making the idea of help-seeking behaviour more normal. It also helps reduce stigma and misunderstanding around the issue and can help change attitudes towards it (Miller, 2011). Attitudes are particularly important as negative attitudes and misinformation regarding suicide and self-harm are pervasive in our society. They can also be unhelpful and counterproductive, so a commitment to tackling these beliefs should be a crucial element of any education programme.

If teachers encourage learning environments in which pupils feel comfortable enough to explore these concepts, attitudes and beliefs openly, they are more likely to be willing to engage in positive discussion. Carefully and honestly answering questions and inviting discussion also conveys the message that the school considers this seriously and is willing to be proactive in doing something about it (Miller, 2011).

In the UK, teaching packs are available from a variety of sources for schools wishing to raise pupil awareness of emotional health, self-harm and suicide. A number of these are listed in the 'resources' section at the end of this chapter.

Example Model: *Developing Emotional Awareness and Learning – DEAL (Samaritans)*

Primarily a teaching resource for secondary school staff that can also be used as part of a whole school approach to emotional health and well-being, the DEAL programme deals with the development of knowledge, skills and attitudes that young people need to cope with challenges in life and look after their emotional health and well-being. It aims to promote the emotional health of young people aged 14–16 through challenging stigma around emotional health problems, developing healthy coping skills and promoting knowledge of sources of support

⇨

and improving attitudes to help seeking. DEAL materials are designed not just for use by PSHE specialists, but also by generalist teachers, Form Tutors or pastoral staff, and can be used as a series of lessons or as part of a collapsed curriculum day. At the time of writing, comprehensive teaching packs can be downloaded for free from the Samaritans website: www.samaritans.org/our_services/work_in_schools/deal_lesson_plans.aspx

The DEAL programme is divided into eight sections: Information booklet for schools; Staff training activities and introduction to the programme; Core PSHE lesson plans; Extended PSHE lesson plans; Citizenship lesson plans; Cross-curricular lesson plans; Factsheets; Interactive 6-part DVD.

The lesson plans include information on how to deliver activities and how teachers can be supported, with clear instructions on how to respond to challenging questions and situations which they may be unsure about. In addition to depression, self-harm and suicide, topics covered in individual lesson plans also cover stress management and problem solving; aggression and bullying; communication and listening skills; emotional health awareness; body language; sources of support and dealing with conflict.

Since its launch in 2006, hundreds of organizations across the UK have implemented the programme. A survey completed by Samaritans (2008) revealed that 86 per cent of people who had used DEAL felt it helped young people to better look after their own emotional health and 83 per cent felt DEAL helped young people ask for help when they needed it.

Skills training for pupils: Gatekeeper and peer support models

Some school programmes incorporate skill-building activities to develop coping and listening skills in pupils, enabling them to support suicidal friends. Gatekeeper or peer support training for pupils is based on the premise and research evidence that teenagers are more likely to confide in peers than in adults when facing a crisis (Aseltine and DeMartino, 2004; Kalafat and Elias, 1994, 1995) and that unprepared pupils may fail to recognize or respond constructively to confidences from an at-risk peer. Research carried out by the Centre for Suicide Research, University of Oxford during 2000–1 found that teenagers were three times more likely to turn to their friends for help before acting (Hawton et al., 2002). This suggests that potential intervention or prevention strategies might well be directed at involving peers and that peers should be provided with information about self-harm and suicide and how to respond appropriately.

The emphasis in this training is on specific steps pupils can take in responding to or intervening with an at-risk peer – including encouraging that peer to confide in an adult (Lake and Gould, 2011). Typically pupils are taught to recognize the signs of depression, self-harm and suicidal behaviour in their peers along with appropriate ways of responding – what to do if they are self-harming or suicidal, or if they suspect or know of someone who is self-harming or suicidal.

Example Model: Signs of Suicide (SOS)

This successful programme, which was developed in the US, has been shown to be effective at increasing help-seeking by pupils concerned about themselves or a friend (Aseltine and Demartino, 2004; Aseltine et al., 2007). SOS teaches young people action steps to take if they think they, or someone they know, is suicidal. It teaches simple and specific instructions for how to recognize the signs of distress and depression, in either themselves or a friend; and how to respond effectively, encouraging help-seeking through the use of a technique known as ACT (Acknowledge, Care and Tell). The 'Tell' aspect of the ACT technique emphasizes that young people should seek help from a trusted adult in responding to suicidal behaviour and teaches them how to turn to them when in need.

The Signs of Self-Injury programme is based on the same principles as the SOS programme. It aims to teach pupils to recognize the signs and symptoms of self-injury, and how to respond appropriately to a friend who self-injures – again using the ACT technique and again emphasizing the importance of seeking adult intervention.

The way in which these types of models are implemented has varied since their inception in the US in the 1980s. All schools in the UK are now required by the Department for Education to have anti-bullying strategies and a number of schools have started to implement peer support schemes, where pupil 'mentors' are trained to support other pupils who are having problems. Recent research has suggested that these schemes are most effective when delivered as part of a whole school approach to good mental health for all, and where mentors are adequately supported and able to refer their peers on to specialist support (Weare and Gray, 2003; Mental Health Foundation and Camelot Foundation, 2006).

According to the Mental Health Foundation (2002) and the Mental Health Foundation and Camelot Foundation (2006), a peer support scheme which is part of a whole school approach may also help schools to meet the demands of the citizenship curriculum, help them work towards the National Healthy School Standard and enable the school to demonstrate commitment to pupils' social and emotional development.

In addition to peer support and gatekeeper training for peers, gatekeeper training programmes for adult professionals who come into regular contact with young people have been developed. Gatekeeper training for school-based personnel is aimed at improving school adults' knowledge and attitudes towards suicide in order to empower those adults to recognize warning signs in pupils and intervene. Training school-based adults in this way has been argued to present a possible way around the barrier of young people's failure to seek help (Lake and Gould, 2011). One example developed originally in the US is QPR. QPR stands for Question, Persuade, and Refer; the three steps gatekeepers are taught to use with potentially suicidal behaviour (and not too dissimilar to the ACT approach in the SOS programme described above). For more information about this model visit: www.qprinstitute.com/. Further information on a number of available models and programmes can be found in the resources section at the end of this chapter.

Research Example: Responses and Prevention in Student Suicide

The dangers inherent in pupils' unpreparedness and failure to respond constructively (or to 'ACT') are exemplified in a recent article by Bell et al. (2012). This article, which reported on research into student suicide in the UK (see Stanley et al., 2007), featured the case of a teenage student and her group of student friends who secretly supported and cared for their self-harming suicidal friend (also a student), for a lengthy period of time while at university, without the intervention of adult or professional help. At the insistence of their suicidal friend, university staff and others responsible for the pastoral care of the students were deliberately kept unaware of the situation which gradually escalated out of control. No one else, apart from the group of friends in question, was aware of what was going on.

⇨

Eventually their friend took her own life. In the weeks and months that followed, the student and her friends were overwhelmingly distraught with feelings of responsibility and guilt, making them vulnerable to mental health problems. They felt that it was their fault that she was dead – a common feeling among those bereaved by suicide. In this extract, reflecting on her experience in the aftermath of her friend's death, one student recognizes how she and her friends were completely out of their depth in trying to care for their friend. They regretted that they had failed to confide in an adult or ask for professional help at the time:

If there's any way of . . . . . getting more information to carers, not just be there for the person but actually having to look after yourself. This is how you look after yourself . . . . Make sure you don't get sucked in. Nowhere is there a warning that if your friends. . . . commit suicide, if you are with them twenty-four hours a day – which can happen – . . . . . . you can end up in a very dangerous situation. And there's no health hazard warning. Nothing, I mean anywhere. I think that's the most important message. . . . . . For eighteen-year-olds, who've got no idea, just don't get too involved, make sure you know where to draw the line. friends have to know that there is a point after which it's too much to expect because eighteen-year-olds are ridiculously loyal to each other. . . . . . . This is about something to do with somebody like me. . . . . what should I have done that I didn't do?, and I should have handed over the responsibility. Somebody should have said to me when they realised it was getting out of hand, you are no longer responsible for this [person] . . . . get the message out there that . . . . if you get involved bad things can happen to you as well. (Bell et al., 2012, p. 63)

Reference

Bell, J., Stanley, N., Mallon, S. and Manthorpe, J. (2012), 'Life will never be the same again: Examining grief in survivors bereaved by young suicide'. *Illness, Crisis, and Loss*, 21(1): 49–68.

This example is poignant for a number of reasons. First, it illustrates the harm that can be done to young people when they do not know how to respond in a very serious situation. The importance of this must never be underestimated, nor should the importance of self-care for care-givers which is also stressed through this example.

From this experience we can draw very clear conclusions about what sort of messages programmes need to convey and what sort of skills young people are helped by. Gatekeeper training and peer support models must equip young people with the skills and awareness to acknowledge when, how and where to seek professional help for their peers (even if this goes against the wishes of those they are seeking to support). However young people also need to know that they could be putting themselves in danger and that they cannot be responsible for the behaviour of their friends. They need to be made aware of how to look after themselves and that it is alright to tell a trusted adult.

Responding to self-harm and suicidal behaviour: Positive pastoral strategies

The discussion so far has focused on the provision of education and training for young people in schools around self-harm and suicidal behaviour. In order not only for teachers to deliver this training, but to have the confidence to respond effectively if they think a pupil in their care is self-harming or suicidal or if a young person makes a disclosure, they need to be adequately prepared and need to know how to respond and help.

The next section will consider ways in which schools and their staff can respond positively and effectively to situations using two main examples. These examples highlight the fear that many adults and other carers have – the fear that by acting they could make things worse. The examples also highlight the complexity of the issue and some of the challenging dilemmas intrinsic to responding to self-harm and suicidal behaviour in schools. Some practical suggestions and implications for positive school policy and pastoral strategies are discussed.

For many people, being told by a young person that they have self-harmed is hard to deal with. In a recent article which explored teachers' reactions to self-harming behaviour among pupils, Best (2006) described a mix of emotions such as anxiety, panic, shock, revulsion and incomprehension. Fearful reactions may be understandable among those where awareness levels are low, but they are also likely to be unhelpful. A helpful response would be one in which teacher does not 'freak out' but is prepared to listen and allow the young person to talk. It is very important not to focus exclusively on the self-harm itself but on the reasons why the young person has self-harmed. A young person disclosing self-harm needs to know that the fact they have been able to disclose shows strength and courage and should be allowed to take the discussion at their own pace. Contrary to popular belief, there is no evidence to suggest that asking questions or talking about self-harm or suicide will increase the probability that it will occur. Talking about it, however, will help them to come to some decisions and an increased understanding of their own behaviour.

Effective strategies also need to reflect the differences and the overlap between suicidal behaviour and deliberate self-harm. In order to distinguish between the two, one has to explore them in depth with the individual. The functions of the behaviour (first-person accounts from the person) or the motivational intention behind it need to be established before intervention can begin. This refers to what the individual intends to accomplish by engaging in the behaviour; in other words, what is the goal of the behaviour? Unfortunately this process may not be as straightforward as it sounds.

As outlined previously, the terms self-harm and suicidal behaviour are often used interchangeably. The relationship between self-harm and suicide is complex. Current literature presents a shifting debate as to whether self-injurious behaviour should be regarded as self-harm or self-help. The fact that an individual history of self-harm is one of the biggest risk factors for suicide (Zahl and Hawton, 2004) supports the view that self-harm and suicidal behaviour are the same thing. In addition, some research has shown that some attempts are aimed at dying, and some may have had intentions to die but had insufficient knowledge of the lethality of the method (Gelder et al., 2006).

On the other hand, many acts of deliberate self-harm are not intended to end the person's life. For some young people, self-harm is practised as a coping mechanism which is, in essence, incongruous with suicide. Support for this view has been found in research which reveals that the intention of many survivors of apparent suicidal acts had not been to die. Testimonies from young people who engage in self-harm reveal a desire to gain temporary relief from a particularly intolerable situation or state, rather than a desire to die (e.g. Mental Health Foundation and Camelot Foundation, 2006). For these young people self-harm operates as an alternative to suicide, a form of self-help (Bell, 2011).

Research has also shown that many people are uncertain about whether they wish to die. Schneidman (1996) writes about the centrality of ambivalence in the suicidal state. Ambivalence involves simultaneously wanting to live and die. This suggests there may be different and shifting motivational positions on the continuum. At one end of the spectrum are those whose behavioural intention is to die. Self-harm for these young people functions as a means to end their life. At the other end of the spectrum are those whose behavioural intention is to maintain life. Self-harm for these young people functions as a coping mechanism – a way of gaining control and temporary relief from emotional pain. Somewhere in between these two positions is ambivalence, where the overlapping features collide. The potential for danger starts here when the boundaries between wanting to live and wanting to die become blurred (Bell, 2011). The consequences may not be intended but a critical point to understand is that individuals contemplating or attempting suicide often do not want to die as much as they want their suffering to end (Miller, 2011).

Walsh (2006) and Miller (2011) point out that eliciting a clear articulation of intent from young people who are engaging in self-destructive behaviour can be difficult. They may be emotionally overwhelmed as well as very confused about their own behaviour and often provide answers that are ambiguous. Assessing intent therefore requires a combination of compassion and investigative persistence (Walsh, 2006). Finding the answers depends on asking the right questions. It is important to establish clearly *when* the behaviour started, *how, how often* and *why*. Again, according to Smith (2004), these will be tricky questions which may not elicit any clear answers.

Direct questions such as '*Do you do this to feel better or to end all your feelings?*' can be a helpful starting point for exploring how it made them feel and what their intentions were / are. Often when people don't know *why*, they may be helped by being asked to think about things which may act as triggers. Is there a precipitating event? What was going on in his or her life at the time? An adult should therefore continue to discuss and explore past experiences with the young person, and should not be afraid to ask the young person directly if he or she has had thoughts of suicide and if there have been previous attempts and what happened. Other important questions include: Is the young person using drugs or alcohol? What are their social supports? Does he or she have a religious or spiritual affiliation? (This could be a protective factor.) Is the young person able to see any alternatives? (More detailed information on possible questions to ask and other related issues can be found in Miller, 2011.)

It can be difficult to cope with a young person's disclosure of self-harm and so it is perhaps not surprising that the initial reaction from an unprepared teacher may well be one of shock and horror. Research suggests that where levels of awareness among teachers are raised, considered and careful reactions are more likely (Berman et al., 2006). The purpose of a positive pastoral strategy is to support pupils, help them to feel better, and, wherever possible, provide them with the best intervention / referral to meet their needs. The sorts of questions suggested here are an important first step in determining the most appropriate referral route and what to do next.

Research Example: Challenges for Pastoral Care in Schools

Raising awareness among staff and pupils is an important first step in dealing with issues of self-harm and suicidal behaviour in schools. Research by Best (2005, 2006) emphasized how raising awareness of the cases of specific pupils in the right way is equally important. One of the things that prevents young people from telling others and seeking help from adults is fear of negative responses and consequences. Disclosing information about specific cases might have undesirable consequences as this example from the *Truth Hurts* report (Mental Health Foundation and Camelot Foundation, 2006, p. 6) shows:

> At school my self-harm was treated very badly. It was treated as a piece of gossip throughout the staff and the head teacher asked me to leave as a result, saying that I was a lovely person but he couldn't have it in his school.

According to Best (2005), the question also of who needs to know and who has a right to know is a vexed one. Teachers need to be cautious that more harm than good is not done by informing others against the wishes of the pupil. Deciding who to inform may well present a number of difficult ethical dilemmas. For example, teachers in one school in a community that was of predominantly one ethnic origin were vigilant to the fact that speaking out about it could make things worse. These teachers were described as:

> . . . routinely avoiding informing the parents because they believed that the response would be harmful and even abusive. Where on-going or previous abuse by parents lies at the heart of self-harming behaviour, informing parents might not be in the interests of the child at all, let alone the first automatic step. (p. 7)

⇨

In another school teachers reported operating a 'need to know' policy in which only those teachers with direct contact or a pastoral responsibility for pupils were informed. Other schools operated a 'pupils at risk' book in the staff room for all teachers to access. Entries in the book indicated that a pupil may be currently under unusual pressure without indicating the nature of the problem. It was hoped that school staff may then make some allowance for unusual moods or behaviour among these pupils (Best, 2006).

The problems associated with potential undesirable consequences suggest that issues of confidentiality need to be respected when young people are clear that they do not want certain others to be told. This raises ethical issues that require professional judgement and discretion and it is not always clear what action should follow: When and to whom should teachers refer cases of self-harm? Do parents have an automatic right to know? If young people have a right to confidentiality, are there any limits to it? Best (2005) also points out that schools may have different policies on disclosure to third parties. Some schools may operate the 'Gillick principle' if they are satisfied that the conditions of understanding and competence are met ('Gillick competence' is a term originating in England and is used in medical law to decide whether a child aged 16 years or under is able to consent to his or her own medical treatment, without the need for parental permission or knowledge. A child who is deemed 'Gillick competent' is able to prevent their parents viewing their medical records. As such, medical staff will not make a disclosure of medical records of a child who is deemed 'Gillick competent' unless consent is given). Other schools might operate a policy of informing parents and other professionals as an automatic first step.

References

Best, R. (2005), 'Self-harm: A challenge for pastoral care'. *Pastoral Care in Education*, 23(3): 3–11.

— (2006), 'Deliberate self-harm in adolescence: A challenge for schools'. *British Journal of Guidance and Counselling*, 34(2): 161–75.

Perhaps two of the most dangerous and misunderstood myths about self-harm and suicidal behaviour are that young people who self-harm are attention-seeking and manipulative and that self-harm and suicide are examples of copycat behaviour. The phenomenon of 'social contagion' – the idea that emotions and behaviour are copied from those around us and can spread rapidly among young people in particular – has long been applied to self-harm and suicidal behaviour. So too has the 'bandwagon effect' – the idea that young people often do and believe things because many other people do and believe the same things (McDougall et al., 2010). Much has been written in the spirit of dispelling these myths and much research attention has been directed at challenging them. However, it is still the case that many professionals believe this, in part, because occasionally it happens. Consider the following scenario:

Case Study: A School Responds to Self-Harm

One girl at a comprehensive secondary school in Year 11 is self-harming (cutting) in a public way at school. Two of her best friends start to do the same thing. Within four weeks there are a number of other girls in the year group doing it. The school's response is to treat the injuries and the girls with a very 'medical model' approach. This means they deal with the physical injuries but with no warmth shown towards the individuals: no eye contact is made, and the behaviour of cutting is not talked about with the individuals. The girls are told that they can speak to the school counsellor about how they feel and other issues which may relate to the behaviour, but only after the behaviour has stopped. It was felt that the girls' behaviour should not be rewarded in any way (i.e. no sympathetic or compassionate attention) lest it should be reinforced and thus become more likely to be repeated. Three months later there were no girls self-harming at school. The strategy appeared to have worked and this approach was incorporated into school policy.

The example above illustrates some challenging issues and dilemmas for schools. On the one hand, if the behaviour is aimed purely at eliciting attention (in a manipulative way), ignoring the behaviour and operating an approach similar to the one described above would seem like an appropriate strategy. However, denying access to support until the behaviour has stopped may seem counter-intuitive and is in many ways similar to approaches used by some drug and alcohol misuse programmes and indeed some rehabilitation programmes for male perpetrators of domestic violence. These approaches have attracted a significant level of criticism.

And how can we tell what the function or intention of the behaviour is? How can we be sure that the behaviour is aimed at eliciting attention (manipulating situations to achieve some other aim / re-claim power / peer group 'dare') and is not a genuine cry for help? If the behaviour is a genuine cry for help, then a different approach to the one outlined above would be necessary.

This scenario highlights a predominant myth that self-harm is a manipulative, attention-seeking group activity. Unfortunately the proliferation of these sorts of

⇨

beliefs can mean that professionals, family and friends are much more likely to treat people who self-harm in a hostile and/or negative manner, and that young people are much less likely to be able to get the support and information they need. It also highlights the complexity of the behaviour and the real dilemmas it can pose for school staff who have a responsibility to consider the pastoral needs of all young people in their care. Public displays of self-harming behaviour such as the one described in this example, although rare, are upsetting for other pupils in the school and the school has some difficult choices to consider in trying to balance the rights and needs of a minority against protecting the rights and needs of the majority.

Questions

1. Do you think the school response in this case was appropriate?
2. Was the school right to incorporate their response into school policy?

Evidence suggests that this sort of attention-seeking, 'copycat' behaviour is rare and transitory. Self-harm may in some cases be a way of asking for attention that is *not* manipulative; in the same way that other people ask for help and attention by crying. Many young people who self-harm do need attention and support but their behaviour may be misunderstood and misinterpreted, as the following comment by one teenager illustrates:

> 'Some people do it for attention, like I did when I first started. That doesn't mean they should be ignored. There are plenty of ways to get attention, why cause yourself pain? And if someone's crying for help, bloody well give them it, don't stand there and judge the way in which they're asking for it.' (Mental Health Foundation and Camelot Foundation, 2006, p. 27)

McDougall et al. (2010) also warn that believing self-harm to be a matter of manipulation or attention seeking is unhelpful and misguided. They argue that it is part of normal human behaviour to seek attention from others and responsible professionals should pay attention to a young person who is distressed enough to want to hurt themselves.

The research and case examples in this chapter highlight the importance of developing a clear and flexible policy for responding to self-harm and suicidal behaviour in schools. This would be one that:

- Is based on awareness and informed understanding of the issues and potential consequences.
- Recognizes the problems of operating a 'one size fits all' model.
- Allows for the important differences in individual meanings and intentions of self-harm to be at the centre of the response.
- Values and respects the wishes of the young person.
- Involves the young person in the decision and referral process and handles disclosure sensitively.
- Recognizes that those who are supporting need supporting too.

Suicide postvention in schools

Finally, unfortunately, even when schools implement rigorous pastoral care and support and awareness and skills training, some pupils may still take their own lives. This chapter began with the stark statistic that, on average, every eight or nine days a young person of secondary school age takes their own life in the UK. In the US, on average, one–two young people of secondary school age currently die by suicide every day. In such situations, the school often becomes a focal point of attention from pupils, parents, staff, wider community and the media. Schools need to be prepared for this and procedures should be in place before a suicide occurs. Schools can also play a vital role in developing postvention procedures which are designed to prevent additional suicidal behaviour (and possible contagion effects) in the aftermath of a suicide (Miller, 2011). A full exploration of school-based postvention is beyond the scope of this chapter. For further details readers are directed to: Miller (2011) chapter 7; Samaritans *Step by Step* (see resources section below).

Conclusion

Self-harm and suicidal behaviour seriously damages the lives of young people; it significantly affects their sense of self-worth and their relationships with families and friends. Self-harm is a response to profound emotional pain. There is no such thing as a typical person who self-harms.

Because of the stigma surrounding it, young people who self-harm can find it very hard to talk about it and are often afraid of how people will react. A common stereotype is that self-injury is about 'attention seeking'. Most young people who self-harm actually do it in secret and for a long time, harbouring feelings of guilt and of shame. They are also scared and confused about their self-harm or about the reasons why they are doing it. The stigma associated with self-harm is unhelpful and prevents young people getting the support and information they need to find more positive coping strategies.

Self-harm and suicidal behaviour among young people is now a major public health issue in the UK and beyond. A public health approach to intervention and prevention in schools is being increasingly viewed as an important and recommended educational practice. This view is based on the premise, and repeated research findings, that psychological wellness is a precondition for pupils' success.

Because school personnel have daily contact with children and adolescents, they are uniquely and ideally positioned to help and support. Schools have a responsibility to respond appropriately as part of their pastoral care provision. Raising awareness among staff and pupils is an important first step in dealing with issues of self-harm and suicidal behaviour in schools. This chapter has discussed how these issues should be addressed in a school curriculum. Regular training, particularly information that can serve as a practical guide to intervention, for staff and personnel is vital.

School-based prevention aimed at educating young people about issues related to self-harm and suicide can also be effective in reducing suicidal behaviour and increasing help-seeking in young people. Young people need to be equipped with the skills and awareness to acknowledge when, how and where to seek professional help for their peers. They need to know that they could be putting themselves in danger and that they cannot be responsible for the behaviour of their friends.

Effective strategies also need to reflect the differences and the overlap between suicidal behaviour and self-harm. It is important to focus on the reasons why the young person has self-harmed and finding the right answers depends on asking the right questions. Where teachers are prepared with appropriate knowledge and skills to be able to talk openly about suicide and self-harm, confident, considered and careful responses are more likely.

The reaction a young person receives when they disclose their self-harm can have a critical influence on whether they go on to access supportive services. Schools need to develop clear and flexible policies for responding to self-harm and suicidal behaviour in pupils. These policies need to be based on an informed understanding of the issues and allow for differences in individual meanings and intentions to be at the centre of the response.

Summary

This chapter has explored:

- Self-harm and suicidal behaviour in children and young people.
- How self-harm and suicidal behaviour should be construed and addressed in a school curriculum.
- What kinds of pedagogical training teachers need to teach on this topic.
- How schools can best support and respond to self-harm and suicidal behaviour in young people.

Notes

1. Suicide was defined using the International Classification of Diseases, Ninth revision, (ICD9) codes E950–E959 and E980–E989 (excluding E988.8 for England and Wales) for the years 1999–2000, and Tenth Revision (ICD-10) codes X60–X84 and Y10–Y34 (excluding Y33.9 where the Coroner's verdict was pending in England and Wales) for the years 2001–2010. From 2007, deaths which were previously coded to Y33.9 are coded to U50.9. In Scotland and Northern Ireland, the ICD-10 codes Y87.0 and Y87.2 are also included. ICD-10 was introduced in Scotland in 2000. These figures represent amalgamated data from statistical sources collated in England, Wales, Scotland and Northern Ireland. Figures from Scotland include deaths registered where cause of death was 'intentional self-harm' or event of undetermined intent between 11–16-year-olds. Figures from Northern Ireland include deaths classified as 'suicide and self-inflicted injury' and 'undetermined injury' between 11–16-year-olds. Figures for England and Wales include deaths given an underlying cause of intentional self-harm or injury / poisoning of undetermined intent between 15–16-year-olds. Deaths where intent is undetermined among 11–14-year-olds in England and Wales are excluded.

Annotated further reading

Miller, D. N. (2011), *Child and Adolescent Suicidal Behaviour: School-Based Prevention, Assessment, and Intervention*. New York: Guilford Press.

This book provides school-based personnel with useful and practical information regarding suicidal behaviour in school-aged children. The author discusses the most important elements necessary for effective school-based prevention, assessment and intervention. Detailed information on possible questions to ask young people in need of support and assessment and other related issues can also be found in this user-friendly text. It also includes a number of useful ready-to-use reproducible handouts and resources for teachers.

Useful websites

American Association of Suicidology (ASS): www.suicidology.org/home

AAS promotes research, public awareness programmes and public education and training for professionals and volunteers. Membership includes mental health and public health professionals, researchers, suicide prevention and crisis intervention centres, school districts, crisis centre volunteers, survivors of suicide and a variety of lay persons who have an interest in suicide prevention.

American Foundation for Suicide Prevention (AFSP): www.afsp.org/

The American Foundation for Suicide Prevention invest in research, educational campaigns, demonstration projects and critical policy work. They also offer assistance and support to people whose lives have been affected by suicide. This website contains a wide range of resources and a brief bibliography on topics concerning suicide that readers may find helpful.

Childline: www.childline.org.uk/

Childline offers information and 24-hour telephone and on-line support:

Harmless (UK based) offer support, information, training and consultancy. A range of useful resources can be obtained from their website: www.harmless.org.uk/index.php

National Self-harm Network: www.nshn.co.uk/index.html

NSHN is a registered charity based in Nottingham, UK. As well as supporting the individual, NSHN aims to raise awareness of self-harm, underlying causes, triggers and the many ways to offer support and provide training to professional organizations, schools, universities, charities, user groups etc. NSHN equally supports friends, families and carers of individuals who self-harm.

Resources for schools

PAPYRUS has produced a DVD and teachers' resource pack for use in schools and colleges. *Don't Die of Embarrassment* deals with issues that young men often find difficult to acknowledge. This learning resource, which includes a video/DVD, teachers' notes and worksheets, needs to be sensitively introduced as part of a wider programme of mental health education. Visit: www.papyrus-uk.org/

Samaritans has developed a school resource called *Developing Emotional Awareness and Learning* (DEAL). DEAL is primarily a teaching resource for secondary school staff and can be used as part of a whole-school approach to emotional health and well-being. Comprehensive teaching packs can be downloaded for free from the Samaritans website: www.samaritans.org/our_services/work_in_schools/deal_lesson_plans.aspx

A report is also available, giving an overview of Samaritans' work in schools and evaluating the uptake of the DEAL programme: www.samaritans.org/pdf/SamaritansinSchools2008.pdf

Step by Step is a Samaritans project to help schools build emotional resilience among staff and young people, and to be prepared for an incident of self-harm or attempted/completed suicide: www.samaritans.org/our_services/work_in_schools/sbs_introduction.aspx

SOS (*Signs of Suicide*) and SSI (*Signs of Self-Injury*) teach young people action steps to take if they think they, or someone they know, is suicidal. Programmes emphasize that young people should seek help from a trusted adult and teach them how to turn to them when in need. For more information on SOS and SSI visit: www.mentalhealthscreening.org/programs/youth-prevention-programs/sos/high-school.aspx

The Basement Project (UK based). This site lists some useful publications and resource packs on self-harm, including points for policy-making and an educational resource on young people and self-harm for schools: www.basementproject.co.uk/publications.html

Mindmatters offers a recent example model of a comprehensive 'whole school' approach from Australia. A number of useful resources are available to download from this site: www.mindmatters.edu.au/default.asp.

Gatekeeper/Peer support models

ASIST (Applied Suicide Intervention Skills Training) is an internationally recognized early intervention programme developed initially in Canada in the 1980s, which aims to equip and prepare caregivers with first-aid intervention skills: www.livingworks.net/

STORM is a suicide prevention training package for developing, through rehearsal, the skills needed to assess and manage a person at risk of suicide: www.stormskillstraining.co.uk/about_storm/our_community_work/

QPR (Question, Persuade, Refer) gatekeeper training (developed initially in the US) is designed for all adults in regular contact with young people: www.qprinstitute.com/

SuicideTalk is a short exploration and awareness-raising session. It provides a structure in which individuals can safely explore some of the challenging attitudinal issues about suicide, and encourages every member to find a part that they can play in preventing suicide: www.livingworks.net/page/suicideTALK.

References

Aseltine, R. H., Jr. and DeMartino, R. (2004), 'An outcome evaluation of the SOS suicide prevention program'. *American Journal of Public Health*, 94: 446–51.

Aseltine, R. H., James, A., Schilling, E. A. and Glanovsky, J. (2007), 'Evaluating the SOS suicide prevention program: A replication and extension'. *BMC Public Health*, 7: 161–8.

Bell, J. (2011), 'Disentangling self-harm and suicide'. *Youngminds*, 112: 26–7.

Bell, J., Stanley, N., Mallon, S. and Manthorpe, J. (2012), 'Life will never be the same again: Examining grief in survivors bereaved by young suicide'. *Illness, Crisis, and Loss*, 21(1): 49–68.

Berman, A. L., Jobes, D. A. and Silverman, M. M. (2006), *Adolescent Suicide: Assessment and Intervention*. Washington, DC: American Psychological Association.

Best, R. (2005), 'Self-harm: A challenge for pastoral care'. *Pastoral Care in Education*, 23(3): 3–11.

— (2006), 'Deliberate self-harm in adolescence: A challenge for schools'. *British Journal of Guidance and Counselling*, 34(2): 161–75.

Department for Education and Skills. (2003). *Every Child Matters*. Norwich: HMSO.

— (2004). *The Children Act*. London: HMSO.

Department of Health (2002), *The National Suicide Prevention Strategy for England*. London: Her Majesty's Stationery Office.

Doll, B. and Cummings, J. A. (eds) (2008a), *Transforming School Mental Health Services: Population-Based Approaches to Promoting the Competency and Wellness of Children*. Thousand Oaks, CA: Corwin Press.

— (2008b), 'Why Population Based Services are Essential for School Mental Health and How to Make Them Happen in Your School', in B. Doll and J. A. Cummings (eds), *Transforming School Mental Health Services: Population-Based Approaches to Promoting the Competency and Wellness of Children*. Thousand Oaks, CA: Corwin Press, pp. 1–20.

Gelder, M., Harrison, P. and Cowen, P. (eds) (2006), *Shorter Oxford Textbook of Psychiatry* (5th edition). Oxford: Oxford University Press.

Hawton, K., Rodham, K., Evans, E. and Weatherall, R. (2002), 'Deliberate self-harm in adolescents: Self-report survey in schools in England'. *British Medical Journal*, 325: 1207–11.

Hoagwood, K. and Johnson, J. (2003), 'School psychology: A public health framework. From evidence based practices to evidence based policies'. *Journal of School Psychology*, 41: 3 – 21.

Kalafat, J. (2003), 'School approaches to youth suicide prevention'. *American Behavioural Scientist*, 46: 1211–23.

Kalafat, J. and Elias, M. (1994), 'An evaluation of a school-based suicide awareness intervention'. *Suicide and Life Threatening Behaviour*, 24: 224–33.

— (1995), 'Suicide prevention in an educational context. Broad and narrow foci'. *Suicide and Life Threatening Behaviour*, 25: 123–33.

Lake, A. M. and Gould, M. S. (2011), 'School Based Strategies for Youth Suicide Prevention', in R. O'Connor, S. Platt and J. Gordon (eds), *International Handbook of Suicide Prevention: Research, Policy, and Practice*. Chichester: John Wiley and Sons Ltd.

Madge, N., Hewitt, A., Hawton, K., de Wilde, E., Corcoran, P., Fekete, S., van Heeringen, K., DeLeo, D. and Ystgaard, M. (2008), 'Deliberate self-harm with an international community sample of young people: Comparative findings from the Child and Adolescent Self-Harm in Europe (CASE) study'. *Journal of Child Psychology and Psychiatry*, 49(6): 667–77.

McDougall, T., Armstrong, M. and Trainor, G. (2010), *Helping Children and Young People who Self-Harm: An Introduction to Self-Harming and Suicidal Behaviours for Health Professionals*. London: Routledge.

Mental Health Foundation. (2002), *Peer Support: Someone to Turn To*. London: Mental Health Foundation.

Mental Health Foundation and Camelot Foundation. (2006), *Truth Hurts: Report of the National Inquiry into Self-Harm among Young People*. London: Mental Health Foundation.

Merrell, K. W., Ervin, R. A. and Gimpel, G. A. (2006), *School Psychology for the 21st Century: Foundations and Practices*. New York: Guilford Press.

Miller, D. N. (2011), *Child and Adolescent Suicidal Behaviour: School-Based Prevention, Assessment, and Intervention*. New York: Guilford Press.

Miller, D. N., Eckert, T. L. and Mazza, J. J. (2009), 'Suicide prevention programs in the schools: A review and public health perspective'. *School Psychology Review*, 38: 168–88.

National Centre for Injury Prevention and Control (Centre for Disease Control) (2012). Suicides among 11–16-year-olds in the US (1999–2009). http://webappa.cdc.gov/sasweb/ncipc/mortrate10_us.html accessed 24.04.2012.

National Records of Scotland. (2012). Suicides and probable suicides among 11–16-year-olds in Scotland (1999–2010). Personal correspondence, February, 2012.

Northern Ireland Statistics and Research Agency. (2012), Suicides among 11–16-year-olds in Northern Ireland (1999–2010). Personal correspondence, February 2012.

Office for National Statistics (2012), Suicides among 11–16-year-olds in England and Wales (1999–2010). Personal correspondence, February, 2012.

Power, T. J. (2003), 'Promoting children's mental health: Reform through interdisciplinary and community partnerships'. *School Psychology Review*, 32: 3–16.

Samaritans (2008), *Samaritans in Schools 2008*. Available online at www.samaritans.org/pdf/SamaritansinSchools2008.pdf.

Schneidman, E. S. (1996), *The Suicidal Mind*. Oxford: Oxford University Press.

Scottish Executive (2002), *Choose Life. The National Suicide Prevention Strategy and Action Plan*. HMSO.

Smith, M. (2004), 'Young Men', in D. Duffy and T. Ryan (eds), *New Approaches to Preventing Suicide*. London: Jessica Kingsley Publishers.

Stanley, N., Mallon, S., Bell, J. and Manthorpe, J. (2007), *Responses and Prevention in Student Suicide*. Preston: University of Central Lancashire.

Strein, W., Hoagwood, K. and Cohn, A. (2003), 'School psychology: A public health perspective. Prevention, populations and system change'. *Journal of School Psychology*, 41: 23–38.

Trainor, G. (2010), *Adolescent Self-Harm* (APSA Practitioner Briefings, 3). Association for Professionals in Service for Adolescents, UK.

United States Department of Health and Human Services (2003), *National Strategy for Suicide Prevention*. SAMHSA National Mental Health Information Center. Available online at www.mentalhealth.org.

Walsh, B. W. (2006), *Treating Self-Injury: A Practical Guide*. New York: Guilford Press.

Weare, K. and Gray, G. (2003), *What Works in Developing Children's Emotional and Social Competence and Well-Being?* University of Southampton for DfES.

Zahl, D. L. and Hawton, K. (2004). 'Repetition of deliberate self-harm and subsequent suicide risk: Long-term follow-up study of 11583 patients'. *The British Journal of Psychiatry*, 185: 70–5.

Zenere, F. J., III. and Lazarus, P. J. (1997), 'The decline of Youth Suicidal Behaviour in an urban multicultural school system following the introduction of a Suicide Prevention and Intervention Program'. *Suicide and Life-Threatening Behaviour*, 16: 360–78.

— (2009), 'The sustained reduction of Youth Suicidal Behaviour in an urban multicultural school district'. *School Psychology Review*, 38: 189–99.

Index

37133028R10129

Printed in Great Britain
by Amazon